SOVIET–
EAST EUROPEAN
DILEMMAS

SOVIET–
EAST EUROPEAN
DILEMMAS:
Coercion,
Competition,
and Consent

Edited by
KAREN DAWISHA
and
PHILIP HANSON

HM Holmes & Meier Publishers, Inc.

Published by Holmes & Meier for the Royal Institute of
International Affairs

First published in the United States of America 1981 by
HOLMES & MEIER PUBLISHERS, INC.
30 Irving Place, New York, N.Y. 10003

Library of Congress Cataloging in Publication Data

Main entry under line:
Soviet–East European Dilemmas
   Includes Index
     1. Europe, Eastern–Foreign Relations–Russia–
Addresses, Essays, Lectures. 2. Russia–Foreign
Relations–Europe, Eastern–Addresses, Essays,
Lectures. 3. Russia–Foreign Relations–1975–
Addresses, Essays, Lectures. I. Dawisha, Karen.
II. Hanson, Philip.
DJK45.R9S67 1981 327′.0947 80–28573

ISBN 0–8419–0697–1
ISBN 0–8419–0698–X (Pbk)

PRINTED IN GREAT BRITAIN

Contents

Foreword by *William Wallace*   vii

Editors' Acknowledgements   ix

Contributors   xi

Abbreviations and Terms   xii

1   **Introduction** by *Karen Dawisha and Philip Hanson*   1

2   **The 1968 Invasion of Czechoslovakia: Causes,
    Consequences, and Lessons for the Future** by *Karen
    Dawisha*   9

3   **The Continuing Validity of the Brezhnev Doctrine**
    by *Peter Summerscale*   26

4   **New Developments in Intra-bloc Relations in
    Historical Perspective** by *Eberhard Schulz*   41

5   **The Political Structure of Eastern Europe as a
    Factor in Intra-bloc Relations** by *George Schöpflin*   61

6   **Economic Reforms as an Issue in Soviet–East
    European Relations** by *Wlodzimierz Brus*   84

7   **Soviet Trade with Eastern Europe** by *Philip Hanson*   90

8   **Economic Factors Affecting Soviet–East European
    Relations in the 1980s** by *Alan H. Smith*   108

9   **Military Considerations in Soviet–East European
    Relations** by *Malcolm Mackintosh*   134

10 **The Warsaw Pact – the Shape of Things to Come?**
    by *John Erickson*   148

11 **Foreign Policy Perspectives in Eastern Europe** by
    Edwina Moreton   172

12 **Stability and Instability in Eastern Europe and their
    Implications for Western Policy** by *Philip Windsor*   195

Appendix: Selected Economic Statistics for the European
    CMEA States in the 1970s   212

Index   222

Tables

5.1 Poland, the GDR, and Hungary 1977–80: percentage increases in the budgets of Ministries of the Interior over the preceding year   81

7.1 Eastern Europe: trade with the USSR as a percentage of total trade 1960–78   92

7.2 Eastern Europe and the USSR: 1978 trade and GNP values   92

8.1 Value of USSR exports to East European members of CMEA 1974–9   114

8.2 Estimated financial and resource transfers from East European members of CMEA to the USSR 1975–9   115

8.3 Value of Soviet imports from East European members of CMEA 1974–9   117

8.4 Soviet imports of machinery and equipment from East European members of CMEA 1977–9   118

10.1 Armament levels: Soviet/non-Soviet Warsaw Pact area 1980   153

11.1 Comparisons of Warsaw Pact states' defence expenditure 1979   187

Foreword

THIS volume is the first fruit of the Institute's revived programme of Soviet and East European studies. After a gap of some years, during which our research programme had concentrated on other aspects of international relations, the decision was taken in the winter of 1978 to return to this field. We did not then foresee how rapidly unexpected developments would throw fresh doubts upon the purpose and extent of détente or on the stability of East–West relations. The invasion of Afghanistan took place after our study group's first three meetings. The troubles in Poland, foreseen in outline in some of the group's discussions, erupted while the papers were being revised for publication, and may only have temporarily abated as the manuscript goes to press.

Other studies of Eastern European developments and of Soviet foreign policy are now under way at the Institute. We hope that this first volume will help to inform the debate about the future of the Soviet bloc and of Western relations with it.

William Wallace
Director of Studies

Royal Institute of International Affairs
September 1980

Editors' Acknowledgements

WE are indebted to a number of people and organizations for help in the preparation of this book. The study group meetings in 1979–80 and a larger meeting with French and German participants in June 1980, from which the essays in this volume grew, were funded by a grant from the Social Science Research Council. The Royal Institute of International Affairs, often known more briefly as Chatham House, provided excellent facilities and support services for these meetings; in this connection we are especially grateful for the assistance, both intellectual and organizational, received from Dr William Wallace, Dr Adeed Dawisha, and Mr Peter Summerscale. Along with the other contributors to the symposium, we owe a great deal to all the members of the study group, who provided many pertinent comments on earlier drafts of the essays that follow. *The Current Digest of the Soviet Press* kindly gave permission for the reproduction of copyright translations from volume xx, numbers 39 and 46. We are thankful to Miss Ann De'Ath of Chatham House who was of tremendous help in collecting together the various drafts of the chapters. Miss Rena Fenteman, who carried out the copy-editing and assisted with the earlier stages of editing, has made an invaluable contribution to the book; we are extremely grateful for her systematic and meticulous work.

K.D.
P.H.

September 1980

Contributors

Wlodzimierz Brus, Fellow of Wolfson College, University of Oxford

Karen Dawisha, Lecturer in the Department of Politics, University of Southampton

Professor John Erickson, Director of Defence Studies, University of Edinburgh

Philip Hanson, Senior Lecturer in Soviet Economics, Centre for Russian and East European Studies, University of Birmingham

Malcolm Mackintosh, Consultant on Soviet affairs to the International Institute for Strategic Studies, London

Edwina Moreton, member of staff of the Foreign Department of *The Economist*

George Schöpflin, Joint Lecturer in the Political Institutions of Eastern Europe, London School of Economics and the School of Slavonic and East European Studies, University of London

Eberhard Schulz, Deputy Director of the Forschungsinstitut der Deutschen Gesellschaft für Auswärtige Politik, Bonn, and Senior Lecturer, Department of Political Sciences, University of Bonn

Alan H. Smith, Lecturer in the Economics of Eastern Europe at the School of Slavonic and East European Studies, University of London

Peter Summerscale, Counsellor in the United Kingdom Diplomatic Service, attached to the Royal Institute of International Affairs as Visiting Research Fellow 1979–80

Philip Windsor, Reader in the Department of International Relations, London School of Economics, University of London

Abbreviations and Terms

billion	one thousand million
CDU	Christian Democratic Union (West German party)
CIA, *Energy*	USA, Central Intelligence Agency, *Energy Supplies in Eastern Europe: a Statistical Compilation.* Washington, DC, Dec. 1979
CIA, *HES 1979*	USA, Central Intelligence Agency, *Handbook of Economic Statistics 1979.* Washington, DC, Aug. 1979
CMEA	Council for Mutual Economic Assistance (in September 1980 the following were members: Bulgaria, Czechoslovakia, the GDR, Hungary, Poland, Romania, the USSR, the Mongolian People's Republic, Cuba, Vietnam)
CoCom	Co-ordinating Committee (of representatives of NATO countries less Iceland plus Japan, responsible for administering the Western strategic embargo)
CPSU	Communist Party of the Soviet Union
CSCE	Conference on Security and Co-operation in Europe
CSSR	Czechoslovak Soviet Socialist Republic
CSU	Christian Social Union (the Bavarian wing of the CDU)
FDP	Free Democratic Party (West German)
FRG	Federal Republic of Germany
GDR	German Democratic Republic
KSS-KOR	Social Self-Defence Committee (Polish dissident organization which started as KOR or the Workers' Defence Committee)
MBFR	Mutual Balanced Force Reduction (negotiations between East and West, proceeding in Vienna through most of the 1970s and into the 1980s)
NATO	North Atlantic Treaty Organization

NSWP	non-Soviet Warsaw Pact
Preisausgleich	literally 'price equalization'; a term used to describe the arrangements (equivalent to subsidies and indirect taxes) whereby, in a traditional Soviet-type economy, the irregular and often large gaps between the domestic and the foreign trade prices of exports and imports are bridged
ROPCiO	Movement for the Defence of Human and Civil Rights (Polish dissident organization)
SDP	Social Democratic Party (West German; German abbreviation SPD)
SED	Sozialistische Einheitspartei Deutschlands (Socialist Unity Party of Germany; East German ruling party)
TNF	Theatre Nuclear Forces
ton	the metric measure unless otherwise specified
WTO	Warsaw Treaty Organization

Other abbreviations and special terms are explained in the text when they first occur.

1 Introduction
by Karen Dawisha and Philip Hanson

THE essays in this volume are revised versions of papers presented in 1979–80 to a Chatham House study group on 'Changing Patterns in Eastern Europe'. The aim of the study group was that specialists in different fields – economics, politics, and strategic studies – should exchange information and ideas on recent and prospective developments in intra-bloc relations in a form accessible to all the participants in the study group and to the interested non-specialist. The essays are therefore 'think pieces' rather than research papers. Each contributor has eschewed both the technical terms and the assumption of specialist background knowledge that might have been appropriate in papers addressed to colleagues in the same field.

The scope of the study group papers and discussion was in large measure determined at the outset. What was not fully spelt out in advance, however, was the emphasis that runs through all the work in this volume: an emphasis on recent and prospective developments in relations between the USSR on the one hand and Eastern Europe on the other. (Throughout the book 'Eastern Europe' means – unless otherwise specified – the Soviet Union's European Warsaw Pact and Council for Mutual Economic Assistance (CMEA) partners: Bulgaria, Czechoslovakia, the German Democratic Republic, Hungary, Poland, and Romania.) This emphasis emerged at an early stage in the work of the study group, and there was general agreement that it was right to treat Soviet–East European relations as the crucial issue.

In focusing on Soviet–East European relations the authors of the chapters that follow have of necessity been concerned also with domestic developments within individual Warsaw Pact countries, with intra-East European relations, and with Soviet and East European relations with the outside world (primarily with the West). They have treated these latter topics, however, principally as phenomena influencing, and influenced by, the developments in relations between

Moscow and Eastern Europe that are the theme of the book.

The periods of time considered have been, for the most part, the Brezhnev era up to early 1980 and the 1980s in prospect. But no rigid time-frame was imposed on the contributors; several have chosen, for the sake of historical perspective, to take a longer backward look.

Somewhat to the surprise of at least some of the participants, the results that emerged, particularly after discussion within the group, were by no means a compendium of the conventional wisdom in each field. In part this is because the contributors all benefited from discussion with the specialists in other fields represented in the study group. Relations between the Soviet Union and Eastern Europe were considered in economic, political, and military contexts; they were also approached by some contributors primarily from a perspective based on research on Eastern Europe, and by others primarily from a 'Soviet' perspective. In the discussion and in the revision of papers, each contributor modified or extended his or her initial analysis in response to information and insights from the other participants: and this interchange reflected differences both in subject and in country specialization.

The chapters on political relations between the Soviet Union and Eastern Europe focus on the evolution of these relations over time and attempt to determine the extent to which the repercussions of past events form the parameters of current and future policies within the bloc. Karen Dawisha deals with the causes and consequences of the 1968 invasion of Czechoslovakia and argues that, although the invasion was designed to halt attempts at fundamental reform inside Czechoslovakia, the source of the crisis extended well beyond that country's boundaries. The crisis emerged out of an exceptionally complicated situation at the international, regional, and domestic levels. For that reason, Dawisha maintains, the Soviet leaders found it more difficult to reconcile their differing perceptions and priorities, and this impeded their formulation of a coherent strategy for dealing with the threats imposed by the Prague Spring. The very lack of consistency in the Soviet management of the crisis made it more difficult for the Czechoslovak leadership to calculate the likelihood of an eventual Soviet invasion. The complete breakdown of communication between the two sides and the mutual misreading of signals which resulted primarily, if not solely, from poor Soviet crisis management, thus ultimately increased the chances of invasion. Turning to the lessons which have been learned from the Prague Spring, Dawisha argues that nearly all the bloc states have drawn different conclusions from the events of 1968. In particular there are large and potentially dangerous areas of uncertainty in East European perceptions of Moscow's resolve to apply the Brezhnev Doctrine uniformly and absolutely throughout the bloc.

In his discussion of the current limitations imposed by the Soviet Union on East European reform Peter Summerscale agrees with Dawisha that, while the USSR may well encounter further crises of authority in Eastern Europe, the Czechoslovak events of 1968 are unlikely to be repeated. Nevertheless Summerscale maintains that the 1968 intervention clearly indicated both that the USSR would not tolerate the development of any new model of socialism and that the defence of 'socialist gains' would henceforth be the collective responsibility of the entire bloc. The promulgation of substantial economic reforms throughout Eastern Europe also indicates that Moscow is more tolerant of developments in this direction, provided that changes in the economic system do not spill over into the political. Summerscale examines the extent to which the Soviet leadership believes the Brezhnev Doctrine to be applicable to relations with socialist states outside the Warsaw Pact, including Afghanistan, Yugoslavia, and Albania. He concludes that, although the Soviet Union may invoke principles of socialist internationalism, the Brezhnev Doctrine serves more as an *ex post facto* justification of policy than as a motivation.

The chapter by Eberhard Schulz examines the phases through which Soviet–East European relations have passed since 1945. It focuses on the three levels of relations, namely multilateral, bilateral between the USSR and individual East European states, and finally amongst the East European states themselves, concluding that, despite improvements in multilateral mechanisms and contacts amongst East European régimes, almost all the issues of crucial significance are still dealt with in bilateral talks with the USSR. In delineating the differences between the various phases, Schulz concludes that the changing nature of the German question has been the single most important cause of shifts in the relations between Moscow and Eastern Europe. Examining the situation that followed the invasion of Afghanistan, Schulz maintains that the impasse in Soviet diplomacy after the invasion, coinciding with similar immobility in Washington's foreign policy during the Iranian crisis, has produced a situation in which the medium powers in both East and West Europe have risen to a position of previously unparalleled influence on their respective super-power patrons. In this way, East Europe's continuing efforts to maintain regional détente in Central Europe are viewed by Schulz as positive phenomena not only in the context of East–West relations but also in the furtherance of East European independence from Moscow.

George Schöpflin examines the role of political culture in Soviet–East European relations, arguing that communist régimes in Eastern Europe, having presided over a dash for modernity in the guise of a quest for a Marxist utopia, have run out of steam. They have lost their purposiveness because they have no policies adequate to deal with the requirements of modern societies. East European attempts to meet these requirements have been thwarted by the constraints imposed on political reform by the Soviet Union, which have forced East European leaders to rely on higher levels of coercion than would otherwise be used by states at similar levels of development.

The intrusion of political considerations into almost all sectors of public life has meant, for example, that the need to base economic decisions on technical criteria has been undermined in communist régimes. The political result is wasteful and non-rational bureaucratization, popular frustration and latent discontent, as well as the further 'decomposition' of Marxist–Leninist ideology as a viable, dynamic body of ideas, and the concomitant risk of competing ideologies such as nationalism, populism, and religion. Schöpflin argues that the alliance with the USSR, generally unpopular in Eastern Europe, further detracts from the legitimacy of bloc régimes and prevents East European leaders, many of whom are perceived as surrogates of Moscow, from establishing a genuine relationship with their own people. He concludes that, although there are significant factors of weakness in communist régimes, provided they can maintain even an unstable equilibrium they should be able to maintain themselves without a major crisis for the foreseeable future. Since the final draft of Schöpflin's essay was written the difficulties in maintaining such an equilibrium have been shown clearly by the challenges to the Polish régime presented in the summer of 1980 by the political demands of striking workers. These demands have reflected, in some detail, many of the sources of weakness of East European régimes to which Schöpflin draws attention.

The three economic papers tend on balance to attribute rather more independence of Moscow to East European economic decision-making than most recent Western commentary would assume. Wlodzimierz Brus argues persuasively that Moscow has not imposed restraints on institutional change in Eastern Europe such as would prevent other East European countries from adopting the sort of limited decentralization exemplified by the Hungarian New Economic Mechanism in its original form. Implicit in Brus' argument is the possibility that Moscow might place constraints on reforms of a more drastic character; the more important point is the one that Brus explicitly makes: that it is primarily domestic factors which inhibit even modest institutional change in Eastern Europe. It is interesting to note, in this connection, that there has been a further round of such changes in the area in 1979 and 1980, with the notable exception (to date) of Poland. These changes have been limited in scope, but the fact that they have been closely bunched in time raises the possibility of prior agreement with Moscow.

Hanson's paper, similarly, provides grounds for arguing that in the 1970s Moscow did not act to reduce the East European countries' relative shift of trade orientation towards the West. True, the whole set of economic and political institutions in the bloc, including CMEA, operates in the long run – as Hanson acknowledges – to set some limits to any such reorientation of external economic relations. But the point is rather that recent and prospective medium-term variations in the share of Eastern Europe's trade with the West seem to lie within those limits. Within an overall framework dominated by the Soviet Union, Hanson argues, Eastern Europe has in some respects done well out of its Moscow connection. Moreover, East–West trade has in important ways complemented, rather than substituted for, intra-bloc transactions. The extent to which East European economic dependence on the USSR is likely to increase as a result of the more 'inward-looking' trade pattern imposed by hard-currency deficits in the late 1970s is therefore less than might be supposed.

Alan Smith looks further forward and in more detail than Hanson at prospects for CMEA integration. Though in general agreement with Hanson, he is inclined to place rather more emphasis on factors making for closer integration of the Soviet and East European economies and for the distribution of the gains from intra-CMEA trade to be 'steered' by Moscow somewhat more effectively than in the past. Not that this necessarily entails gains for the Soviet Union at the expense of Eastern Europe. His analysis of resource transfers within CMEA in the late 1970s suggests that the less-developed, non-European member states may have been the main beneficiaries of changes in that period.

In Western discussion of intra-CMEA economic relations much attention has recently been paid, and with good cause, to the question of energy supplies. It was precisely because this question has received so much attention that we felt it would be redundant to include, as a separate chapter in this volume, yet another review of the energy issues. The need was rather to relate the energy issues to other intra-CMEA economic issues, and this – particularly Alan Smith's chapter – is what has indeed been done. If we were to identify one economic topic that would merit more extended treatment than it is given here, it would be the economics of military co-operation within the bloc. The problem is that this is a generally neglected subject on which most of the spade work still remains to be done; it was not within the study group's remit to undertake pioneering research on substantially 'new' topics. We can only express the hope that this gap in Western study of the area will be filled sooner rather than later.

The chapters on military relations within the bloc focus both on the strategic importance of Eastern Europe to the Soviet Union and the underlying tensions and interactions within the Warsaw Pact. Malcolm Mackintosh presents a picture of military relationships between the Soviet Union and Eastern Europe which suggests that the 'permanent factor' in Soviet thinking is the retention of military control over the communist countries of Eastern Europe in order to support the existing political domination of the area. Further, Eastern Europe continues to satisfy the Russian and Soviet desire for a buffer zone to protect the Soviet frontier and also for a concentration area for any Soviet offensive against Western Europe. Mackintosh considers the various East European components of the Warsaw Pact to be highly trained, well armed, and generally reliable while recognizing that the Soviet leaders must take the diverse, and often anti-Russian, nationalisms of its East European allies into account in calculating their military posture within the territory of the Pact and in pursuing their general aims within Europe as a whole.

John Erickson's chapter is in agreement with many of the points raised by Mackintosh but it puts somewhat greater emphasis on the Soviet desire to create a truly integrated standing force, albeit under Soviet command. Because of this desire, the Soviet leadership is working towards the increased military effectiveness of its East European allies, not only by means of closer and more effective command integration but also by the development of rough comparability in firepower and mobility between Soviet and selected non-Soviet units. After detailing shifts in East European weapons procurement and providing much new and interesting detail on defence production in Eastern Europe, Erickson maintains that earlier Western predictions of continuing disparities in Soviet and non-Soviet capabilities have failed to materialize. Erickson concludes that, far from losing its importance, the Warsaw Pact has taken on increased significance.

Edwina Moreton, in discussing the differing foreign policy perspectives of the Soviet Union and its East European allies, deals with a subject previously ignored in Western literature. There have, it is true, been few cases where individual Pact members, with the exception of Romania, have publicly challenged Moscow. Beneath this surface, however, there is a number of issues likely to cause ripples in Soviet–East European relations in the 1980s. This chapter argues that because of the emphasis the Soviet Union places on cohesion within the alliance and as a result of the serious implications of some of these issues, the continued co-ordination of public statements may well disguise an active bargaining process within the alliance, tending towards mutual influence rather than simple Soviet fiat. Among the issues discussed are East German influence on Soviet–West German relations, Romania's defiant position on several occasions, East European attitudes to the Sino–Soviet conflict, and Soviet policy towards Africa and the Third World. Equally, a whole range of intra-bloc policies has produced conflicting positions, including Soviet interference in the domestic affairs of East European states, and both CMEA and Warsaw Pact policies. The chapter concludes that the growing complexity of international relations is likely to produce more frequent consultation and mutual influence within bloc countries, combined with a greater division of labour within the alliance, albeit in the context of a co-ordinated framework largely determined by the Soviet Union.

In the concluding chapter Philip Windsor brings together two underlying themes of the preceding essays and discusses their implications for Western policies. The two themes are the sources of stability and the sources of instability in intra-bloc relations. He argues that the limits which Moscow seeks to impose on social and political change in Eastern Europe have been clarified by the Brezhnev Doctrine, and that this clarification is in itself a source of stability. At the same time, he argues, one of the key limitations imposed by Moscow – the maintenance of the leading role of the Party – is a source of instability. This is so, broadly speaking, for the reasons adduced in chapter 5 by George Schöpflin. Windsor, however, is more inclined than Schöpflin to stress the differences with respect to political stability among the various East European nations.

He draws particular attention to a worrying set of linkages between the especial instability of Poland and the relations between Moscow, Bucharest, and Belgrade: these linkages could, in the worst case, lead from an internal East European upheaval to an East–West confrontation. Windsor concludes that the West's interests do indeed lie in the promotion of stability and even – in some respects – of integration in Eastern Europe, but that this need not be incompatible with the promotion of liberalization. No doubt the subtle policy-mix that he prescribes is intended for the Western alliance as a whole to pursue. It seems at present to be an approach that finds more favour in Western Europe than in Washington.

It would be wrong to suggest that there is any key, central proposition about Soviet–East European relations on which the contributors converged. One could reasonably say, however, that on balance these essays tend to attribute rather more elements of strength to Soviet–East European relations – particularly in the near future – than many Western commentators would allow. At the same time – and this is only superficially a paradox – most of the contributors do not believe that the Soviet Union is very likely in the 1980s to be able greatly to strengthen the institutional ties between itself and its Warsaw Pact allies or dramatically to increase the latter's economic dependence on Moscow.

2 The 1968 Invasion of Czechoslovakia: Causes, Consequences, and Lessons for the Future
by Karen Dawisha

IT is now more than a decade since the hopes raised during the Prague Spring were ended when Soviet and allied troops invaded Czechoslovakia. The repercussions of those events continue to influence Soviet–East European relations, in both tangible and intangible ways, yet the lessons to be drawn from the Prague Spring and the subsequent invasion are by no means uniform for all participants and observers. Views about the salience of 1968 as a watershed in Soviet–East European relations depend very much on the conclusions drawn about the scope and nature of the crisis which gave rise to the invasion, the way in which the Soviet Union managed the crisis, and the extent to which the lessons of 1968 were uniformly incorporated as part of the learning process for leaders in both the East and the West.

The External Setting
In examining the scope and nature of the crisis it is necessary first to underline the fact that, while the invasion was designed to halt attempts at fundamental reform inside Czechoslovakia, the source of the crisis extended well beyond that country's boundaries. The Soviet leadership went into 1968 without a clear and pre-agreed 'general line' on either internal or external policy issues. This inevitably fostered within the Politburo differing and contradictory sets of policy priorities for dealing with what was by any standards an unusually complex situation, not only in Czechoslovakia, but internationally and within the Soviet Union as well.

Thus, on the international level, the growing American involvement in Vietnam, the military *coup* by right-wing colonels in Greece, and the occupation by Israel of Arab territory during the 1967 June war were cited repeatedly as evidence of increased aggressiveness in the Western camp. Thus for some Soviet leaders there was no question of negotiation or co-existence with the West, which was seen to be going through a period of increased expansionism, adventurism, and militarism. Yet this view was not universally shared in Moscow. President Johnson's decision not to seek renomination for the Presidency and the growth of the public outcry in the West against American actions in Vietnam were interpreted by other leaders as a sign of increased weakness and disarray in the Western alliance. Additionally, President Johnson's own interest in obtaining a breakthrough on strategic arms limitation prior to his departure from office convinced many in Moscow, notably Kosygin and Gromyko, that genuine negotiation with the West was possible on a whole range of issues.

It took several months for a consensus to emerge within the leadership on East–West relations. By April it had been agreed that, although the bombing of North Vietnam and other actions indicated increased aggressive intent, setbacks in Vietnam and elsewhere showed the weakness of Western capabilities. By August it was abundantly clear that American preoccupation with Vietnam and Johnson's interest in SALT, coupled with the paralysis at the top resulting from the presidential campaign, would militate against a NATO military response to any Soviet invasion. Indeed it has repeatedly been suggested that the USSR received more or less explicit signals from Washington to this effect from June onwards.[1] A joint statement announcing an imminent summit on SALT was to have been made in Washington and Moscow on the very morning of the invasion, indicating at best the compartmentalization of decision-making in the Soviet Union and at worst a cynical assessment in the Kremlin that Johnson would 'sacrifice' Czechoslovakia for SALT. The haste with which the US administration attempted to reschedule talks after the invasion would seem to indicate that the Soviet leaders did indeed correctly assess the nature of American priorities.

Of equal importance in shaping the international environment in which the Czechoslovak events developed was the West German policy of 'building bridges' to Eastern Europe. A favourable response to this policy had already been elicited from many European leaders in 1967 and most notably had led to the establishment of formal diplomatic relations between Bucharest and Bonn. The Soviet response to the West German policy was once again marked by contradictory tendencies. Some Soviet leaders expressed the belief that the existence of 'realistic elements' within the West German leadership made contacts with the West Germans highly desirable. In particular, the secret exchange of notes with the West Germans – begun in October 1967 – for the renunciation of force, was seen by some in the Soviet leadership as a positive step towards the solution of outstanding problems in Central Europe. However, Bonn's attempts to establish direct links with Eastern Europe were interpreted by hardliners, not only in Moscow but also in East Berlin and Warsaw, as designed primarily to weaken the unity of the socialist bloc and further isolate the GDR. The June 1967 Karlovy Vary conference had imposed minimum preconditions for the establishment of relations with the Federal Republic, and when in 1968 the Dubcek leadership appeared to transgress this pre-agreed bloc policy, the East German and Polish leaderships, in particular, expressed the fear that their vital interests were being undermined. As a result, not only was pressure put on the Czechoslovaks to reverse their policy, but by July 1968 the Soviet Union too was forced to forgo, for the time being, its own contacts with Bonn.[2]

Demands for the tightening of control over the bloc emanated not merely from hard-line elements in Eastern Europe but also from the Soviet military. The continuing calls within NATO for the adoption of a strategy of 'flexible response' introduced the need to develop contingency plans for a longer period of conventional warfare before any escalation to a nuclear exchange. This necessitated greater attention in Moscow on the preparedness and reliability of front-line forces, particularly in those bloc states bordering the Federal Republic. Because the Soviet Union had its own troops stationed in Hungary, Poland, and East Germany, Czechoslovakia increasingly was cast as the 'weak link' in the Warsaw Pact. Negotiations for the permanent stationing in Czechoslovakia of Soviet troops began under Novotny and became more frantic in 1968 with the Prague leadership's very reluctance to agree to such stationing or even to large-scale Pact manoeuvres proving, at least in the eyes of the Soviet military planners, the absolute necessity of a direct Soviet presence along the Czechoslovak–West German border.

If Soviet concern to prevent Prague from establishing closer links with Bonn was reinforced by Polish and East German pressure and by Moscow's own desire to contain the disruptive effects of Romania's more independent stance on a wide range of foreign policy issues, many leaders in Moscow were equally concerned that the more reform-minded elements of the communist movement should not be alienated. Plans to convene an international communist conference in November 1968 were already well advanced by the time the Prague Spring began to evoke disquiet in Moscow, and up until this time it was hoped that the conference would serve to forge a united front against the Chinese. The argument that Chinese 'dogmatism' was the greatest threat to Soviet-defined communist ideals inevitably lost ground throughout 1968, not only as a result of the Prague Spring but also following unrest amongst Polish students in March and the upsurge of New Left ideas during 'les événements' in Paris and elsewhere. Thus while some Soviet leaders, notably Suslov and Ponomarev, were keen to prevent the alienation of the 'revisionist' wing of the movement, the threat to Soviet ideological leadership emanating from the Prague reform ultimately took priority over hopes of a broad united front against the Chinese position.

The change in the Soviet 'general line' to combat revisionism and the 'subversive efforts of bourgeois propaganda' was directed not only against Prague but also against dissidents within the Soviet Union itself. By 1968 it was becoming fully apparent that the new Soviet leadership had no intention of tolerating the more unorthodox tendencies which had arisen during the Khrushchev era. So at the very time that intellectual life was undergoing a renaissance in Prague, Solzhenitsyn, Sakharov, Ginzburg, and the entire scientific and literary community in Moscow were being subjected to renewed censorship and restriction.

From the Soviet point of view, one of the most worrying aspects of this situation was the mutual support and links which were developed between the Prague and Moscow intelligentsia from the very outset of the reform movement. The fact that a letter from Alexander Solzhenitsyn to the Soviet Writers' Union attacking official censorship was read out, not in Moscow, but at the June 1967 Czechoslovak Writers' Congress, created a novel, and from the Soviet standpoint, alarming precedent whereby Soviet dissidents might find an official outlet in a friendly socialist country for material censored in the USSR.

The lifting of press controls in Prague thereby threatened the Communist Party's monopoly over information both in Czechoslovakia and throughout the bloc. East Germany and the Soviet Union reacted early in 1968 by banning or selectively censoring materials coming into their own countries from Prague, but clearly such a policy was not likely to be either effective or desirable on a long-term basis.

Soviet fears of 'spill-over' from Czechoslovakia were particularly acute in relation to another source of dissent – namely, the nationalist and even separatist sentiments in the Ukraine, and, to a lesser extent, also in the Baltic Republics. The problems in the Ukraine were exacerbated by the Czechoslovak reform movement in two ways: on the one hand, the small Ukrainian minority in the Presov region of Slovakia began to take a lead in calling for the revival of Ukrainian culture both in Czechoslovakia and in the Ukraine itself. Broadcasts to the Ukraine from Radio Presov and symposia devoted to Ukrainian culture thus posed a direct challenge to the Communist Party in the Ukraine and particularly to its First Secretary, Pyotr Shelest. Equally, however, the provisions for federalization proposed in Czechoslovakia during 1968 presented a more indirect, but no less radical, threat to the Soviet Union's own nationalities policy.

The importance of outlining in some detail the broader set of circumstances surrounding the Soviet and bloc reaction to the Prague Spring lies in the fact that because the crisis emerged out of an unusually complex and contradictory situation at the international, regional, and domestic levels, Soviet leaders found it more difficult to reconcile their differing perceptions and priorities. This difficulty hindered the formulation of a coherent strategy for dealing with the threats posed by the Prague Spring. The very lack of consistency in the Soviet management of the crisis made it more difficult for the Czechoslovak leadership to calculate the likelihood of an eventual Soviet invasion. The complete breakdown of communication between the two sides and the mutual misreading of signals which resulted primarily, but not solely, from poor Soviet crisis management thus ultimately increased the chances of invasion.

It should not be inferred from the above that the bloc crisis was somehow a 'terrible mistake' or that the two sides had no irreconcilable differences. It is to suggest, however, that no nation, not even (contrary to Polish opinion) Czechoslovakia, invites invasion and suppression. The conscience of that country and of its emigré community has been dominated over the last decade by the single question: how could it have been avoided? What might the Dubcek leadership have done to keep the reform movement within acceptable parameters? What precisely made the Soviet and bloc leaders decide that the situation in Prague had so deteriorated that 'socialism' could be saved only by invading?

Causes of Bloc Concern

Much has been written about why the Soviet Union and some of its East European allies responded so negatively to the reform movement. On an ideological level, the USSR repeatedly expressed its concern that the Czechoslovak Communist Party was surrendering its leading role. A protracted polemic developed between Prague and Moscow about the continued viability of Lenin's views on Party leadership, with several of the leading Prague reformers – notably Mlynar, Kriegal, and Cisar – suggesting that Lenin had revised Marxism to fit specific Russian circumstances and that these circumstances did not pertain to conditions in Czechoslovakia. The reformers' view that they had the right to an independent interpretation of Marxism represented a fundamental challenge to the legitimacy of the Soviet model and to the ideological cohesion of the bloc, based as it was on East European acceptance of the universality of Soviet-defined Marxist-Leninist precepts.

Yet Soviet concerns that the Czechoslovak Communist Party was surrendering its leading role were not based solely on fears that the Soviet model was being displaced or that Soviet ideological supremacy was being challenged. At the heart of Soviet worries were views about power and control. The cornerstone of communist rule in all communist states is the leading role of the party. Translated from abstract to concrete terms, this means monopolistic party control over all branches of the government, the legislature, and the judiciary. In 1968 this system of Party control was steadily being dismantled in Prague. The non-communist parties within the National Front began to participate more fully in the political life of the country, a precedent with particularly dangerous implications for other East European countries, such as Poland, with similar multi-party structures. Additionally, Party control over the National Assembly underwent substantial erosion in Czechoslovakia during 1968. Votes of no confidence were passed on leading officials, open and free debates marked Assembly sessions, and a system of Assembly committees with rights to subpoena and examine witnesses began to function.

Also central to the exercise of the Party's leading role is the control of the organs of state power, namely the police, the military, and the judiciary. In all communist states this control is exercised through the Central Committee apparat. However, in 1968 the power of the so-called Eighth Department for State Administration was severely reduced, and following the dismissal in July, under Soviet pressure, of its reformist head, General Vaclav Prchlik, the Department was abolished altogether, with responsibility for supervising the organs of state security transferred to the government. These events took place against the backdrop of wholesale purges of conservative and pro-Soviet officials from the Party apparat, the Ministry of the Interior, the Ministry of Defence, and other sensitive departments. The loss of Party supervision over the organs of state power removed also the key mechanism through which the USSR exercised influence inside Czechoslovakia.

Through reliance on loyal officials within the central Party apparat, the Soviet Union had been able to manipulate and monitor events throughout the country with comparative ease. With the diffusion of power and the decline in the central Party apparat's control of events, the Soviet Union realized that if the reform movement was allowed to continue, it would become much more difficult, if not impossible, to exert the same degree of influence over day-to-day affairs inside Czechoslovakia. The argument over the leading role of the Communist Party should not, therefore, be seen as a sterile ideological polemic between Moscow and Prague, but rather as an absolutely vital and irreconcilable conflict over the issue of control, including not only control by the Party of the state but also, through that mechanism, Soviet control over Czechoslovakia.

A central feature in the exercise of the Party's leading role is the control over information. The abolition of censorship in Czechoslovakia opened the floodgates for the free expression of opinion, which inevitably led to criticisms of the Party's monopoly of power and the Soviet Union's hegemonic position in the international communist movement. As discussed above, the Soviet leadership felt threatened by these developments both because they were beyond Soviet control and because of the near-impossibility of preventing information published in the Czech press from finding its way into other socialist countries. Thus articles about the direct involvement of Stalin and his lieutenants in ordering the show trials throughout Eastern Europe in the early 1950s had a dramatic effect in Moscow and elsewhere in the bloc, as did articles commemorating the execution of Imre Nagy, the leader of the 1956 Hungarian uprising.

A further principle of Party leadership under attack during the Prague Spring was democratic centralism. Involving as it does the strict control of lower Party echelons by the central Party apparat and the strict subordination of the minority to the majority, democratic centralism was challenged by the growth of grass-roots participation. Party conferences at local and regional level voted out long-standing conservative Party officials, the Prague City Party Committee went into permanent session to protect the gains of the reform movement from reversal by the central Party apparat, and momentum grew for the convocation of an extraordinary Party congress to oust Central Committee members blocking reform. Moreover, the draft Party statutes which were to have been approved by the extraordinary Fourteenth Party Congress included provision for minority factions to publicize their views even after their proposals had been rejected by a majority vote. Such a situation had not existed within the communist movement since the Resolution on Party Unity, passed at Lenin's insistence at the Tenth Party Congress in 1921, had condemned 'the perniciousness and impermissibility of factionalism of any kind'. To have allowed the Czechoslovaks to include such a statute in their Party rules would have seriously weakened the monolithic unity of the Party and would have served as a dangerous example to other Communist régimes, such as Poland and the USSR, where divisions within the Party are deep but kept in check by the principles of democratic centralism.

While the threats to the leading role of the Party, the challenge to Soviet control, the lifting of press censorship, and the revision of democratic centralism were the main points of the reform movement clearly unacceptable to Moscow, yet other aspects of the Prague Spring also warranted attention. The extent to which events in Prague were undermining the unity and security of the socialist bloc was a major issue of debate, not only within the Soviet Union but also within Eastern Europe. Because of its central position linking the northern and southern sectors of the Warsaw Pact, any decline in Czechoslovakia's reliability as an ally would have created untold problems in formulating bloc military strategy, and would have divided the Pact into two isolated northern and southern sectors.

Border security also became a matter of some contention in Prague's relations with its allies soon after reports started circulating in April that some of the electrical and barbed wire fences on the frontier with Austria had been removed. This measure, combined with the virtual lifting of any restrictions on obtaining entry visas to Czechoslovakia, led to Soviet claims that foreign agents could now infiltrate into Czechoslovakia and other bloc countries with impunity. Of greater importance, Prague's more relaxed attitude toward border security also created new opportunities for East European citizens to cross illegally to the West. The Soviet Union and East Germany, it could be argued, had not withstood all the international ignominy surrounding the construction of the Berlin Wall in 1961 in order to see another uncontrolled exit route created elsewhere in Eastern Europe. The East Germans reacted to this situation by erecting barbed wire fences along their own border with Czechoslovakia and by refusing, along with the USSR, to grant tourist visas for travel to Czechoslovakia. Despite these measures, the Czechoslovak authorities admitted that in the first six months of 1968 an unusually high number of people, mainly from the GDR, had been apprehended while trying to cross to the West. Clearly, such a situation was unacceptable in the long run.

While economic reforms in Eastern Europe were not contested *per se* by Moscow during this period, the belief in Czechoslovakia that political changes were an essential feature and even a prerequisite for the success of economic reforms did in fact cause alarm in the Soviet Union. Furthermore, Czechoslovak determination to obtain a $500 million convertible currency loan worried Moscow, both because Prague was willing to negotiate even with the West Germans and the World Bank (after attempts to obtain the required amount from Moscow had, not surprisingly, failed) and because the Soviet Union rightly believed that such a loan would gradually lead to the reorientation of Czechoslovak trade towards the West and the concomitant diminution in that country's role as a technology supplier to the USSR and other less-developed CMEA members.

In retrospect, it seems hardly possible that the Dubcek leadership failed to appreciate the seriousness with which the reform movement was viewed in Moscow and other East European capitals. The substantial, and even revolutionary, nature of the changes being made in Prague threatened to dismantle the system so carefully constructed to maintain the control of the Communist Party, and with it the influence of the Soviet Union and the unity of the socialist bloc. Dubcek himself was subsequently forced to admit that the Prague leadership 'did not always take sufficient note of the strategic and general interests of the USSR and the other four members of the Warsaw Pact as a real, objectively existing and limiting factor of the possible pace and form of our own political development.'[3] And yet, up until the very moment of the invasion the Czechoslovak leadership firmly, if not unanimously, believed that the Soviet Union was prepared to allow the reform movement to continue. That they were mistaken is clear, but why is more difficult to discern.

Crisis Management

Any number of reasons can be found to explain why the crisis was managed so poorly on both sides as ultimately to result in invasion. Dubcek's naiveté, contradictory signals from the Soviet bloc, Czechoslovak conviction that the overwhelming support for their programme both from within the country and from abroad would convince the USSR that the risks of invading were too high – all of these were factors which contributed to the failure of both sides to find a solution short of a military occupation. Yet there are two aspects of the crisis which bear further consideration because of their wider repercussions for the subsequent development of intra-bloc relations, namely the process of consensus-building by Moscow which preceded the invasion, and the extent to which the lessons learned, or mislearned, from the 1956 Hungarian uprising influenced the outcome of events in 1968.

Examination of the process of consensus-building makes it clear not only that the Soviet leaders were initially cautious in their reaction to events in Prague, but also that they were divided on the best policy to reconcile conflicting priorities. Soviet management of the crisis was severely affected by the continual need to work out a consensus within the leadership on the next course of action. The contradictory trends in East-West and intra-bloc relations, outlined above, further impeded the emergence at an early stage of a clear policy on Czechoslovakia.

Any argument for invasion first had to surmount the difficulty that the formally enunciated principles governing relations amongst communist states included, up to 1968, non-interference in domestic affairs and respect for state sovereignty. The bilateral agreements between the USSR and Czechoslovakia and the terms of the Warsaw Pact Treaty sanctioned the entry of Soviet troops on to Czechoslovak territory *only* in the event of a *direct* military attack on Czechoslovakia by the Federal Republic of Germany or forces allied with it. Thus the absence at the beginning of the crisis of anything approximating to the Brezhnev Doctrine of limited sovereignty complicated the process of consensus-building both within the Soviet leadership and amongst the communist states.

Many analyses of the invasion attach relatively little importance to this process of consensus-building, arguing that the top Soviet leadership was not worried about the need to be able to justify its actions whether within the Party, to its own public, or to the wider communist movement. Central to this view is the belief that the Brezhnev Doctrine as enunciated in Kovalev's *Pravda* article of 26 September 1968 was merely an *ad hoc* and *ex post facto* justification of an invasion which had failed to be legitimized by other means. That the invasion could not be justified by any universal standards is undoubted, and the promulgation of the Brezhnev Doctrine did nothing to alter the contempt with which the Soviet action was held inside Czechoslovakia and elsewhere. However, the point is that, while Kovalev's article was immediately significant because of the invasion, all the substantive elements of the doctrine had in fact appeared before Soviet and allied troops entered Prague.

The laying of the theoretical foundation for the use of force against Czechoslovakia was the product of a protracted debate within the leadership which spanned the six months prior to the invasion. Non-interference in internal affairs was first dropped as a stated principle governing relations between socialist states not by Kovalev in September, but as early as the Dresden meeting of bloc states in March. The redefinition of security to include not only security against direct external military attack but also against efforts by the West to subvert socialism from within occurred at the end of March when Brezhnev declared that imperialism, 'not daring to engage in a frontal attack on the world of socialism, is trying to weaken the ideological and political unity of the working people of the socialist countries. In so doing, it is chiefly gambling on nationalist and revisionist elements.'[4] Since the security of the socialist bloc is the primary responsibility of the USSR, if that security was to be threatened by Western reliance on 'nationalist and revisionist' elements then it was only a short step to accepting the need for more active Soviet assistance in guaranteeing the security of the bloc from *internal* as well as *external* threats. The resolution adopted by the CPSU Central Committee plenum in early April did indeed commit the Party 'to do everything necessary for the steady political, economic and defensive consolidation of the socialist commonwealth.'[5] The *right* of the Soviet Union to use all means – including military force – to prevent the 'erosion' of socialism anywhere in the bloc was first advocated later in that month by V. V. Grishin, the First Secretary of the Moscow City Party Committee and a candidate member of the Politburo. Grishin also dropped all references to non-interference and advocated proletarian internationalism, fraternal mutual aid, and the 'harmonization of the national interests of each fraternal country with the general interests of the world socialist system' as the principles which should henceforth govern intra-bloc relations.[6] However, it was several months before the principles expressed by Grishin were formally enunciated as bloc policy. As late as mid-July, for example, Prime Minister Kosygin was still advocating non-interference in the internal affairs of Czechoslovakia.[7] But his views were overruled at the Warsaw meeting of bloc leaders from the USSR, Poland, Bulgaria, Hungary, and the GDR. At that conclave, the 'five' sent a letter to the Czechoslovak Central Committee making it clear that the leading, controlling, and monopolistic role of the Communist Party could in no way be dismantled without posing a serious threat to socialism within that country and consequently to the security of the entire bloc. The final component of the Brezhnev Doctrine was then added at the Bratislava meeting in early August when the bloc states (excluding Romania but including Czechoslovakia) declared that proletarian internationalism included not just the *right*, but the positive *duty*, of all socialist countries jointly to defend socialism wherever it was threatened. With this communiqué, all the major elements of the Brezhnev Doctrine were 'in place'. The process of consensus-building had taken nearly six months, but by the beginning of August no one within the Soviet leadership or within the bloc could any longer argue that an invasion would be inconsistent with stated Soviet principles.

The gradual process of developing the theoretical basis for the invasion had the effect of prolonging the crisis, and, perhaps as a result, also of misleading the Czechoslovak Praesidium into believing that the Soviet Union was not prepared to pay the cost of invading. However, the Soviet leadership showed a uniform commitment to take high risks and incur high costs to keep Czechoslovakia within the socialist camp. One of the Czechoslovak participants in the bilateral talks in May reported that the Soviet leaders had told them that Czechoslovakia would not be allowed to leave the bloc 'even at the risk of a third world war'.[8] Brezhnev repeated these words after the invasion when he told the Czechoslovak leaders that the immutable composition of the socialist bloc 'would have been defended even if there had been a danger of a new world war breaking out. Even with this risk the Soviet Union was prepared to invade Czechoslovakia.'[9] Clearly, the Czechoslovaks had miscalculated the high risks the Soviets were prepared to take to maintain the status quo.

Prague also seems to have miscalculated the extent to which the Soviet leaders believed that the reform movement was leading inexorably to a situation in which Czechoslovakia would no longer be a member of the socialist bloc. Moscow was evidently unimpressed by Prague's continuing declarations of loyalty to the Soviet Union, focusing more on the structural changes being made and the reorientation of Czechoslovakia's external policy to the West.

Here the irony of learning processes bears some examination. All the participants continually looked to the example of the Hungarian Uprising to determine whether 'counter-revolution' had progressed as far in Prague. The Dubcek leadership was convinced that because it had no intention of withdrawing from the Warsaw Pact, as Nagy had done before Soviet troops entered Budapest for the second time, the USSR ultimately would not invade. This view was reinforced by the belief that because the Party supported the reform movement, rather than being the focus of attack as in Hungary, there was no question of a Soviet invasion against the wishes of a Party that was in control of the situation. Thirdly, there was no armed uprising in Czechoslovakia as there had been in Hungary. These were the lessons which Prague chose to derive from 1956.

The Soviet leaders also looked back to 1956. Some, including Brezhnev as late as June, were comparing the Prague Spring not to the Hungarian uprising but to the Polish events of 1956, which of course had not ended in invasion.[10] But not until the notorious 'Two Thousand Words' manifesto from Prague intellectuals, promising armed support for the continuation of the reform movement, did the Soviet press begin to draw alarming parallels with Hungary. Even so, the absence of violence in Prague and the dominant position of the Party created problems in defining the Prague Spring as an open counter-revolution on the 1956 Hungarian model. The turning point came when the Soviet leaders decided that just as they were being vigilant in preventing a repetition of 1956, so were their enemies, with the result that the counter-revolutionary forces were resorting to covert acts rather than overt armed struggle. In particular, this 'quiet counter-revolution' – to use the Soviet description – had as its main objective not an open attack on Party rule but the steady infiltration and internal subversion of the Party. Thus, once the parallel with 1956 had been dropped and the Soviet leadership had become convinced that the Party and other key sectors were under the influence of revisionists, with the result that 'loyal Communists' could not maintain control, it became very much easier to argue that an invasion was required almost to protect the Party from the very Communists within it. This doctrine of 'quiet counter-revolution' was formulated before the invasion; but like the Brezhnev Doctrine it was enunciated more explicitly, also by Kovalev, only afterwards. He stated that the Soviet Union would no longer wait, as it had done in 1956, for 'the shooting and hanging of Communists' before coming to the assistance of 'the champions of socialism'.[11] Thus the lessons of 1956, while uppermost in the minds of the Czechoslovaks, did not aid them in calculating the chances of invasion. As for the Soviet Union, the decision to invade was made that much easier once it had been agreed that there was very little to learn from 1956, since the situation in 1968 was so radically different.

The Lessons of 1968

If we continue with the question of learning processes but move forward in time, what are the lessons which can be derived from 1968 and how far might their careful study prevent another Soviet invasion? The obvious lesson is that the leading role of the Party, with democratic centralism as its key organizational principle, must be maintained as the cornerstones of Party rule, thus effectively eliminating the possibility of any substantial reform of political structures in the foreseeable future. The fact that the USSR did not object to the purely economic aspects of the Prague reforms, on the other hand, has signalled to the East Europeans that this is one area of development which could progress without Soviet interference. This trend has led to the widespread belief in Eastern Europe that anything short of capitalism itself could be reintroduced, provided it was done under the leading role of the Communist Party. However, as Wlodzimierz Brus argues in chapter 6 below, the almost inevitable spillover of economic reforms of a more than limited, 'Hungarian' character into the political sphere could produce a repetition of 1968 even without an open commitment by the local leadership to structural political change. Thus East European leaders must be especially cognizant of the risks of implementing economic reforms which threaten the political status quo. But because of the great difficulty of successfully reforming a centrally planned economy without affecting the political controls necessary for its operation, the risks of incurring a negative Soviet reaction remain high, and such leaders might be misled by an over-simplistic extraction of the lessons of 1968.

In the realm of Soviet risk-taking, too, different interpretations have been formulated. While it is apparent that the Soviet Union was willing to, and did in fact, take high risks and incur substantial costs in invading Czechoslovakia, the general lesson to be derived from its action is open to dispute. Some would say that the USSR would come to the 'assistance' of any East European country where socialism was threatened, even if, as already stated, this involved the risk of a third world war. However, a powerful counter-argument has since emerged in Eastern Europe which suggests that the Soviet decision to invade was influenced by two factors – the almost certain knowledge, gained from Western signals, there was virtually no risk of a third world war, and secondly, the calculation that Czechoslovak resistance would be minimal and that the invasion would indeed be welcomed by certain sections of the population. Yugoslavia is one adherent to the belief that the USSR would not have invaded Czechoslovakia if this had risked a global conflict. The Yugoslavs have sought to deter an invasion of their own country by obtaining American security guarantees and making it clear that an invasion of Yugoslavia would escalate to a global confrontation. Romania has also followed a similar policy, based on the conviction that the Soviet Union would be much more cautious about invading Romania if a sure knowledge of Romanian armed resistance was part of the Soviet risk calculation. Equally, Poland's long history of anti-Russian nationalism, combined with its perception in Moscow as a country with a strong martial tradition, has long been used to explain the special understanding extended to Poland's problems by the Soviet leadership. Finally, given Czechoslovakia's special strategic position in Central Europe, it is commonly believed that the Soviet leaders were prepared to pay a higher cost to keep Prague within the bloc than they would be for example if similar problems were to occur in Romania or Bulgaria. As a result, while the USSR may wish the East European régimes to believe that the invasion of Czechoslovakia demonstrated Moscow's absolute commitment to the 'immutability of the borders of socialism', it would appear that several of these régimes believe this commitment to be far from absolute. There is therefore a large and potentially dangerous area of uncertainty in East European perceptions of Moscow's resolve to apply the Brezhnev Doctrine uniformly and absolutely throughout the bloc.

In assessments of the lessons which Western countries derived from the invasion it has often been noted that, although the invasion widened the splits in the international communist movement, its impact on East-West relations was practically negligible. The invasion did act, however, as a kind of *tabula rasa* upon which Ostpolitik and détente – Soviet-style – could be written. It succeeded where the 1967 Karlovy Vary Conference had failed in making it clear to East and West alike that any bridges which might be built across divided Europe would have to pass through Moscow. By interpreting the Soviet action as an attempt not only to stamp out domestic reform in Prague but also to regain control over bloc external policy, it is possible to eliminate much of the contradiction between the act of invasion and the subsequent promotion of East-West contacts. In the first half of the 1970s American recognition of the symbolic relationship between déténte and Soviet hegemony in Eastern Europe was enshrined in the so-called 'Sonnenfeldt doctrine'. More recently, under the influence of President Carter's National Security Advisor Zbigniew Brzezinski, the West has once again begun to pursue a policy which encourages greater East European independence from Soviet dictates.

It remains to be seen whether any of the lessons of 1968 will cast their long shadow over Soviet-East European relations in coming years. It is certainly possible that, in a future crisis, the participants may decide that there are no lessons to be derived from the Prague Spring, occurring as it did in a past decade and under different circumstances, thus proving the wisdom of Hegel's view that 'what experience and history teach is this – that people and governments never have learnt anything from history, or acted on principles deduced from it'. To take Hegel one step further, however, one of the tragedies of the Prague Spring was that Dubcek did try to draw the correct lessons from 1956, while crucially failing to realize that the Soviet decision to invade Czechoslovakia would be, and was, made on an evaluation of costs and risks at the time, and not on the basis of abstract lessons deduced from the Hungarian experience. Thus, by implication, future Soviet actions in Eastern Europe are more likely to be determined not by the experience of the Prague Spring but by the USSR's own assessment of the 'correlation of forces' existing at that moment.

Notes

1 The issue of Soviet–American signalling prior to the invasion of Czechoslovakia is further discussed in Karen Dawisha, 'Soviet Security and the Role of the Military: the 1968 Czechoslovak Crisis', *British Journal of Political Science*, 10/3 (July 1980), pp. 341–64.

2 The publication by *Izvestia* on 12, 13, and 14 July 1968 of the notes which had been exchanged secretly between the USSR and the FRG on the renunciation of the use of force put an end to any improvement in bloc relations with West Germany until 1969. The unusual step of publishing the full texts of the notes also served to allay East German fears of Soviet perfidy. That the USSR should feel compelled to placate the East Germans is itself an indication of the unusually strong position of Ulbricht within the bloc at this time.

3 Address to the Czechoslovak Central Committee plenum, *The Times*, 2 Sept. 1968.

4 *Pravda*, 30 Mar. 1968.

5 *Pravda*, 10 Apr. 1968.

6 *Izvestia*, 23 Apr. 1968.

7 In his press conference in Stockholm on 13 July, *Pravda*, 15 July 1968.

8 Speech by Bil'ak to the 1969 Czechoslovak Central Committee plenum, *Svedestvi*, 10/38 (1970), pp. 284–5.

9 Zdenek Mlynar, *Nachtfrost* (Cologne, Europäische Verlagsanstalt, 1978), p. 301.

10 Brezhnev's remarks were made to a visiting Czechoslovak parliamentary delegation headed by Josef Smrkovsky and reported in an interview with Josef Zednik, the Vice-Chairman of the Czechoslovak National Assembly. CTK in English, 17 June 1968, BBC *Summary of World Broadcasts*, pt II, EE/2799/C/2.

11 *Pravda*, 11 Sept. 1968.

3 The Continuing Validity of the Brezhnev Doctrine
by Peter Summerscale*

THE Czechoslovak events of 1968 are unlikely to be repeated: while the Soviet Union may well encounter further crises of authority in Eastern Europe, the form that these take will doubtless be different. Nevertheless it may be useful to consider the continuing implications of the Brezhnev Doctrine for autonomy in the area. To what extent would the considerations underlying the Brezhnev Doctrine be a determining factor in Soviet policy? And what would be the influence of the rather differently conceived international undertakings in the 1975 Helsinki Final Act? What is the applicability of the doctrine outside the Warsaw Pact? It may also be useful to consider the way in which perceptions about the Brezhnev Doctrine may have altered on the Western side.

Karen Dawisha has argued in her chapter that the Brezhnev Doctrine was a good deal more than an *ex post facto* justification of a clumsily managed exercise in intra-bloc discipline: its main elements were already in place when the Warsaw Pact Five dispatched their forces to Czechoslovakia. In his now celebrated article in *Pravda* of 26 September 1968 Kovalev took matters a stage further by setting out in comprehensive form the reasons for the military intervention. This was complemented shortly afterwards by the authoritative statement of the Soviet position by Leonid Brezhnev in his speech of 12 November 1968 to the Fifth Congress of the Polish United Workers' Party.[1] Kovalev argued that socialism was being undermined in Czechoslovakia by revolutionary forces which were gaining encouragement and support from the 'imperialists'. On the question of sovereignty he contended that:

> There is no doubt that the peoples of the socialist countries and the Communist Parties have and must have freedom to determine

* In the views expressed here the author is writing purely in his personal capacity.

their country's [*sic*] path of development. However, any decision of theirs must damage neither socialism in their own country nor the fundamental interests of the other socialist countries nor the worldwide workers' movement, which is waging a struggle for socialism. This means that every Communist Party is responsible not only to its own people but also to all the socialist countries and to the entire Communist movement. Whoever forgets this in placing sole emphasis on the autonomy and independence of Communist Parties lapses into one-sidedness, shirking his internationalist obligations....

The sovereignty of individual socialist countries cannot be counterposed to the interests of world socialism and the world revolutionary movement.[2]

The common interests of 'world socialism' are elaborated as follows:

People who 'disapprove' of the actions taken by the allied socialist countries ignore the decisive fact that these countries are defending the interests of worldwide socialism and the worldwide revolutionary movement. The socialist system exists in concrete form in individual countries that have their own well-defined state boundaries and develops with regard for the specific attributes of each such country. And no one interferes with concrete measures to perfect the socialist system in various socialist countries. But matters change radically when a danger to socialism itself arises in a country. World socialism as a social system is the common achievement of the working people of all countries, it is indivisible, and its defense is the common cause of all Communists and all progressive people on earth, first and foremost the working people of the socialist countries.[3]

Kovalev's article also included an interesting commentary on international law as conceived by communists. He argued that the type of international law governing relations between socialist states was distinct from international law as conceived by bourgeois theorists:

Those who speak of the 'illegality' of the allied socialist countries' actions in Czechoslovakia forget that in a class society there is and can be no such thing as nonclass law. Laws and the norms of law are subordinated to the laws of the class struggle and the laws of social development. These laws are clearly formulated in the documents jointly adopted by the Communist and Workers' Parties.[4]

In his Warsaw speech, Brezhnev emphasized the crucial importance of a bloc Communist Party's maintaining its 'leadership role':

Experience shows most convincingly the exception and, one might say, decisive importance for successful construction of socialism that attaches to ensuring and constantly consolidating the leadership role of the Communist Party as the most advanced leading, organizing, and directing force in all societal development under socialism. . . .

It is not for nothing that the enemies of socialism have chosen precisely the Communist Party as the prime target for their attacks. It is not for nothing that the revisionists of every stripe who are conductors of bourgeois influence in the workers' movement invariably seek to loosen and weaken the party and undermine its organizational basis – the Leninist principle of democratic centralism – and that they preach relaxation of party discipline. It is not for nothing that they circulate 'theories' stating that the party should 'separate itself' from guidance over the development of society in the areas of economics, state life, culture and so forth. Such a situation, of course, would be very convenient for those who dream of turning development in all these areas backward – in the direction of capitalism.[5]

Brezhnev also argued that the socialist states were subject to 'common natural laws' of socialist construction:

It is common knowledge that the Soviet Union has really done a good deal to strengthen the sovereignty and autonomy of the socialist countries. The C.P.S.U. has always advocated that each socialist country determine the concrete forms of its development along the path of socialism by taking into account the specific nature of their national conditions. But it is well known, comrades, that there are common natural laws of socialist construction, deviation from which could lead to deviation from socialism as such. And when external and internal forces hostile to socialism try to turn the development of a given socialist country in the direction of restoration of the capitalist system, when a threat arises to the cause of socialism in that country – a threat to the security of the socialist commonwealth as a whole – this is no longer merely a problem for that country's people, but a common problem, the concern of all socialist countries.

It is quite clear that an action such as military assistance to a fraternal country to end a threat to the socialist system is an extraordinary measure, dictated by necessity; it can be called forth only by the overt actions of enemies of socialism within the country and beyond its boundaries, actions that create a threat to the common interests of the socialist camp.[6]

Events since 1968 have appeared to demonstrate a strongly felt Soviet need to obtain acceptance, in the East if not in the West, of the main principles underlying the Brezhnev Doctrine. The 1970 Soviet-Czechoslovak Treaty of Friendship and the 1975 Soviet-GDR

Treaty of Friendship (which, interestingly, was signed, just two months after the signature of the Helsinki Final Act) referred to the need to take joint measures to preserve the 'achievements of Socialism'. In the Soviet-GDR treaty the two countries 'declare their preparedness to take the necessary measures to protect and defend the historic achievements of socialism and the security and independence of both countries.' Similar Brezhnev-Doctrine language was incorporated in other bloc agreements – though in none with Romania, which has continued resolutely to oppose the doctrine. It also featured in the 1977 'Brezhnev constitution', where reference is made to the need for 'comradely mutual assistance on the basis of the principles of socialist internationalism'.

The Soviet invasion of Afghanistan has evoked parallels with the Brezhnev Doctrine. While the Soviet leaders have not reasserted the doctrine in explicit terms, Soviet justification of the invasion as a response to its 'internationalist duty' in defending the achievements of socialism is based on the same concept of 'socialist internationalism' as that at the core of the Brezhnev Doctrine. The circumstances were, however, very different from those surrounding the intervention in Czechoslovakia in 1968, and, as will be argued below, these differences are of some importance.

The main significance of the Brezhnev Doctrine lies in the fact that in 1968 the Soviet leadership, with evident strong encouragement from the East Geman and Polish leaders, found it necessary to make a formal redefinition of the limits of autonomy in Eastern Europe. The circumstances of the Soviet military intervention in Hungary in 1956 had already established an important precedent, demonstrating beyond doubt that the Kremlin would not permit the secession of a member of the Warsaw Pact. There is ample evidence that in 1968 Dubcek had this precedent very much at the forefront of his mind, and that he was determined to avoid the obvious danger which any move towards secession from the Warsaw Pact would pose. But the lesson of 1956 was less clear in other areas. In Hungary in that year the Soviet forces had intervened in circumstances in which the Hungarian Communist Party had disintegrated and in which there appeared to be a real and imminent threat of the reinstatement of capitalism.[7] In 1968 the external threat was far more oblique, and the immediate question, at least in the eyes of the Dubcek leadership, was the extent to which a national variation of socialism that diverged substantially from the Soviet model would be acceptable to the Kremlin and to the less secure leaderships elsewhere in Eastern Europe.

Between Stalin's death in 1953 and the events of 1968 there was considerable ambiguity in the Soviet position regarding possible variations in national approaches to the development of socialism. The 1955 Belgrade Declaration recognized 'differences of concrete forms' of socialist development. In Khrushchev's speech at the XX Party Congress, the Soviet Union recognized the legitimacy of 'separate roads to socialism' but, as was evident from the subsequent polemics with Yugoslavia, it did so with misgivings and reservations, and was unwilling to accept that this implied the abandonment of the Soviet Union's leading role in the communist movement.[8] The Soviet leaders were particularly concerned to ensure that the communist parties of the Warsaw Pact states did not conclude from Moscow's grudging acceptance of Yugoslavia as a socialist state that the Yugoslav approach was appropriate elsewhere in Eastern Europe.

The Brezhnev leadership's attempt, since the spring of 1968, to redefine the limits of autonomy, has also contained a fair measure of ambiguity. The main message of the Brezhnev Doctrine has been that the borders of the socialist commonwealth are inviolable and that its members have common interests and obligations towards one another; as stated by Brezhnev in his Warsaw speech, it is the common concern of socialist countries to determine whether in any given country there exists a risk of 'deviation' from the 'common natural laws of socialist construction', which might risk the restoration of the capitalist system. But these 'common natural laws' have themselves never been spelt out. Similarly, no clear explanation has been offered of the process by which members of the socialist commonwealth are to determine whether a 'deviation' may be taking place. The one entirely clear lesson of the events in Czechoslovakia was that in the view of the Soviet Union and of the four other Warsaw Pact countries which joined in the invasion, the 'undermining of the leading role of the Communist Party' was a cardinal sin.[9] Less explicitly stated, but also evident, was that a free press which printed frank criticism of the practices and policies of other Warsaw Pact states was considered unacceptable. It was also obvious that the Dubcek régime's assertion of an independent foreign policy in relation to Western Europe was viewed with disfavour.[10] Not altogether surprisingly, however, no precise definitions of the limits of tolerance were offered on points such as these, either in 1968 or in succeeding years. Despite the implication that any decision to intervene in fraternal countries should be a collective responsibility, there seems little doubt that the decisive factor will be the judgement of the Soviet leaders as to whether vital Soviet interests are threatened.

Occurrences since 1968 have not dispelled the ambiguities. Of some interest was the Soviet response to events in Poland in December 1970 when a change of leadership was effected following workers' riots on the Baltic seaboard. The Soviet leaders were on this occasion prepared to allow the Polish Central Committee to work out its own solution, and to throw their weight quickly behind the new Gierek/Jaroszewicz leadership once Gomulka had been forced out. Soviet troops in Poland were confined to barracks throughout the crisis. The Soviet leaders resisted the temptation (to which they had readily succumbed at the time of the East German riots in 1953 and the Polish strikes in 1956) to present the riots as the work of counter-revolutionaries. Instead, they appear to have come to the conclusion that Gomulka's handling of events had been somewhat inept, and that a change of leadership offered a way out of the crisis. Although there is no evidence of direct Soviet intervention in the affairs of the Polish Central Committee, the point has rightly been made that Soviet failure to support Gomulka in itself had an important influence on the outcome.[11]

The Soviet Union reacted with similar restraint in 1976 when Poland underwent a second crisis sparked off by workers' disturbances. On both occasions it supplied economic aid promptly in order to assist in the tasks facing the Gierek leadership. However, neither of these episodes presented the magnitude of the threat perceived by the Soviet Union to exist in Czechoslovakia in 1968, since they did not involve experimentation with radically new forms of socialism.

The third crisis which Poland experienced in the summer of 1980 was more serious in that the strikers who brought the Gdansk shipyards to a halt included a number of patently political points among their demands. The recognition they won of the right to form trade unions which are independent of control by the Polish United Workers' Party is something which, if preserved, could have the most far-reaching implications. The Soviet reaction to events, while restrained, betrayed a number of signs of disquiet, including the *Pravda* editorial of 2 September which accused the strikers of threatening the interests of the Polish state and of undermining socialism. The language, which linked the strikers with 'anti-socialist' elements supported by Poland's enemies from outside, was reminiscent of the warnings issued to the Czechoslovaks in 1968. However, it was evident that the strikers and the Workers' Defence Committee (KOR), as well as the Polish government, were throughout sensitive to the implications of the Brezhnev Doctrine; in a press conference after release from prison, the KOR leader Kuron spoke of the 'limits set by Soviet tanks'.[12] The recognition, in the agreement which the Gdansk strikers concluded with the government, of the leading role of the Communist Party, and of the need to preserve Poland's alliances, was important in this context.

Soviet calculations may also have been influenced by the fact that there were influential elements within the Polish United Workers' Party favouring reform. But perhaps most important is Soviet realization of the immense problems which any attempt to achieve 'normalization' through military intervention would create, especially in response to pressure from within the working class, in a country as fiercely nationalistic as Poland. The Polish situation remains volatile and potentially explosive, and much will clearly depend on the degree of restraint exercised on all sides.

The Soviet Union has faced a different type of problem in dealing with the maverick behaviour of Ceausescu's Romania. The Romanians have often publicly differed with the USSR on foreign policy and defence issues. Romania broke ranks in the bloc in 1964 by adopting an independent position in the dispute with China, and in 1967 both by establishing diplomatic relations with the Federal Republic of Germany before other Pact states had done so, and by maintaining diplomatic relations with Israel notwithstanding the 1967 Arab-Israel war. Since then she has continued to cultivate close relations with China, while also developing a special relationship with Yugoslavia. For the Soviet Union, perhaps the most wounding Romanian action was Ceausescu's public denunciation of the invasion of Czechoslovakia, delivered just after this took place. In the world communist movement, Romania has joined forces with the Eurocommunists and others in blocking attempts to gain acceptance for the 'leading role' of the Communist Party of the Soviet Union. In the defence field, Romania has refused to participate in joint Warsaw Pact manoeuvres, and has frustrated Soviet attempts, e.g. in Budapest in March 1969, to engage the Warsaw Pact in the dispute with China.[13] More recently, in November 1978, Romania refused to commit herself to an increase in defence spending as requested by the USSR. On that occasion she again reportedly opposed Soviet attempts to engage the Warsaw Pact against China (this time through co-ordinated aid to Vietnam). In 1980 the Romanian industrial co-operation agreement with the EEC represented a new gesture of individualism.

However, Romania has stopped short of adopting positions which have seriously threatened basic Soviet security concerns in Europe. Romania's less than orthodox approach on some defence issues has been facilitated by the fact that she is outside the strategically vital 'northern tier'. The Romanians have also shown sensitivity to Soviet *amour propre*, and have sought to avoid actions which directly challenge Soviet prestige. Still more important, the authoritarian mould of Romanian internal policies has posed no challenge to the authority of the Soviet model of communism; it may indeed be held to present the least danger from any bloc member state. At no time has the authority of the Romanian Communist Party appeared to be seriously at risk.

The Romanians have in fact balanced their independent posture in the World Communist Movement with at least the trappings of ideological conformity with the WTO fraternal states, for example through participation in conferences of representatives of Communist Party Central Committees. Romanian recalcitrance had been hurtful to the USSR in its periodic impairment of smooth co-ordination within the Warsaw Pact apparatus. However, Romania has remained within the WTO, and has not challenged the principle that there should be close consultation between the fraternal parties and governments. Similarly, although the Romanians have on not a few occasions blocked Soviet attempts, and also attempts by other East European states, to deepen CMEA integration,[14] they have not questioned the utility of CMEA as such. Romania was able to secure various concessions in the course of negotiation of the 1971 CMEA 'Comprehensive Programme for Integration'; these included the recognition of the Romanian interpretation of state sovereignty, and the rights of the less developed states. But the fact of Romania's participation in this major programme of integration must itself be a source of satisfaction to the Soviet Union, given especially that Romania had hitherto opposed the very principle of integration.

One major lesson which the Kremlin has evidently learnt is the value of close and frequent contact between representatives of bloc countries as a way of monitoring trends within bloc parties. Since 1968 the USSR has arranged matters so that there are now more frequent meetings at all levels within the WTO. Especially valuable have been the now regular meetings of the Political Consultative Committee. Also important have been the annual meetings of Pact leaders with Brezhnev in the Crimea. The Soviet leaders probably feel considerably more confident today than they did in 1968 about their ability to understand trends of thought – and also the impact of personalities – within the bloc. Conversely, other bloc leaders probably have more acute awareness of Soviet preoccupations and changing priorities.

Ambiguities notwithstanding, the Kremlin may not be unrealistic if it assesses that the 'rules of the game' which apply to the limits of autonomy and divergence are today better understood in Eastern Europe than in 1968. The circumstances of the 1968 intervention indicated clearly enough that (a) the Soviet Union would not tolerate within the Warsaw Pact the development of a new model of socialism which substantially departed from its own, and (b) when it came to justifying intervention to correct such a departure the determining factor should be the collective wisdom of the 'socialist commonwealth' (in the articulation of which the Soviet Union can naturally expect to wield considerable influence). Since 1968 there has been nothing to suggest that Soviet thinking on either of these points has significantly altered. As regards economic policy, Soviet tolerance of a certain diversity of economic policy – as evidenced in the Hungarian New Economic Mechanism – has suggested that this is an area where the limits of tolerance may be more flexible (see the essay by Wlodziemierz Brus, below). But it is probably also significant that the Hungarian régime has been at pains to ensure that economic reform is not seen as the precursor to major political change: the economic has been carefully insulated from the political. The Polish leadership, which must take into account the politically motivated nature of some of the demands in Poland for economic reform, may reckon that it would be sailing closer to the wind if it were to make major concessions in this area.

Although it can be argued that the Soviet intervention in Afghanistan represents an extension of the Brezhnev Doctrine beyond the confines of Europe, the significance of this adventure for Soviet policy towards Eastern Europe should not be exaggerated. The intervention in Afghanistan is a Soviet and in no sense a collective Warsaw Pact operation. The main justification advanced by the Russians in international fora has been that they were fulfilling treaty obligations, in response to a direct request for Soviet assistance; the invocation of 'socialist internationalist' responsibilities may have been primarily designed for the ears of communist parties who were beginning to question the degree of Moscow's commitment to the cause of national liberation movements.[15] There is, however, a clear parallel with both Hungary in 1956 and Czechoslovakia in 1968 in the sense that in each of these cases military force was employed to forestall developments which it was feared would lead to the overthrow of a loyalist communist régime. Perhaps the most interesting aspect of the Afghan affair has been the evidence of continuing Soviet readiness to employ military force as an instrument of policy, at any rate in areas close to Soviet borders, notwithstanding the strong reactions likely to be aroused not only in the Western world but also amongst many world communist parties and amongst the non-aligned. In this context the major novelty of Afghanistan is that the Soviet Union intervened there to preserve a gain of socialism of less than two years' standing, whereas in the other two cases intervention was in order to maintain control in an area already widely accepted as being a special Soviet preserve.

It is in any event unlikely that in launching its intervention in Afghanistan, the Soviet Union saw more than marginal relevance to Eastern Europe. Its reinvocation of the Leninist principle of proletarian socialist internationalism will have come as little surprise to other communist parties, and can hardly in itself be held to betoken a new departure in Soviet attitudes towards the Eastern European camp, or towards Yugoslavia. Within the former, the emphasis remains on a common responsibility to preserve socialism against the intrigues of imperialism. Yugoslavia is a special case, given especially that Western states have adopted a deterrent posture contrasting with their more resigned approach to the rest of Eastern Europe. While the ambiguities of the Brezhnev Doctrine are such that it could be applied with respect to any 'socialist' state, Soviet policy is in practice likely to be much influenced by the Western attitudes, together with Yugoslavia's standing in the non-aligned group.

Similar considerations apply to the possibility of the Brezhnev Doctrine's being invoked in the case of Albania. Albania's non-membership of the Warsaw Pact is one such factor. Another is that

Western countries are likely to be extremely sensitive to any risk that the Soviet Union might, by intervening in Albania, aim to acquire for itself port facilities in the Adriatic. So long at least as Yugoslavia retains its non-aligned status there can be no doubt that she would strongly oppose the possibility of Soviet intervention in Albania, and this would constitute a further deterrent to military action.

The Soviet Union will in addition, both in the cases of Yugoslavia and Albania and in its application of the Brezhnev Doctrine within the Pact itself, need to take account of the implications of the signature of the Helsinki Final Act in August 1975. The Declaration of Principles in the Final Act contains a number of principles, most notably those on Sovereign Equality, Refraining from the Threat or Use of Force, and Non-Intervention in Internal Affairs, which are, to put it at its lowest, difficult to reconcile with the Brezhnev Doctrine (at any rate in the Western view, shared by the neutrals and the non-aligned participating states in the CSCE, and also by Romania). Principle VI on Non-Intervention contains the specifically anti-Brezhnev Doctrine stipulation that it shall apply to all signatory states 'irrespective of their mutual relations'. The Soviet Union for its part has attempted to place a rather different construction on this Principle, arguing that it should be regarded as primarily a prohibition on criticism of internal practices of the governments of the signatory states (allegedly a persistent Western offence). The Soviet Union is, however, well enough aware of the views of Western states and of others, including Romania. It is also aware that there is a strong likelihood that the armed intervention in Afghanistan will be raised during the next review of the implementation of the Final Act, due to take place in Madrid at the beginning of November 1980.[16]

Soviet signature of the Final Act did not of course signify the abandonment of the Soviet Union's determination to maintain control of the East European hinterland. But it does constitute a new constraint on Soviet policy in Europe that is likely to exert a certain influence on Soviet policy-makers. Legalistic arguments about interpretation of the Final Act, which is not legally binding but rather a set of undertakings, may not carry much weight with policy-makers. But what is incontestable is that a repetition of the 1968 experience would provide fresh arguments for those in the West who question the Soviet Union's sincerity in applying the Helsinki principles, and hence its commitment to détente on terms acceptable to the West.

While such a repetition might have less impact on US-Soviet relations than Afghanistan has had, the impact in Europe would probably be substantial.

The Soviet Union would again, as in 1968, need to take account of likely reactions in the world communist movement. Further damage would almost certainly ensue if collective pressures were brought to bear on a Communist Party leadership striving to develop an independent road to socialism. But this may not be a decisive consideration. The ground lost in 1968 is not likely to be retrieved, whether or not there are new armed or other interventions, and the Soviet Union will doubtless remain more concerned about its relations with Eastern European communist parties than about its popularity with West European communists who (apart from the Chinese) have so far been the main trouble-makers. If radically new attitudes were to emerge within the East European leaderships, this would seem likely to have a greater impact on Soviet thinking.

The Soviet leaders would also have to reckon with the possibility that Western countries might in the future adopt a rather higher profile than that adopted in 1968. The American attitude in 1968 was coloured by its preoccupation with Vietnam. A US administration today or in the foreseeable future would probably not be any more prepared than in 1968 to use physical means to try to deter Soviet armed intervention in Eastern Europe. But the United States and other Western states might today be more disposed to try, by diplomatic means, and conceivably by economic sanctions, to dissuade the Soviet Union from contemplating overt intervention that would infringe the sovereignty of an East European state. The Helsinki Final Act would provide justification for discussion with the Soviet government on this issue (even though the latter would doubtless try to represent this as interference in internal Soviet bloc affairs). However, the Afghanistan precedent would appear to offer little encouragement for the belief that diplomatic action, even when supported by economic sanctions, is likely to have a decisive – or early – effect.

The Soviet Union resorted to force in 1968 with considerable reluctance. An important factor in its attitude at that time is likely to have been the assessment that it would encounter minimal armed resistance in Czechoslovakia. In future contingencies it seems probable that the Soviet Union will attach considerable importance to this aspect. If there were a strong prospect of encountering armed resistance, which might result in substantial casualties, this would strengthen the hands of those in the Soviet establishment counselling caution. But the use of military force is not a necessary component of the Brezhnev Doctrine but rather a measure of possible last resort. The doctrine itself could still be invoked in order to apply collective pressure of a non-military kind, e.g. in the economic field.

The Romanian attitude continues to pose some awkward problems. There are firstly the obvious implications of repeated Romanian declarations of readiness to fight to defend Romanian national territory. But perhaps more important is Romania's specific rejection of the view – which appears still to be a basic tenet of Soviet policy – that the Warsaw Pact should perform a policing role in Eastern Europe. The Romanians consider that the Pact's role should be confined to countering the threat of military aggression from the West. The events of 1968 showed that the Russians were prepared to ignore Romanian sensibilities in a crunch and to mount an intervention in the name of the Warsaw Pact despite Romania's non-participation and indeed opposition. But this is clearly an uncomfortable position to have to adopt.

Given the magnitude of the constraints, there is clearly every incentive for the Soviet Union to avoid the need for further military intervention on the 1968 pattern. It also has incentive to avoid other forms of intervention which might attract international publicity and be represented as intervention in internal affairs in the definition of Principle VI of the Helsinki Final Act. The Soviet leaders may derive a degree of encouragement from the fact that, in addition to the improvement in the consultative mechanisms of the Warsaw Pact, the formal definition of the rules of the game in the Brezhnev Doctrine was not put to any serious test in the twelve years between 1968 and the events in Poland in the summer of 1980. Comfort may also be found in the reflection that (from a Soviet viewpoint) the Prague events came close in a number of respects to constituting a 'worst-case' scenario; against all odds, the Dubcek leadership maintained unity in the face of mounting pressures, and it was impossible plausibly to present the intervention as response to a request for help even from a faction of the leadership. It might be thought to be less difficult to defend a situation in which a threatened leadership sought Warsaw Pact intervention. If, alternatively, intervention were to be contemplated to resolve a struggle between competing factions (as might have happened in Poland in 1956 if Khrushchev had opted for a less statesmanlike approach), this would be poorly received in many quarters but might not give rise to the same degree of protest as was encountered in 1968.

The major post-war crises in Eastern Europe (in 1956 and 1968) occurred not long after a change of leadership in the Soviet Union. The Brezhnev leadership has, since 1968, developed a policy towards Eastern Europe, with the Brezhnev Doctrine its sheet anchor if not its touchstone, in which cohesion and integration are balanced with a certain degree of diversity. So far this policy may be claimed to have enjoyed a measure of success, although positions adopted by Romania have posed problems for the Soviet Union, and the events in Poland in the summer of 1980 have demonstrated the danger that spontaneous developments within a bloc country can spark a crisis without warning.

It will be interesting to see whether a post-Brezhnev leadership is disposed further to extend the limits of tolerance or whether it develops a more restrictive interpretation. The doctrine is in fact personally identified with Brezhnev only outside the Soviet Union, and there seems little reason to doubt that it will survive his death. It could be that new disturbances in Eastern Europe following the advent of a post-Brezhnev leadership will give rise to a new doctrine on the limits of sovereignty. At the time of writing, however, there is little to suggest that Eastern Europe is an area where a new generation of Soviet leaders will wish to make early innovations. What seems most probable is that, with or without Brezhnev at the helm, the essential elements in the Brezhnev Doctrine may still have quite a few years' life as a convenient justification for the preponderance of Soviet influence within the bloc, and as a way of ensuring that its members march at least roughly in step. In the actual formation of policy the Soviet leaders will doubtless continue to be influenced above all by practical rather than doctrinal considerations; in this respect the Brezhnev Doctrine may be of marginal importance. But it will serve as a continuing reminder of the preparedness of the Soviet Union to use force – where force seems likely to be successful – if it believes that its essential interests are threatened.

Notes
1   Text in *Pravda*, 13 Nov. 1968.

2 *Pravda*, 26 Sept. 1968: *The Current Digest of the Soviet Press (CDSP)*, 16 Oct. 1968, p. 10.

3 Ibid., p. 11.

4 Ibid., p. 12.

5 *Pravda*, 13 Nov. 1968: *CDSP*, 4 Dec. 1968, p. 3.

6 Ibid., p. 4.

7 Significantly, Tito himself accepted the existence of such a threat and reluctantly concluded that although the first Soviet intervention in Hungary had been mistaken, the second could not have been avoided. Veljko Micunovic, *Moscow Diary*, trans. David Floyd (London, Chatto & Windus, 1980), p. 135.

8 Boris Meissner has shown that, at the time of the Khrushchev speech, Suslov took a highly restrictive view of the scope for independent development. Meissner, *The Brezhnev Doctrine* (Kansas City, Mo., Park College, 1970), pp. 15–16.

9 Brezhnev's speech at the 5th Congress of the Polish United Workers Party on 12 Nov. 1968, quoted in *Pravda*, 13 Nov. 1968. As stated in this speech, the need to maintain the Party's leading role had earlier been spelt out in the Warsaw letter to the Czechoslovak Communist Party one month before the invasion. *Pravda*, 18 July 1968.

10 It is worth recalling that a large part of Kovalev's well-known *apologia* for the invasion concentrated on the alleged threat that Czechoslovakia was allowing itself to be sucked into the Western orbit. *Pravda*, 26 Sept. 1968.

11 Z. A. Pelczynski in A. Bromke and J. W. Strong, eds., *Gierek's Poland* (New York, Praeger, 1973), pp. 16–23.

12 See e.g. *The Daily Telegraph* report of 2 Sept. 1980.

13 The crucial 1969 events are well described in Thomas W. Wolfe's *Soviet Power and Europe, 1945–1970* (Baltimore, Md, and London, Johns Hopkins Press for the Rand Corporation, 1970), pp. 496–8.

14 The most notable Romanian obstruction was the blocking in 1962–4 of Khrushchev's attempt to introduce supranational planning into CMEA. M. Kaser, *Comecon: Integration Problems of the Planned Economies*, 2nd edn (London, OUP for Royal Institute of International Affairs, 1967), pp. 92–129.

15 Such an inference can be drawn from the fact that this argument has appeared primarily in Marxist journals such as *New Times*, intended for this type of audience. See in particular *New Times*, no. 3 of Feb. 1980.

16 Although Afghanistan is of course outside Europe and is not a CSCE participating state, the issue can be legitimately raised in CSCE discussions in the context of the provision (at the end of Principle X in the Declaration of Principles) stating the participating states' 'intention to conduct their relations with all other States in the spirit of the principles contained in the present declaration'.

4 New Developments in Intra-bloc Relations in Historical Perspective
by Eberhard Schulz

A New Pattern after Six Phases of 'Normal' Intra-bloc Contradictions?

EARLY in 1980 there evolved a situation in which, for the first time since World War II, the maintenance of a minimum of East–West contacts was left to the medium-rank powers in Europe. This unexpected phenomenon cannot be explained by the assumption that states which had hitherto been political dwarfs had changed into giants. It derived from the apparent inability of the two superpowers to manage the crisis following the Soviet invasion of Afghanistan. This crisis was perceived by the Central European states as a threat to their very existence, and it seemed to be caused by mutual misperceptions and by domestic trouble in Moscow and Washington rather than by the sudden emergence of an unbridgeable contradiction in objective national interests between the two superpowers.

As far as West Europeans were concerned, the tendency of some governments to stress the parallelism of vital interests in East and West Europe was not caused, contrary to the widespread view in Washington, either by anti-Americanism or by any desire to shift the disadvantageous consequences of punishing the Russians on to the transatlantic ally, thus protecting the benefits Europe had derived from détente. Nor was there any proclivity towards neutralization or 'finlandization', least of all on the part of the West Germans; they are the most exposed to military threats by virtue of their geographical position and are more immunized against communist temptations than their European allies owing to the fact that one-third of the German nation is under Soviet domination. Rather, the Europeans mostly felt that the North–South dimension of the conflicts in South Asia and the Middle East was underestimated in Washington. They were also at odds with the White House view that punitive actions or pressure might change Soviet attitudes and deter future Soviet military intervention rather than produce actions directed against vulnerable points on the Western side, such as West Berlin.

It was by no means surprising that the cautious and subtle diplomacy, pursued notably by the West Germans in this situation, met with keen interest in Eastern Europe, though not yet in the Kremlin. The divergence of attitudes within the Warsaw Pact was clearly discernible. Moscow maintained (at least in private conversations) that it had to remove instability in a sensitive region that was adjacent to its own territory and exposed to dangerous collusion by Peking and Washington, and that the Pentagon would have taken similar action if a communist *coup* had been imminent in Mexico. Any legitimate American interest was strictly denied by Soviet officials, who suggested that it was up to Washington to ratify the SALT II agreement and to put an end to the hysterical hostility towards the Soviet Union.

The first reaction of the East Europeans to the Soviet intervention in Afghanistan was – without exception – perplexity. This was followed by a strong apprehension lest a combination of Soviet stubbornness and American 'overreaction' might lead to a global armed conflict or at least to economic sanctions which might hit their economies in an extremely critical phase when economic growth in their countries could not keep pace with booming consumer demand. The more or less covert attempts by the East Europeans to signal their wish to maintain or even expand their relations with the West were not matched by any comparable Soviet flexibility. While some observers in the West predicted Soviet endeavours to evade sanctions by striving for 'business as usual' with the West or at least by using other Warsaw Pact members as proxies for the same purpose, the Kremlin leaders appeared unable to make any move. No instructions were given to the East Europeans except that they were to take the Soviet side in their propaganda. This demand they had – in various degrees – to comply with.

In this situation the East European leaderships tried to keep a low profile. It was the East German state which reversed its normal attitude of acting as the spearhead of the Warsaw Pact against the West. Surprisingly the Soviet ambassador to East Berlin, Pyotr Abrasimov, in an interview on West German television on 6 February, did not *expressis verbis* exclude a meeting between the two German leaders Schmidt and Honecker which had previously been scheduled for the end of February. When this meeting eventually had to be postponed a couple of weeks later by a telephone conversation between Schmidt and Honecker after the GDR foreign minister Oskar Fischer had met his Soviet colleague Andrei Gromyko in Moscow, this was done by the East Germans in unusually conciliatory terms. In striking contrast to his often very harsh statements, Abrasimov in his interview abstained from any threats against West Berlin. When in early March the Soviet Consulate General in West Berlin was hit by a bomb the Soviet government came out with only a mild protest.

From the invasion of Afghanistan until Gromyko's visit to Paris in April 1980 the USSR sought to ban high-level contacts between its allies and the West. While Hungary and Czechoslovakia, for example, acceded to this pressure, the East Germans seemed to be eager even to intensify communication with the West German side. One might speculate that the Soviet Union eventually let them pursue this aim when the East Germans argued that the Warsaw Pact could thereby exploit and possibly widen the apparent rift in the Western alliance. But Soviet officials made it plain in private talks that the East Germans (this time, apparently, largely in accord with am- bassador Abrasimov) had annoyed the Kremlin leaders by their insistence on the necessity to maintain their relations with the West and by urging the Russians to do likewise. Some people within the Soviet leadership are even reported to have become suspicious of Honecker for his (from their point of view) excessively normal be- haviour towards Helmut Schmidt. So the East German government gladly seized the opportunity to protest against the 'interference in the internal affairs of the sovereign GDR' when the NATO foreign ministers (in Ankara) for the first time in several years mentioned the German problem in their official communiqué. This protest was designed to signal to Moscow, to their East European partners, and to the whole world that the East German wish to maintain relations with the West, and the FRG in particular, had nothing in common with any readiness to talk about German reunification and that the East Berlin leadership was aware of the dangers implied in its unusual initiatives towards the West. Obviously the East German leaders did not wish to strain Moscow's indulgence and to raise suspicions amongst their East European neighbours.

Looking back at thirty-five years of Soviet predominance in Eastern Europe, one may say that the development of intra-bloc relations there has been shaped by three main factors: Russian political culture; the German question, including the stance the West took towards this problem; and – at least in the initial phase – Tito's aspirations for hegemony in South-east Europe. While Yugoslavia's heresy made itself felt in Eastern Europe time and again, the immediate danger to Soviet predominance was removed when Yugoslavia was ousted from the 'socialist camp' in 1948.

The general framework of long-term East European developments is, no doubt, primarily defined by the lack of Soviet flexibility and the cleavage between Russian and East European political cultures. But, regarding the short-term moves, one is struck by the strong impact Western policies have had on intra-bloc relationships in Eastern Central Europe (i.e. the GDR, Poland, Czechoslovakia, and Hungary as opposed to the Balkan nations, which largely followed different policies). The emerging North Atlantic Treaty Organization and the various integration processes in Western Europe were inevitably mirrored or answered by programmes and initiatives in Eastern Europe, but it was the FRG's political doctrines which were considered by the East Europeans as the factor primarily shaping their conception of their national interest within the framework of the hegemonial sphere of the Soviet Union. So, while general lines were drawn by historical traditions, political cultures, and systemic forces, the changing patterns after a first phase of consolidation may be explained to a considerable extent by moves or developments in the West in the different phases (which partially overlap).

From this point of view the following six phases may be discerned up to 1979. *The first phase: 1944–9.* This is the period of communist takeover in the Central and South-east European countries (including the Eastern part of Germany) under Moscow's auspices, and of the elimination of Western influence (including that of former communist emigrés in Western countries) and of Tito's sympathizers. *The second phase: 1949–55.* Full dependency on Stalin's Soviet Union and unchallenged Soviet domination were established, though these tended to decrease after the elimination of Beria and his closest collaborators in the summer of 1953. There were also the destabilizing effects of Soviet overtures towards Bonn between March 1952 and September 1955 to prevent the rearmament of the FRG, and of Khrushchev's reconciliation with Tito in summer 1955. *The third phase: 1955–64.* Following the decisions on a West German defence contribution in 1955, cautious signals came from Prague, Warsaw, and Budapest towards Bonn at the expense of East Berlin. These were ignored or misinterpreted by the West, and paralleled by Soviet attempts to come to terms with Bonn between 1955 and 1964, and by the alarming consequences of Khrushchev's zigzag course in ideological and international affairs (culminating in the invasion of Hungary). *The fourth phase: 1964–9.* During this period Moscow (heavily instigated by East Berlin) sought increasingly to apply the Ulbricht Doctrine as a wall against the undermining of East European 'monolithism' and the isolation of the GDR by Schröder's 'Eastern policy of small steps' after his establishing crypto-diplomatic trade missions in Warsaw, Budapest, Bucharest, and Sofia. This line of Soviet policy was initiated with Khrushchev's demotion; was fully exercised after the resumption of diplomatic relations between Bucharest and Bonn in 1966–7; and was most drastically enforced by the execution of the Brezhnev Doctrine against Czechoslovakia till the end of the sixties. *The fifth phase: 1969–74.* There was a far-reaching convergence of East European and Soviet objective interests (but not along the lines preferred by Ulbricht) during the early phase of Richard Nixon's SALT policy and Willy Brandt's 'new Ostpolitik' from 1969–70 until 1973–4. In both of these Western policies there was a 'Sonnenfeldtian' element: not only with respect to guaranteeing the territorial *status quo* in Central Europe, but also, implicitly, with respect to accepting the political hegemony of the Soviet Union over its buffer zone. This enabled the East Europeans (with the exception of Czechoslovakia) to enlarge their relations with the West while lessening their dependence on the Soviet Union. *The sixth phase: 1974–9.* In this most recent period East European dependence on the Soviet Union re-emerged for a number of reasons: contradictions in the FRG's Ostpolitik, unfortunate developments for the East Europeans in the world market (indebtedness, insufficient exports, deteriorating terms of trade), and, last but not least, destabilizing effects arising from détente and notably from the Final Act of the CSCE (human rights, basket 3) and its follow-up process and from MBFR.

The Three Stages on which Relations are Played

Before elaborating a little more on the characteristics of those phases it seems to be in order briefly to note some basic features which underlie the fabric of intra-bloc relations. It goes without saying that we have to discuss three different stages where relations take place. The first is the multilateral network of the WTO and CMEA; the second is the threads connecting the single countries, with the Russian spider in the centre; and the third consists of the bilateral links between the smaller members of the 'socialist camp'.

It would certainly be naive to take the notion of the new 'brotherly' quality of 'socialist' international relations, based on the principle of 'proletarian internationalism', too seriously, but it is exactly the common ideological and organizational heritage of the nineteenth and early twentieth centuries' workers movement which tied the first generations of East European leaders together. Most of the old communists from Georgi Dimitrov to Walter Ulbricht had been persecuted by the bourgeois authorities and worked together in the framework of the Comintern under Stalin's immediate supervision. While they had lost their faith in the goodness of communism and become cynics long ago, during the purges or afterwards, they had preserved a feeling of traditional loyalty and comradeship which sometimes even grew sentimental when they grew old. None of them believed any more in the sole truth of the holy ideological dogma; but their perceptions of the outside world – shaped by isolation in the prison of their bourgeois nation-state or in the 'internationalist' microcosmos of the closed Russian society and confirmed by the ban imposed upon them by the public opinion of the 'free world' – were not open to change any more. They knew that their legitimacy lacked strong roots in their nations and that they therefore had to rely for their survival (politically as well as physically) on Soviet power. None of them, with the sole exception of Josip Broz Tito (and some years later the Albanian Enver Hoxha, who was sheltered against Soviet interference by Yugoslavia but threatened by Tito's hegemonic ambitions), dared to challenge the Muscovite order.

In striking contrast to the 'internationalist' prescriptions of Marxism-Leninism, each of the East European leaders began, after their take-over, to construct, copying the Russian model, an autarkic 'socialist' nation secluded from their brother-states, and it took two decades for CMEA after its formal foundation in 1949 to develop meaningful economic links between the member states. For the first generation of communist leaders the 'socialist camp' remained compartmentalized. The official notion of 'monolithic unity' which was uncritically accepted in Western public opinion had in fact nothing in common with reality except Soviet domination and scarcely differentiated hostility from the West.

The extent of political leeway varied considerably among the different member states and in general according to the prevailing political atmosphere. Josef Stalin had an obvious preference for relying on the Soviet army, which was widely deployed in Eastern Europe. At the same time, however, he took advantage of a close network of police, intelligence, 'political advisors', and, last but not least, of his ambassadors who could in their capacity as members of the Central Committee of the CPSU make use of the party channels leading independently from the diplomatic bureaucracy immediately to the power centre in the Kremlin. Whatever freedom of manoeuvre East European leaders enjoyed they were not allowed to admit counter-revolution, to neglect the 'principle of democratic centralism', which means the communist authoritarian system, or to leave the 'socialist community'. Moreover they had to abstain from forming within the camp sub-groups of member states in which the Soviet Union was not represented.

This scenario has not fundamentally changed. The present generation of East European communist leaders has become more national, and while multilateral co-ordination at first sight seems to dominate the scene now, this is in reality an artificial or artistic stage where real life is presented by actors who do not decide the course the drama takes. All meaningful decisions are prepared bilaterally between the Kremlin and the respective national leadership behind the multilateral scene. This applies to such important acts as meetings of high-level party functionaries, e.g. secretaries of the Central Committees, as well as for the military activities of the WTO.

When the Kremlin leaders, exceptionally, concede a really multilateral preparation and arrangement of a conference – as they did in view of strong opposition to the usual Stalinist procedure for the conference of twenty-nine European communist parties in East Berlin in 1976, which was convened to adopt a common strategy against the West and confirm the leading role of the CPSU – the unanimous approval of Moscow's point of view will not be reached. This is what happened in East Berlin in spite of preparatory negotiations of several committees over a period of twenty months. In East Berlin the autonomous communist parties enforced the omission of the notion of 'proletarian internationalism' since the Soviets were claiming the right to decide upon when, how, and against whom the 'fraternal aid' was to be provided. The Kremlin leaders' contempt for the decisions of such conferences (decisions taken, in the East Berlin case, after numerous rounds of painful and protracted negotiations) was shown by the head of the Soviet delegation while he was still in East Berlin: he used the disputed term as if it had in fact been adopted by all participating parties. A somewhat different pattern prevails in the CMEA, where most decisions are taken on a bilateral basis.

In sum, one can maintain that as a rule it is not in the multilateral scene that important political problems are decided. Issues of crucial significance are tackled in bilateral talks with the Kremlin. The multilateral activities of the bloc countries are devoid of political substance and remain primarily ceremonial performances in a Byzantine style, which is, curiously enough, taken extremely seriously by the actors – probably because this offers them some kind of compensation and satisfaction for lacking freedom of political manoeuvre. The multilateral stage contains, however, a certain political weight in so far as it provides – at least theoretically – part of the legitimation for the communist ruling élites because one of the basic features of Marxist-Leninist ideology is the promise of a true 'proletarian internationalism' exercised by the 'vanguard of the working class' and it must, therefore, not be sacrificed, if only to preserve a Potemkin façade.

The second stage is the most important one. From the very beginning Stalin was eager to manage bloc cohesion by using Soviet national means and bilateral ties. But he did not interfere very much with the mutual relations of the smaller states. Suffice it to mention that the Poles finally refrained from their territorial claims against Czechoslovakia only in 1958. Stalin strictly vetoed any multilateral venture which was not fully controlled by the Kremlin, such as the Dimitrov-Tito project of a Balkan federation, and his successors have kept to his approach. This does not, however, mean that the Soviet leaders have always been strong enough simply to impose their will on their smaller partners. The East European communists do have a certain political leeway, and it depends largely on their skills how much they can make use of it below the final threshold of arousing concern with the Kremlin leaders about their vital interest – a threshold which Alexander Dubcek clearly, if unwillingly and, indeed, unconsciously, transgressed. This stage has been dealt with lucidly in other papers and will not be elaborated here in detail.

The most interesting insights into the fabric of 'socialist internationalism' are provided by the third stage. While anxious to prevent disruptive developments in their hegemonial sphere, Soviet leaders have often abstained from interfering – and on some other occasions have been surprisingly slow to intervene – in the bilateral issues among their clients. It was on this stage, therefore, that Western influence made itself felt most perceptibly. The two vehicles of such influence were (partly and temporarily linked together) the German question, notably the Western stance towards the GDR, and the famous bridge-building theory developed primarily by Polish and Czech emigrés in the United States and by some politicians in the FRG including the former CDU foreign minister Gerhard Schröder and the SPD refugee leader Wenzel Jaksch. Different in origin but similar in effect was one of the two main currents of Gaullist Ostpolitik in France which aimed at promoting the independence from Moscow of East European nations such as Romania and Poland. The crucial question in this context is to what extent the Soviet Union and the East-European states observed loyalty towards their allies and bloc discipline in view of flattering or advantageous Western overtures. This will be analysed for the different phases in the following section.

Conflicting National Interests in the Six Phases up to 1979

First phase: struggles about the 'socialist camp' under Soviet control 1944–9
The region incorporated in the Soviet sphere at the end of the Second World War was extremely heterogeneous. Most of the peoples there had strong anti-Russian and anti-Soviet traditions. Some of the nations had formed part of Adolf Hitler's alliance against the Soviet Union and changed alliances more or less at the last moment, and thus were regarded as 'enemy countries'. Only the Bulgarians had a clear russophile record due to tsarist assistance in their liberation from Turkey. Czechoslovakia was the only nation with a relatively strong indigenous communist party. Polish resistance against German occupation was split between pro-Western and pro-Soviet armies.

The only nations not primarily liberated from German occupation by the Red Army were the Yugoslavs and the Albanians (who were largely subordinated to Yugoslav influence when the war ended). Tito was firmly resolved not just to maintain independence from the Soviet Union but also to take the leadership in the Balkans. He kept the Albanians under control, negotiated a 'Balkan federation' with the Bulgarian leader Dimitrov, and backed the Greek communists in their civil war even when Stalin had decided, in view of active British resistance, to abandon them. Tito certainly enjoyed the sympathy of communists beyond his own country but it is disputed whether people like Traycho Kostov in Bulgaria or Laszlo Rajk in Hungary, who were executed as his 'agents', really favoured a South European socialist camp under Yugoslav leadership. In any case the major features of this first post-war period were Stalin's attempt to edge Tito out and Yugoslavia's eventual expulsion from the 'socialist camp'. At the end of this phase the Albanians had escaped Yugoslav domination and joined Stalin's side, while all tendencies in the bloc sympathetic to Yugoslavia were eliminated.

At the same time the East European states were transformed to 'peoples democracies' and all remnants of the former bourgeois ruling classes were deprived of political influence. This was particularly complicated in East Germany, where the frontier between the Eastern and Western Zones of Occupation had not yet been effectively closed. But more important was the fact that the East European countries which had fallen victim to German aggression in the Second World War had a keen interest in getting compensation for damage done to them rather than in establishing an Iron Curtain. The latter was, however, the inevitable consequence of Soviet policy in Eastern Europe and of the Berlin blockade, the more so since Stalin prevented the East Europeans from participating in the Marshall Plan and had nothing more to offer than a meaningless (at the time) CMEA. Strong Soviet military superiority in Europe, however, provided a firm guarantee against this becoming an argument against Moscow.

Second phase: from Stalin's ambiguity to his successors' manoeuvring on the German question 1949–55

It has already been mentioned that bilateral relations between the minor communist countries during the second phase were close to nil. The same is true for the multilateral stage. The main foe appeared to be Tito's Yugoslavia which had been expelled from the 'socialist camp' in 1948. The full dependence of all the other countries on

Moscow was dramatically demonstrated by the presence of Soviet troops (except in Bulgaria) and the parallelism of purges and show-trials against alleged agents of the 'Tito clique' and 'Western imperialism' (with some marked differences: no trial in Poland and no death penalty in the GDR). Economically, the richer East European countries were severely exploited by the poor and most heavily devastated Soviet Union.

The main political problem during this phase consisted in the uncertain status of the GDR. Stalin had apparently not yet taken a decision as to the future of Germany. While having favoured a partition of Germany in Teheran and Yalta he clung to the Four-Power régime in Potsdam (except for the Eastern territories). He claimed part of the reparations from the Western Zones of Occupation and showed interest in a special régime for the Ruhr. While ordering the East German communists to reshape society in the Soviet Zone of Occupation according to the Soviet model, he agreed to a partial restoration of the Berlin régime after the blockade in 1949 and backed the East German propaganda slogan 'Deutsche an einen Tisch!' (Germans to the negotiating table). Then, surprisingly for the East Germans, who were already in the full swing of preparations for the II Party Conference of July 1952 which was to proclaim the 'construction of socialism' in the GDR alone, Stalin took the propaganda seriously and offered – more or less sincerely – the reunification of Germany in a diplomatic note to the three Western powers on 10 March 1952. This kind of Soviet manoeuvring on the German question persisted until early 1955 when it became clear that the inclusion of the FRG in NATO was not to be prevented any longer.

This Soviet behaviour on the German question had very strong repercussions on intra-bloc relationships all over Central Europe. The East European governments had formally to recognize the German Democratic Republic when it was proclaimed in October 1949. But the traumas of German atrocities were not yet healed and the Poles insisted that the new leaders, who had still claimed the Eastern territories for Germany in 1946, immediately, solemnly and for ever to accept the Oder-Neisse frontier. It must have come as a shock to the Poles and Czechs when Stalin in 1952 offered the reunification of Germany and when, one year later, the East German communists were urged by the Kremlin leaders to prepare to confine themselves to the role of a parliamentary opposition in a reunified German state where the overwhelming majority strictly resented any waiving of claims for the Eastern territories.

The basic line of Soviet policy in Eastern Europe appeared to be blurred. In 1945 Stalin had abandoned the idea of incorporating the East European countries as federated states of the Soviet Union. But what was his and his successors' stance towards the nation state? Would they release East Germany from the camp and would they do so with other East European countries? These questions were accentuated when the Kremlin agreed to conclude the Austrian State Treaty. There was a high degree of uncertainty in Eastern Europe which was increased by the 'new course' introduced by Georgi Malenkov and his colleagues in the Soviet Union and too swiftly adopted by Ulbricht – which led to unrest throughout the GDR on 17 June 1953. Eventually, however, the Soviet Union remained master of the situation although it had to provide credits to East European countries from time to time, beginning in 1955, in order to reduce domestic troubles in the region.

Third phase: the explosive results of Khrushchev's zigzag course 1955–64
It was as early as 1955 that Prague, and, a little later, Warsaw sent the first cautious signals to Bonn indicating that they had acknowledged the permanent existence of two German states and wanted to establish bilateral relations of their own. These were sold in the East, of course, as actions designed to back the diplomatic recognition of the GDR by the Western countries. This was also the interpretation in Bonn, where the government combined the establishment of diplomatic relations with the Soviet Union (as a result of Konrad Adenauer's trip to Moscow in September 1955) with the proclamation of the Hallstein Doctrine, which practically forbade not just the acceptance of a second German state but also the establishment of diplomatic relations with the East European countries which had recognized the GDR. It remained unnoticed by Bonn at that time that loyalty to the unloved East German brother-state served Prague and Warsaw to a certain degree as a pretext to come to terms with the much more important West German state. After all, they had not consulted East Berlin about their moves, and, like the Soviet Union, they had not established the precondition that Bonn had to recognize the GDR first. The principal source of this opportunist behaviour, so dangerous to bloc cohesiveness, was the Soviet Union,

which did not care very much about East Berlin's vital strategy when it saw a chance to come to terms with Bonn, although reunification was ruled out after 1955.

On the other hand Nikita Khrushchev repeatedly used opportunities to instigate crises over West Berlin. To a certain degree Ulbricht may have felt that activities of that kind might work in his best interests, notably to bring about the separate peace treaty with the GDR which he was aiming at. In the final outcome, however, the Soviet Union drew back and left him with a dangerous flow of people using the loophole of West Berlin to 'drain' away to the West. So the Warsaw Pact had eventually to take the blame for deciding to erect the Berlin wall. Khrushchev's anxiety not to be drawn into dangerous conflicts (e.g. by the Chinese shelling of Quemoy or their border conflict with India), even if self-inflicted by an adventurist policy such as the Cuban crisis, largely contributed to the Sino-Soviet rift, and, in its aftermath, the secession of Albania.

The main event, however, which marked this second phase was Khrushchev's denunciation of Stalin at the XX Party Congress in February 1956. In 1955 he had already reconciled the Soviet Union with Yugoslavia. Both actions came as shocks to the Stalinist East European leaders, who felt their legitimacy fading away and became deeply demoralized. There was no mention of the fact that the accusations against Kostov, Rajk, Rudolf Slansky, and many other victims of Stalin's terror had been fabricated. In a very vague manner Lavrenty Beria was made responsible for having slandered Tito. Nor was there any word about the nasty terms which leaders like Ulbricht, Matyas Rakosi, Gheorghe Gheorghiu-Dej or Valko Chervenkov had used against Tito in favour of their own position in the party. The revolts in Poland and Hungary were an outcome of Khrushchev's destabilizing action – here, again, he pursued a zigzag course. In 1958, when he had realized that his hopes to bring the Yugoslavs back into the 'socialist camp' would not come true, he condemned the new Yugoslav constitution. After a more conservative XXI Party Congress (1959) he resumed his criticism of Stalin at the XXII Congress (1961). Khrushchev's ideological instability indeed enhanced destabilization all over Eastern Europe. His economic reformism, beginning with the administrative changes of 1957 and leading to debates in which the liberal views of economists like Evsei Liberman were elicited, was more or less echoed in other communist countries (e.g. the 'New Economic System' in the GDR). His crude proposal to introduce supra-national planning encountered unsurmountable resistance from the Romanians and others. His 'goulash communism' proved unrealistic and his campaigning for maize did not earn him more than the nickname of 'kukuruznik'.

At the same time periods of cultural thaw spread over Eastern Europe culminating in 1963 in a very lively debate on Franz Kafka in Czechoslovakia which was perceived as so threatening in the GDR that a Politbureau member in East Berlin protested in Prague about 'addled eggs' which the Czechs had put into the socialist nest.

Fourth phase: from the Ulbricht Doctrine to the Brezhnev Doctrine 1964–9
When Khrushchev was overthrown nothing was more badly needed in the 'socialist camp' than consolidation. This was what the Brezhnev team aimed at in this fourth phase through a cautious and, indeed, conservative approach. Brezhnev took account of Ulbricht's bitter complaints and immediately jettisoned the rapprochement with Bonn which Khrushchev had initiated in the summer of 1964. He did not allow Czechoslovakia to follow Poland's, Hungary's, Romania's, and even Bulgaria's acceptance of West German trade missions. He tried to restore, by means of various large-scale communist conferences, Soviet predominance in the world-wide communist movement as well as within the bloc. By such methods he succeeded in halting the FRG's 'Ostpolitik of small steps', which, with the circular 'peace note' in 1966 and the establishment of diplomatic relations with Romania in 1967, had damaged East European solidarity. On the other hand the repeated announcements of readiness to send 'volunteers' to Vietnam remained idle verbiage.

On the basis of the harsh declarations of the conferences of the communist parties of Bucharest (1966) and Karlovy Vary (1967) Brezhnev allowed his ambassador to the FRG to engage in confidential talks about possible arrangements between Moscow and Bonn but he stopped the contacts abruptly in July 1968 when he recognized that the internally split grand coalition was not in a position to take decisions.

His major setback, however, occurred in Czechoslovakia where, in the aftermath of Khrushchev's secret speech, reformist tendencies directed primarily against the immobile leader Antonin Novotny had grown stronger during the sixties. Economic pressures and national tensions between Slovaks and Czechs, combined with vain hopes of a new political flexibility in Bonn's grand coalition, paved the way for Dubcek, who incredibly overestimated Soviet political mobility and overlooked the dangers his experiments produced for the whole Soviet system, notably for Ulbricht's GDR, Wladyslaw Gomulka's Poland, and Pyotr Shelest's Ukraine. Soviet apprehensions of possible interference by Bonn in the CSSR by financial or other means was devoid of any substance, but this added to the Kremlin's feeling that Dubcek was betraying them. 'At the request of loyal communists' law and order were restored, as had been done in Hungary in 1956, but this time with the 'brotherly assistance' of East Germans, Poles, Hungarians, and Bulgarians. All of these except the Bulgarians had already assisted Hitler in dismantling Czechoslovakia in 1938–9 – a tragic irony of history.

While the Soviet procedure against the deviators was not unprecedented the reinterpretation of 'socialist internationalism' was now canonized. The Brezhnev Doctrine was born. It introduced new apprehensions and strains into intra-bloc relations and finally undermined the credibility of the official ideology. A fundamental problem was created: on what legitimacy could the communist élites base their rules once ideology had disqualified itself?

Fifth phase: the benefits of détente 1969–74

A first answer to the question was, again, provided by the West. Richard Nixon and Henry Kissinger brought about a settlement of the Vietnam issue and a certain détente in US relations with both the Soviet Union and China, which might alleviate the burden of armaments. At the same time the small coalition in Bonn came up with its 'new Ostpolitik', which seemed:

(a) to sanction Soviet hegemony over Eastern Europe and thereby satisfy the Kremlin;

(b) eventually to settle the territorial disputes with Poland and Czechoslovakia, thus making them less dependent on Soviet protection;

(c) to recognize the GDR as a separate state, thereby relieving its 'brother nations' from the annoying burden of loyalty towards East Berlin;

(d) to eliminate the Berlin question as a stumbling block from practical politics; and

(e) to clear the way for East–West economic co-operation which, again, would lessen the dependence of the East Europeans on the Soviet Union.

No East European felt worried about the fact that the price for these benefits was to be paid initially by Ulbricht, though the GDR, at first glance, appeared as the main winner. It is true that the GDR was upgraded and, indeed, acknowledged as a state for the foreseeable future; and this, to be sure, fitted in with Gomulka's as well as Edward Gierek's and Gustav Husak's best interests. Ulbricht, however, saw his plans regarding a separate peace treaty and the inclusion of West Berlin into the GDR finally buried. Ulbricht had to go, and fell into oblivion. His successor desperately but courageously used the chance of a big leap forward in trade with the West, notably with the FRG, to improve the living standards of the population and thereby overcome a number of complications in the GDR's development.

The 'Comprehensive Programme' which the CMEA had approved in 1971 after two years of tricky bargaining did not open up any bright perspectives since it consisted of little more than a conglomeration of largely incompatible elements and idle phrases. Brezhnev was none the less obsessed by the vision of large American, Japanese, and West German investment in Siberia which would eventually enable him to modernize the Soviet economy without having to resort to structural and managerial reforms with the enormous risks involved, and the East Europeans would follow suit, co-operating with the West and keeping a low political profile. In the latter respect Romania, once again, constituted the exception to the rule. It was favoured by its geographical situation, which largely precludes Western influence, and by the tough patriarchal régime of Nicolae Ceausescu and his energetic wife Elena. At least the Romanians had no objections to SALT, which the USSR surprisingly enough agreed to engage in. Fairly soon it became evident that Brezhnev was pleased by the prospect of reaching global parity with the United States which would, inter alia, strengthen Soviet hegemony in the alliance, as was rightly observed by Helmut Sonnenfeldt. SALT seemed to the Kremlin to be certainly more promising than MBFR, which might raise the question of reducing Soviet troops (instead of those of their allies) and thereby, from Moscow's point of view, endanger Soviet predominance in, and the stability of, Eastern Europe.

Sixth phase: novel tensions from the backfiring of détente 1974–9

There was a fantastic upswing in the early seventies but the bill was presented soon afterwards and the venture proved much more expensive than anybody had expected. Suddenly the problem of legitimacy came to the fore again and the situation appeared more puzzling than at any previous time. As long as the Germans had to shoulder the burden of détente it was not extremely difficult for the director in Moscow to co-ordinate the parts the single actors were to play. In the mid-1970s, however, all East Europeans and the Russians were asked for cash, and now the harmony was more and more outmatched by the cacophony of antagonistic selfish interests. The reasons were twofold: the outcome looked bleaker than the initial dreams, and the costs jumped up alarmingly.

Probably the most remarkable spillover of the intra-German and Berlin negotiations was Honecker's idea, put to Gierek in November 1971, of opening the East German–Polish frontier on 1 January 1972 and of introducing freedom of movement for the first time in the 'socialist camp'. The proposal was accepted, and a little later Czechoslovakia, albeit on a bilateral basis, joined the two forerunners. But the dream of 'the first time real freedom was introduced since administrations were technically able to close frontiers', as a Polish writer put it, did not last. Centralized economic planning on the basis of arbitrary national price systems, unable to satisfy rapidly changing consumer demands, enforced the reintroduction of financial restrictions. To make things worse, the Soviet Union kept its frontiers as closed as ever and the new idea was not allowed to spread all over the 'socialist camp'.

But the idea of freedom was there, and grew stronger and stronger during the CSCE process which Moscow had envisaged as completely different from its eventual outcome. Dissidents, though small in number, raised their voices, and, for the first time since 1945, transcended the national frontiers. As the Stalinist repressive system had vanished in the meantime, the national organs of state security had to act much more on their own and respect the feelings of their populations. The leaders who had relied on *panem et circenses* during the early seventies had to switch to nationalism as the only remedy when economic growth rates declined, keeping the possibilities for rising living standards far behind consumer expectations. Now again, the problem which came to the fore was how to restrain anti-Sovietism, which traditionally had been the main expression of nationalsim, the more so since anti-Germanism had lost momentum through Bonn's new Ostpolitik. The Kremlin's patience became strained to the utmost by the hazardous escapades which Ceausescu chose as a means of refurbishing his national prestige in view of the bad living conditions of the workers, notably the miners, and his harsh autocratic régime. For some time even the eventuality of 'brotherly help' extended under the flag of the Brezhnev Doctrine could not be excluded.

For all practical purposes a rethinking of the economic mechanisms became imperative. The quantitative sources of growth had been largely exhausted. There was a continued deterioration of the terms of trade as a consequence of the booming prices both for oil (which lessened the financial strains in the Soviet Union) and for the badly needed Western high technology. The Hungarians were greatly relieved when they realized that Moscow would not veto the introduction of more flexible methods. In 1972–5 there had been some evidence of Soviet interference in Hungary's reform policy. The dismissal of Reszo Nyers from the Politburo and from responsibility for economic policy seems to have been engineered by Moscow, but the Hungarians had no illusions about the latent unrest in their own population and Janos Kadar's main concern was that a possible renewed upsurge among the Poles (as in 1976 when Piotr Jaroszewicz tried sharply to increase the prices for the most-wanted foodstuffs) might spread to Czechoslovakia and Hungary and get out of control. This anxiety was shown in the Hungarian reaction to recent events in Poland, when trade union reform was hurriedly introduced to forestall a recurrence in Hungary of the Polish troubles.

Back to the Starting Point: Change or Return to Familiar Patterns?

None of the political theories which have been developed since the end of the fifties about the end of the bipolar global system, the crystallization of a pentagonal pattern, or the growth of medium powers to political maturity, including the change of the German economic great power to a political one, has altered the simple truth that Europe is basically split into two antagonistic blocs. While in Western Europe there exist very strong and vivid criss-cross relations between the single states this is not so in Eastern Europe, where, as in a cobweb, the Muscovite spider controls all the vital threads. Because of Soviet military power, Moscow's hegemony is not challenged. Even when initiatives have been developed by smaller allies, as was the 'Rapacki plan' by Poland, they could not be transmitted to the West before they had received Soviet approval, which in the case of the Rapacki plan was hard to obtain. The basic reason for Poland's difficulties in securing Moscow's agreement was not the substance of the proposition but the mere fact that the Soviet leadership had not been accustomed to a real division of labour which would allow for the input of innovative ideas by their alliance partners.

The novel situation which we faced in early 1980 was the complete immobility of Soviet diplomacy after Moscow had entered the blind alley of seizing Afghanistan. Like the Americans in Vietnam, the Russians have had the experience that it was fairly easy (militarily) to get in, but extremely difficult (politically) to get out; and while the Americans – obsessed with the hostages in Iran and apparently powerless to force a Soviet withdrawal from Afghanistan – fled into an escalation of helpless gestures, the Russians showed every intention of remaining in that blood-stained country and answered with an escalation of self-encapsulation and hostile propaganda.

This development created a twofold danger for the East Europeans. The first one was that of an armed East–West conflict which would threaten their physical survival, and it is here where (besides tactical and propagandistic considerations) the NATO decisions of December 1979 came in. American strategic capabilities had never been regarded as directed against East European nations, nor had the French or the British which were seen more as an insurance against dangerous moves of the Soviet superpower. What the NATO decisions amounted to was – in the eyes of many East Europeans – a first step towards delivering strategic weapons to the Germans. Until now NATO's nuclear arsenal deployed on the continent was clearly confined to theatre missions. A Pershing II would constitute a qualitative change – not only because it might hit Soviet targets without any warning time and thereby make the Russians think about preventive actions, but also because the Germans might demand some control over these systems at a time when the provisional character of the treaties with Eastern Europe – for whatever reasons – was being stressed in Bonn much more strongly than since the early 1970s.

The second concern of those East Europeans might look more convincing to a Western observer: it is that the Americans might enforce a return to the Cold War with larger restrictions in the CoCom list, the non-availability of further credits, and, last but not least, a heavier burden of armaments at a time when the rift between consumer demands and growth in productivity had become wider than ever and the obligation to provide economic assistance to countries like Vietnam, Ethiopia, or Cuba cut deeply into their resources

Only the attempts to revive the temporarily frozen contacts with the medium powers in Western Europe and to persuade the Soviet Union at least to tolerate a resumption of talks with the West offered the East Europeans certain prospects of overcoming the impasse. Astonishingly enough, the Soviet leaders, though initially seeking to ban all high-level East–West contacts, did not respond entirely negatively to this effort and left the initiative for a while to their allies. In the meantime they have apparently recovered from their paralysis. Helmut Schmidt's visit to Moscow at the end of June 1980 offered them the opportunity to come up with new proposals, limited though these were, in the field of arms control. The Kremlin, to be sure, will not treat the Europeans on an equal footing in the future. Even so, the experience, unprecedented since World War II, of serious talks between the Central European powers across the European dividing line will leave behind a slightly changed atmosphere. The climate within the bloc will not be the same any more. Above all these considerations, however, hangs the Damoclean sword of Brezhnev's succession. This is what concerns the East Europeans more than anything else. But they have not the slightest idea what will come out of that – except that it is highly unlikely that Russian political culture will change in the foreseeable future and allow a 'liberalization' in Eastern Europe. The political upheaval in Poland in the summer of 1980 has resulted in a most serious challenge to Moscow's limited tolerance of social reforms – which in Russian history have never been easily accepted. The consequences will very soon become apparent. The most unfortunate feature of the Warsaw Pact is that the leading power, which is so overwhelming in weight, is at the same time the most backward and reactionary one.

5 The Political Structure of Eastern Europe as a Factor in Intra-bloc Relations
by George Schöpflin

THE basic problem faced by all East European governments is that, after thirty years in power, they have run out of steam. After the countries of Eastern Europe had become part of the Soviet sphere soon after the Second World War their governments undertook a rapid – perhaps overrapid – modernization on the Soviet model, and, to differing degrees, they have achieved this modernization only in extensive terms, whether in politics or economics. The ruling parties have proved to be singularly unfitted to introduce intensive development and have shown their greatest success in holding on to power. In other words, having presided over a dash for modernity in the guise of a quest for a Marxist utopia, the communist parties have lost their purposiveness because they lack policies commensurate with the requirements of modern societies.[1]

This may be seen in various facets of the 1970s. The most significant problem is certainly the Soviet constraint, which has effectively prevented any East European party from attempting *political* modernization since the invasion of Czechoslovakia in 1968. It has left these régimes in the grip of an accelerating process in which political communication is deteriorating, political fragmentation is intensifying, the level of political commitment by the people to their rulers is declining, and political aspirations are growing. Between the mid-1950s and 1968 it was possible to assume that any East European party was fairly free to pursue political reforms as long as the country affirmed its loyalty to the Warsaw Pact and maintained a relatively liberal interpretation of the political monopoly of the party. The Soviet response to the Czechoslovak reforms destroyed that assumption, and, with it, there vanished the prospect of effective reform of the system.

At the same time this inability to deal with the requirements of modernity is manifesting itself increasingly in the economic field. As a general proposition, it can be argued that the more developed an economy is the greater the need for high information flows, flexibility, adaptability, and decision-making at lower levels. On all these counts, communist systems perform badly. Such methods of work demand a greater decentralization of power and the removal of political considerations from decision-making. This last has two aspects that are worth spelling out. Political considerations can mean that a particular decision might run counter to the interest of the party and is therefore vetoed; rather more insidious is the fear of a decision-maker seeking to use technical criteria that, in the event of an error, he will be held politically responsible. This is a particular risk in communist societies, where the rules of the political game are arbitrarily altered. An illustration may be taken from Yugoslavia, where, prior to December 1971, the managerial élite had a great deal of power, but after the recentralization of 1972, it could be held politically accountable for economic decisions taken before the clamp-down.

To secure its power, the party feels constrained to continue the deployment of a high level of coercion, including the off-stage threat of the Soviet Union, and this runs counter to the needs of modernization. And there is no way to avoid this problem, given that the communist parties have failed to find a formula that would enable them to shift their political order to a basis of consent, i.e. political integration. This in turn has led to a reliance on economic performance – the steady rise in living standards – as the central component of legitimacy. Whenever economic performance is threatened, the political consequences are far-reaching. The clearest example of this was Poland in 1976, when the authorities gravely undermined their own position through a simple economic decision, price rises. Given the nature of the tacit compact between the rulers and the ruled, price rises were, in fact, very far from being a simple economic decision, but had for some time been transformed into a matter of the gravest importance for the country. A large part of Poland's political stability rested on price stability, because there existed no adequate political linkage between the government and the people.[2] By 1980 the relationship between the Polish workers and the leadership had changed to such an extent that the former began to insist on direct access to the political process.

A measure of movement away from exclusively political criteria in decision-making has, of course, taken place and since the 1950s – with variations from country to country – skills and technocratic criteria have been introduced. This in essence has been the meaning of the change from Stalinist to neo-Stalinist modes of rule and it has necessarily been paralleled by the acceptance of a measure of competition in society, whereas under Stalinist concepts of monolithism a conflict of interests was held to be illegitimate and usually criminal. But this change is by definition limited. Political factors continue to influence economic decisions in a far wider range of issues than in a Western society, so that the party's claim to rule in the name of rationality is repeatedly undermined, and, what is worse for the party, is perceived as having been undermined. Furthermore, given the intimate link between party control and economic decision-making, there is no institutional machinery for resolving competing claims on resources in ways that are accepted as just by the majority. On the contrary, if debates are perceived as having been manipulated, responses to a decision will be those of cynicism and apathy. In a word, there is no machinery of competitive politics and popular control of institutions. The political result is wasteful and non-rational bureaucratization, popular frustration, and latent discontent.

That in turn reinforces all-or-nothing attitudes: people demand that the party should provide for all their aspirations and when it fails to do that, as it must, it is rejected totally. Naturally this process is assisted by the utopian values of Marxism propagated by the party, even when they are not taken seriously, for they can be and are used as a pretext. Thus one of the gravest sources of weakness in East European states can be seen to be the absence of intermediate institutions with the function of mediating between society as a whole and the ruling élite. The inability or unwillingness of the ruling élite, the party, to do much about this serves only to perpetuate political illiteracy, which then promotes unrealistic expectations, thereby reinforcing the entire cycle of inadequate integration.

To the above may be added the complex of problems associated with the process of rapid modernization. A very large proportion of the population of Eastern Europe – East Germany and the Czech lands are an exception – is either first generation off the land or consists of peasant-workers or still retains some link with rural lifestyles. The process of eradicating peasant values (e.g. in time keeping) and replacing them with industrial values is difficult and creates major traumata. The rapid change undergone by Eastern Europe has brought into being societies that are extensively but not intensively modernized, in that the bulk of the new working class may earn industrial wages and is thus above starvation level for the first time in history – an enormous achievement – but lives and works under poor conditions with few prospects of improving its circumstances. (For a more detailed discussion see 'Social Immobility' below.) Change is associated with enforced initiatives from above, the destruction of age-old values, and is thus viewed with disfavour; when existing achievements appear to be threatened, reactions can be very strong. This was the lesson of Poland in December 1970 (the riots in the Baltic coast towns) and of Romania in 1977 (the Jiu valley miners' strike). The danger of ruling over rapidly changing societies is not immediately obvious. There is no real threat of a revolutionary outburst triggered off by persistently poor conditions. The danger lies in situations in which the political leadership is divided or is under some form of pressure, allowing itself to be stampeded into using coercion either to enforce its will or as a demonstration of its strength. It is at moments of that kind that the long-term undercurrent of discontent can spill over into the streets and set off much greater changes. This was one of the lessons of Hungary in 1956, for the revolution erupted not when conditions were worst but after they had improved and had made possible the hope of more improvements; an irresolute leadership then used force at a time when the crowds were already in the streets – with catastrophic consequences.

The Decomposition of Ideology
The second broad factor contributing to instability in Eastern Europe and thus to certain difficulties in Soviet–East European relations has been the slow but inexorable decay of the official Marxist-Leninist ideology as a viable, dynamic body of ideas.[3] With a few exceptions political, economic, and social thinking is in no way informed by Marxism, and Marxism attracts no loyalty either from among the intelligentsia or from the rest of the population. A vague commitment to egalitarianism is the main exception. Thus the gap between the official value system of collectivism and the dominant value system is growing. This aggravates the problem of political communication and promotes cynicism and apathy (socialization is discussed below).

While at the popular level there was probably never any widespread support for a Marxian revolution, its rejection by the intelligentsia is a relatively new phenomenon. It can be traced directly to the impact of the Soviet invasion of Czechoslovakia, which demonstrated the failure of revisionism in that attempts by a ruling party to reshape Marxism-Leninism to something more in line with local needs and conditions formally were rejected as being unacceptable. From that point on, the Marxist intelligentsia, which included sections of the party, was forced to conclude that it had no option but to accede to the formal requirements of sustaining Marxism-Leninism, though knowing that it had degenerated into a set of empty phrases.

This disintegration of Marxism has left it with two interlinked functions in the political process. One of these is that Marxist language serves as a recognition code, as a shared mode of communication within the bureaucracy, which helps to sustain morale.[4] It plays a part in sustaining the cohesiveness of the ruling élite, which knows that it is a small minority and that its rule is short on legitimacy. Tied in with this is the much more important role played by Marxist-Leninist jargon as a means of perpetuating and strengthening the party's monopoly of information. By insisting that political communication is couched in a phraseology almost empty of meaning the party can prevent the emergence of alternative ideas and concepts in officially sanctioned publications. In this way Marxist-Leninist jargon functions as a protective screen, ensuring that competitive ideologies or political debates are expressed only in a semi-intelligible form, if at all. Finally, precisely because Marxism-Leninism is empty of real significance, that which is communicated is inexact and this imprecision is valuable in maintaining an atmosphere of uncertainty in which the party finds it easier to manipulate opinion and promote depoliticization. Thus although the adherence to Marxist-Leninist expression is a source of weakness, in that communication is made poorer thereby, the resulting uncertainty is exploited by the party in its insistence on the sole right to communicate politically. Contrariwise, the central function of *samizdat* is to break the monopoly and to ensure the spread of competing concepts and ideas.

The decomposition of Marxism-Leninism as an effective ideology with the stated aim of transforming society into a secular utopia does raise the question of what the real ideology of the ruling élite is. There appears to be no single overall set of concepts that have replaced

Marxism-Leninism, but the political ideology of communist parties can probably be reduced to two basic components: efficiency and nationhood. The party arrogates to itself its right to rule by claiming to be the sole repository of rationality and thus the best and most efficient agent of modernization. The fact that this is not the case is immaterial. The party seeks to ensure that its claim to be the agent of rationality is not challenged. In fact, such challenges are beginning to be found in *samizdat*, e.g. a Polish document prepared by a brains trust of economists very largely destroyed the party's pretensions to economic efficiency. Similar conclusions can be drawn from several of the Charter 77 documents and some Hungarian material. Hence one is forced back to the earlier proposition that the most signal success of communist parties in Eastern Europe has been to cling on to power despite their minority support. In practice, the claim to rationality founders on everyday experiences, and Marxism-Leninism, as currently understood and deployed, tends to be both wasteful through bureaucratization and a drag on progress, because it is anti-innovative, static, and prevents the information flows necessary to political, economic, and social dynamism.[5]

Competing Ideologies

If Marxism-Leninism has been transformed into a not very effective guide to efficiency and is incapable of meeting the challenge of its pretensions – that of being a transcendental philosophical system – clearly a vacuum of sorts is bound to arise. This vacuum is being filled by a variety of competing ideologies. Nationalism is the most important of these, firstly because it was the original mass political ideology of Eastern Europe, and, secondly, because the party itself has found itself constrained to use it as an instrument of mobilization and an instrument of legitimization.

There are considerable dangers in the mounting expression of nationalism in Eastern Europe because nationalist ideologies are generally strongly dynamic and because they have targets that cannot be met. The 1918–20 peace settlement, confirmed after 1945, left behind three types of states in Eastern Europe: nationally and territorially satisfied states with gains to defend; nationally and territorially dissatisfied states with substantial numbers of co-nationals outside their frontiers; and multi-national states in which the first two types of national problem have been reproduced and exacerbated by national competition within the state framework. Transcending these intra-East European national problems is the perception of the Soviet Union in national terms as the foreign overlord. These make up a complex of problems which communist governments have been largely unable to solve, and, indeed, have to some extent made worse by inappropriate policies. National friction is not so dangerous as to bring about disintegration on its own, but in a crisis triggered off by other factors it can cause explosions. Thus in Hungary in 1956 the internal problem of the relationship between the Stalinist ruling élite and the liberalizing revisionists was instantly transformed into a Hungarian–Soviet national liberation struggle by the deployment of the Red Army to restore law and order. Similarly the fear of Soviet intervention acts as a severe constraint on the Polish government, in that there is an expectation that reprisals against the working class-cum-opposition could produce large-scale disorders and that, in turn, would provoke Soviet military intervention. That, it is predicted, would unleash an uncontrollable Polish–Soviet conflict. By the same token, of course, the Soviet constraint is just as effective on the opposition.

As far as intra-East European national problems are concerned, the use of nationalism as a *de facto* source of legitimacy has produced anti-minority policies in Romania (Hungarians) and Bulgaria (Turks, Moslems). In Czechoslovakia the partial satisfaction of Slovak national demands after 1968 has provided the Husak régime with a useful popular base, but this has been at the cost of alienating many Czechs, particularly in the bureaucracy, who strongly resent the growth of the Slovak presence in Prague. Yugoslavia provides some of the most intractable and potentially debilitating national problems. Two of these are worth further examination. About 40 per cent of the Albanian nation lives in Yugoslavia, mostly in the Kosovo province but also in Dzamija, the western districts of Macedonia marching with Albania. The Albanians of Yugoslavia have a very high birth rate, a growing intelligentsia with a separately identified political consciousness, and their own political aspirations. It is not at all certain that the Yugoslav state can contain these. In periods of stability the problem may not be acute, but during times of unrest Albanian nationalism in Yugoslavia could play a serious disintegrative role by finding a focus in a quest for unification with Albania. Even if such efforts were contained, they could gravely destabilize Yugoslavia at a time when political stability would be at a premium. Even if such a worst-case scenario fails to eventuate, an inability on the part of Yugoslav policy-makers to secure the loyalty of the Albanians, to promote an overriding commitment to a Yugoslav state rather than to Albania, leaves a question mark over their aspirations. On the other hand, any attempt to upgrade the political level of their participation in Yugoslav politics – by establishing the Kosovo as a seventh republic, for example – would create problems with the Serbs and Macedonians, who would be reluctant to accede to this increase in the status of the Albanians.

Yugoslavia's other problem concerns the Serb–Croat conflict. The nature of this has frequently been missed. It does not merely consist of Croatian resentment of the federal government perceived as Serbian or of Serbian hostility to Croatian nationalism perceived as separatism. Rather, the core of the problem is the substantial Serbian minority in Croatia, the *precani*, about 14 per cent of the population of the Croatian republic. By reason of their adhesion to the Partisans during the Second World War the *precani* have come to play a disproportionate role in Croatian affairs, especially in the police, the armed forces, and the secret police. This is the real focus of Croatian resentments and this is felt to be the case by the *precani*, one representative of whom recently declared in private that 'the Serbs of Croatia will not become the Palestinians of Europe'. The fear of mass reprisals is obviously very real. It is likewise present among the Serbs of Serbia, who perceive Croatian pressure for national self-fulfilment as a process that would be completed at the expense of their co-nationals. In this atmosphere of suspicions and latent hostilities, destabilization could be easily triggered off. The Soviet Union is well aware of this and has potential, or even actual, allies among the *precani*, from whose ranks the majority of Cominformists have come. Nor is the Yugoslav army, upgraded with the political function of safeguarding the country's national integrity, the most welcome agent, viewed as it is by Croats as an instrument of Serbian power.

Overlapping with nationalism in some areas, populism should nevertheless be distinguished from it. Traditionally a section of the intelligentsia in Eastern Europe has been attracted to populist politics, often as a reaction against modernization, and has sought to mobilize the people directly, without reference to institutions. Populism, a vague concept at the best of times, has tended to evolve into peasantism in Eastern Europe and it is this variant of it that continues to hold the support of some intellectuals. The ideology they propound includes some or all of the following propositions: the need to commune and communicate directly with the people, the repository of all that is desirable in society, and a corresponding hostility to a complexity of social structures; a distrust of politics, of the political game, as a means of resource allocation and an equivalent trust in 'basic common sense' as expressed by the community; a latent isolationism and neutralism; and a messianism that expects and demands total change (redemption), which paradoxically goes hand in hand with a static and uniform concept of the ideal society. In East European conditions populism has tended to favour the peasantry and to be hostile to 'the city', but there are indications that today some populists include the urban proletariat in their ideal community. In this sense, they reject class-based concepts of society. A strong sense of belonging, from which outsiders are excluded; this emerges as nationalism or even xenophobia, notably anti-Semitism.

It is impossible to state with any claim to accuracy how influential populism is in Eastern Europe. It has been almost wholly overlaid by Marxism, of which it may, indeed, be one component. Nevertheless if it is possible to extrapolate from past trends, then populism is likely to inform a section of the intelligentsia in most East European countries. Elements of it exist in Hungary, Poland, Croatia, Romania, and probably Bulgaria, but which precise demands populists would articulate is hard to determine. The sole exception to this is that populists have been ready to form alliances with communist parties where they have perceived the communists as defenders of the nation. On this basis populists would presumably be ready to form an alliance with anyone.

Another competing ideology is religion. Indeed, religion is unique in this context because it has not only its own ideology but also its own ostensibly autonomous institutional structure. These two may be distinguished, in that ecclesiastical institutions have been an easier target than a religious *Weltanschauung*. Even at that, some communist parties have failed in their efforts to restrict the churches to sacrament, and church activities may include caritative and social work and some education. In Poland and East Germany the churches constitute institutional foci of opposition, and the Roman Catholic church in Poland has been emerging in an increasingly overt struggle against the state in its demands for freedom of expression and the right to criticize certain government policies. Religious ideology can actually overlap with Marxism, notably in Christian concern for social justice, but a religious world-view is otherwise profoundly hostile to Marxism. This trend has been particularly important in Poland, where there now exists a sizeable neo-positivist (lay Catholic) intelligentsia with a potential constituency in an overwhelmingly Roman Catholic society. In other Roman Catholic societies this trend is much less evident, but recent survey material on levels of religiousness shows that at least half these societies regard themselves as in some way religious (not to be equated with church-going). Roman Catholic intellectual currents are known to exist in Czechoslovakia, Hungary, and Croatia but there is a dearth of information about their strengths and aims. The Romanian and Bulgarian Orthodox churches are on the whole too closely identified with the state to permit analogous developments.

The opposition that has recently begun to evolve includes adherents of the ideologies outlined above but can be said to be basing itself on an ideology of human rights.[6] The core of this is the argument that the Marxist-Leninist formulae of 'the class struggle' and 'the revolution' are no longer sufficient ground for legitimacy and that communist governments must at the very least abide by their own legality. It has been a repeated feature of the emergent opposition movements to demand that the régime refrain from acts of illegality and that its activities be firmly based on the legal provisions of the state. This non-normative approach is the outcome of a very significant development of the early 1970s, namely the recognition of the non-viability of official Marxism by the politically active Marxist intelligentsia; the subsequent acceptance by it that Marxism did not have an intellectual monopoly in society; and the consequent ability of such ex-Marxists and revisionist Marxists to co-operate with the non-Marxist majority of the intelligentsia. This broad front of opposition activists can thus agree on a political ideology – it is not as specific as a programme – that accepts democracy today as a more meaningful objective than utopia tomorrow, a development that may turn out to be one of the most important ideological changes in post-war Eastern Europe.

The form of action chosen by the opposition has been *samizdat*, which is defined here as unofficially circulated writings with a political objective. Hence *samizdat* in this sense differs from literary or even non-literary material circulating only among friends without being intended for a wider readership. The essence of *samizdat* is that its authors accept the possible consequences of this wider circulation. Having broken the information monopoly of the régime, the opposition's next step has been to establish its own competitive institutions outside the official framework and thereby challenge the leading role of the party – its monopoly of political initiative. In Poland this process is already well under way, with the activities of the KSS-KOR and ROPCiO human rights groups. Charter 77, despite denying that it is an organized movement or institution, does in practice operate in analogous ways. The principle underlying the activities of these bodies is that, because of the decay of ideology and the rigid constraints imposed by the Soviet Union, political change from inside the system has become impossible – hence those seeking change have to act upon the system from without.

The prospects for the opposition movements and their chosen *modus operandi* are difficult to define. Much will depend on factors outside their control, notably the economic success of East European governments, the morale of the ruling élite, and, above all, whether they succeed in striking roots in sections of society other than the intelligentsia. The indications for the moment are that in Poland the opposition has found some common ground with dissatisfied workers and peasants and that this has gone hand-in-hand with a marked decline in the authority of the party; the tacit backing of the church has proved to be a key factor in all this. But this is hardly the same as the capacity to mobilize mass support, the essential component for transforming relatively marginal intellectual activity into something with political weight. Nor is there any sign that the morale of the party is being undermined, albeit the Polish opposition movement must certainly have some sympathizers within the party.

The Czechoslovak opposition is significantly more marginalized and isolated, despite some support from individual workers; the authorities have, in effect, succeeded in meeting the challenge of Charter 77 for the time being by massive police harassment and by relying on the apathy of the population. Relative economic well-being has helped the Czechoslovak government in this strategy, but this cannot be guaranteed for the future.

In Hungary, where the economic situation is likely to be one of definite deterioration during the 1980s, the intelligentsia is scarcely at the stage reached by its counterparts in Poland and Czechoslovakia. So far activity has been restricted to *samizdat*, the bulk of which is theoretical rather than directly political.

With the exception of occasional documents it would be misleading to discuss other East European countries in anything like these terms. There has been no sign of any organized or semi-organized group operating in East Germany, despite a considerable ground-swell of dissatisfaction over bans on emigration and the fairly well-established position of the church. In Yugoslavia, although there are certainly contacts among dissidents, *attentisme* is the order of the day; there have been isolated but unconfirmed reports of activity in Bulgaria; and in Romania opposition, as sketched out above, can be found only within the Hungarian minority and the small group of persecuted Baptists.

The Failure of Integration

What makes the opposition so much of a potential threat is not its immediate significance but the long-term failure of communist modernization. Some of this has already been discussed above, notably in the context of Marxist-Leninist ideology; two other factors require discussion at this point – social fragmentation and problems of political socialization. When communist parties took power after 1945 they did so in societies with ineffective social communications, in which there was no sense of a single political identity or loyalty among the majority of the population. Politics was, in fact, the preserve of a small élite, either an amalgam of the gentry and the bureaucracy or the bureaucracy on its own. The peasantry was very largely outside the ambit of politics and the inability of peasant parties to make any kind of impact on the political process was the best indicator of this. Thus the political structure of the countries of the area was made up of fragments of society, each with its own political concepts and aspirations, but cut off from one another and without any wider sense of community. Nationalism failed to cement these fragments as it had little relevance to day-to-day political problems and could be deployed only in situations of crisis.

Communist modernization transformed the lay-out of these fragments – the old gentry has largely vanished – but it has failed to bring about integration. Different sections of society – the bureaucracy, the intelligentsia, the peasantry, and different sections of the working class – continue to be informed by their own political identities and interests, which may conflict or overlap. In this sense, society and the state are not coextensive, despite the vastly superior instruments of control at the disposal of the state. Thus in situations of crisis, the authorities can find themselves totally isolated because they lack adequate communications with the people affected by their policies. This makes it difficult to calculate the impact of policies, because there is always the risk of an unforeseeable overreaction. For most of the time communist parties can rely on the apathy of a depoliticized population, but they cannot rely on this method of rule at all times and they recognize at some level their isolation from society.

They have sought to overcome this isolation by promoting their own official value system derived from Marxism-Leninism, but they have not achieved any great success in the internalization of this. On the contrary, the evidence is that the traditional – dominant – values of individualism survive strongly, that political aspirations are informed by dominant values, and that, in practice, there is a vast gap between official and dominant values. A gap of this kind self-evidently constitutes a serious weakness in the fabric of society, for it must serve to discredit the government and its actions. Once again, in a crisis this could have far-reaching consequences, as it already has had on several occasions.

Social Immobility

Another factor of weakness likely to increase in importance in the 1980s derives from the failure of communist societies to fulfil the promise of their rhetoric in an area close to the centre of Marxism-Leninism, that of social equality. The last twenty-five years have seen a slowing-down of social mobility and ever greater rigidity in social stratification.[8] In the immediate aftermath of the communist takeover, there was a substantial break-through of persons of working class and peasant backgrounds to higher positions in society, whether in terms of power or of privilege; this has ceased. Indeed, upward social mobility appears to be appreciably slower in communist societies – with the central control of the means of mobility (education) in the hands of the state – than in the West, where alternative routes are more readily available (private enterprise). It is worth adding that the stoutest defenders of the existing class lines are those who were promoted upwards by the communist takeover.

For the first three decades of communist rule this dispensation has not resulted in any visible disadvantages. The creaming-off of the peasantry and the workers meant that the most talented leaders of these strata were co-opted into the system. At the same time, the massive industrialization of the 1950s had the by-product of swamping the old working class (where this existed) with new arrivals from the countryside. Both these processes contributed to social stability in Eastern Europe. As a general proposition, first-generation workers retain many of their peasant characteristics. They are aware that for the first time in their lives they are above starvation level and that they have a disposable income. They lack the traditions of sustained organization and the aspirations to control the broader social and political environment. Hence industrial unrest in Eastern Europe has generally been short-lived and it can be readily defused by welfare concessions. While this generation of workers probably still forms the majority, it is being replaced by a younger generation that takes disposable incomes for granted and will not be so ready to accept authoritarian controls.

In other words, the quality of the working class in Eastern Europe is changing. Increasingly there is hereditary transmission of class status, and, given low mobility, the possibility of the emergence of class politics seems strong. The problem for East European rulers is that they are poorly placed to accommodate demands made on such a basis, as the Polish events of 1980 suggested. While they have on the whole bought off the intelligentsia – the cost of which was relatively low – the price of meeting working-class demands is bound to be higher. This is true both in economic terms and politically, especially the latter in the light of the poor record of East European systems in the area of political renewal and institutional change. The evidence of the last few years in Poland suggests that the Polish working class is aware of its political power (the removal of Gomulka in 1970) and that demands for autonomous working-class institutions are likely to increase rather than decline. In that sense, the demands of the Gdansk shipyard workers are only a foretaste of the kind of pressure that communist governments will have to face in the 1980s. The problem with this is that the existence of genuinely autonomous institutions would be a direct breach of the party's political monopoly, the leading role, and would not be countenanced by the Soviet Union either.

One of the factors of social development which communist planners have been strangely slow to recognize is that development – economic, social, cultural – is continuously costly.[9] In other words, as a society becomes industrialized and the role of the individual in it more specialized, the state itself must play a greater part in providing the economic backing. In concrete terms, if a factory is established in a town, then it will draw on neighbouring villages for its labour force. That will immediately impose a social cost in the provision of adequate transport (roads, buses). Then, the new industrial workforce will itself acquire greater expectations of the system, from medical care to main drainage. On the whole, communist planners have performed poorly by these criteria. In the Stalinist phase infrastructure was neglected in favour of 'productive' investment. This lopsided development has left its mark on later changes – the acute urban housing shortage that is a feature of every East European country is one instance. And even in the 1960s and 1970s planners found it difficult to make provision for all-round development. Thus the politically inspired decision to build a 'people's car' in Poland, the Polski Fiat, has not been matched by the road and services network that mass motoring demands.

Above a certain level of development an ever greater section of society will gain a perspective of these socio-economic decisions taken by the state and will want a measure of control over how they are taken and resources allocated. Pressures of this kind are clearly political and they can, of course, be contained for long periods of time. The next two decades in Eastern Europe should show whether they can actually be contained indefinitely. The experience of Czechoslovakia in the 1970s suggests that a determined government can buy off these pressures for political control through economic benefits and through diverting potential *political* enterprise into *economic* enterprise in the secondary economy. But it is not clear if this is a durable feature of these societies or a temporary one, specific to Czechoslovakia and governed by that country's experience. In any event, the political structure of Eastern Europe, its societies and polities, is such as to make political pressures of this kind extremely difficult to absorb. Equally the underlying political expectations of a greater share of power are likely to be just as difficult to satisfy.

Relations with the Soviet Union

One aspect of Soviet–East European relations – the Soviet constraint on political renewal – has already been discussed. But there are other facets of this relationship that can contribute to political weakness or intensify it in a crisis. The first of these is that, as long as East European communist governments depend on Soviet power for their survival, they will find genuine legitimacy that much more difficult to achieve.

At the popular level, subordination to the Soviet Union is not accepted as legitimate. Indeed, it is constantly exacerbated by the way in which the Soviet Union exercises its power in Eastern Europe: the insistence on the glorification of the Soviet Union and the high level of Soviet interference in East European affairs. Evidence for this deep resentment of the Soviet Union's political role in Eastern Europe has, of course, been most obvious at times of crisis, like Hungary 1956 and Czechoslovakia 1968. But it can also be deduced from the three decades of resistance to the learning of Russian or from the contempt that is popularly shown, say, to Soviet films. This popular hostility is expressed most clearly in crowd behaviour at sporting fixtures, an obvious surrogate for rather more significant conflict. The 1969 Soviet–Czechoslovak ice-hockey tournament was only the best-known example of this; others have included boxing matches between Romania and the Soviet Union and football matches between the Soviet and just about every East European team. Nor do East Europeans find it pleasant to have to accept economic subordination to the Soviet Union. There is widespread suspicion – not invariably justified – that the Soviet Union exploits East European countries in bilateral trade (some of this is the legacy of the 1950s), notably in ever-higher prices charged for Soviet raw materials. A good deal of this resentment has merged with more traditional anti-Russian sentiments. The national ideologies of every East European nation (including Bulgaria) contain such elements, and in the case of several there is the added complication of irredenta (Romania being the clearest case). Finally, the Soviet connection is also regarded as undesirable by those sections of the intelligentsia (not necessarily a majority), which perceive the distortions imposed on East European developments by the very strict definition of security and interest adopted by the Soviet Union. This is what underlies the call made by sections of the Polish opposition for the 'finlandization' of Poland.

Leadership

The nature and quality of leadership in Eastern Europe may also play a role in weakening the political fabric. Several aspects of this question are noteworthy. In the first place, there is now only one European communist leader of the first revolutionary vintage still in office – Enver Hoxha. All the others have come to office through some succession mechanism, which has varied from major to minor crises. Only one leadership succession arose through resignation – Ochab to Gomulka in 1956 – from which it is fair to draw the conclusion that leadership succession remains a time of uncertainty for East European polities.

Just as it is comparatively difficult to persuade a top leader to step down (Ulbricht or Gomulka), it is equally difficult for the new leader to establish himself in the short term. During the immediate post-succession period – until the new leader has consolidated his position within the system – the system itself will be exposed to disturbances of greater or lesser intensity. This points towards one of the important features of leadership in Eastern Europe – that the personality of the leader, rather than the office, is an important source of stability.[10] For example, it took Gierek at least three years to eliminate all other possible contenders for power and to ensure that no one could emulate his route to the top office by building up a local power base, as he had done in Silesia.

This raises another issue in connection with the emergence of a successor. Leaders appear quite consciously to pursue policies that will keep the powers of their subordinates divided and this has the inevitable consequence of a greater or lesser power struggle in the aftermath. Parallel with this, a long-established leader does gradually acquire a genuine authority (Kadar) and even legitimacy (Tito). But this is largely personal and does not accrue strictly to his office and least of all can it be transmitted (post-Tito Yugoslavia). The significance of this for the 1980s is that all Warsaw Pact leaders in Eastern Europe (Ceausescu and Kania excepted) are approaching their seventies and the chances are high that one or two will leave politics 'for biological reasons' in the coming years.

The Soviet Union also plays a role in this process, in that there is evidence to suggest that the East European politburos are an informal part of the central Soviet *nomenklatura* and that the Kremlin actively participates in decisions on promotions and demotions. In 1969 the Czechoslovak party discovered that Soviet acquiescence in the ousting of Novotny in 1967 did not mean Soviet abandonment of the claim to choose new leaders. Romania is fairly certainly an exception to this. While it is unclear whether the Soviet role is merely interdictory or whether the Kremlin has the *de facto* power to insist on the promotion of individuals, it is obvious that in certain circumstances this could mean that a candidate with strong local qualifications and a good chance of achieving rapid consolidation might be overruled as unacceptable to Moscow (Smrkovsky). The converse of this is also possible, where the Kremlin might insist on the promotion of a highly unsuitable candidate (Gero).

Another aspect of this problem concerns the qualities brought to the office of leader. The present generation of leaders can be said to have acquired its experience in politics rather than in administration. In other words, they all have some knowledge of the pre-communist period, when they were obliged to confront alternative ideas and modes of thought. Although the nexus might be difficult to demonstrate, it ought in theory at least to make them more open to a consideration of alternatives, to political innovation, to persuasion rather than command. But that generation is slowly passing and is being replaced by those whose formative years were spent in administration largely in the communist system. In a fairly crude way, therefore, we might reasonably speak of a dichotomy between 'politicians' and 'administrators' (Husak *v.* Strougal, for example); the qualities of the latter seem on the whole to be those of consistency and adherence to orderly procedures, rather than those attracted by political alternatives. In the Soviet Union this division was vividly illustrated by the switch in styles from Khrushchev to Brezhnev.

Corruption and Social Violence

Among the most obvious manifestations of this failure of socialization is the high level of corruption that has for all practical purposes become institutionalized in Eastern Europe.[11] It is hardly an exaggeration to argue that the social norm is corrupt, that even the smallest acts of service are performed only against a *douceur*, or that abuse of powers is rife. Evidence for this is legion. In 1978 a man was found to have amassed 17 million lei and 8kg of gold from illegal wine dealing in Romania. He had operated for a decade and had been able to buy off the lower levels of authority, including the party and the judiciary. Similar stories of large-scale corruption sanctioned by public opinion are common to every East European country. In Czechoslovakia, for example, in certain jobs income from bribes is higher than the official salary. In Hungary a manager built villas for his children out of enterprise funds, and, when called to account for this, replied that he had only acted out of paternal love. The wider conclusion to be drawn from the prevalence of corruption is to confirm the failure of socialization, and, equally important, to demonstrate the weakness of state control over large areas of society. Thus while individual political initiative might well attract dire penalties, in the economic sphere far more damaging activities are overlooked.

The emergence of the secondary or black economy in the last few years (or more precisely the availability of a great deal of new information on the subject) shows the nature of this damaging effect fairly clearly. On the one hand, by permitting individuals to exercise their entrepreneurial talents and thereby to maximize their incomes, East European governments are buying themselves a measure of stability, in that the ambitions of potential trouble-makers are channelled into individualist consumerism. On the other hand, the existence of this individualism undermines the officially propagated ideology of collectivism; it seriously distorts the ostensible rationality of the system; and it contributes greatly to the inequalities that are already such a striking feature of East European societies. It is hardly a matter for surprise, therefore, that when the East European consumer is faced with inadequate supplies he is likely to turn to violence. Here again the best evidence is from Poland, where the erosion of the system is furthest advanced. Nor is the popular mood likely to take kindly to the results of the energy crisis. Fuel shortages and power cuts are a regular feature of East European winters.

Thus in this somewhat indirect fashion, corruption may actually be linked with the apparent growth of social violence ('apparent' because it may only be that such cases are more widely reported than in the past). Some instances may be fairly directly political, like the Jiu valley miners' strike in 1977. Others are transformed into political acts by the intervention of the police. The riot at the Alexanderplatz in East Berlin in 1977 came about because the police moved in to restore order at a pop concert, and, in the rampage that followed, political slogans were shouted. Similarly the riot at the Unirei market in Bucharest in 1978 erupted because of police intervention. Other stories from East Germany tell of motorcycle gangs who bait the police for their evening's entertainment. This suggests that an enormous change in attitudes has taken place. The police no longer inspire the total dread of the 1950s in the younger generation, which has no memory of that time. This decline in the authority of one of the principal coercive instruments of the state has potentially serious implications for law and order.

The Role of the Police

Parallel with these processes there have been important developments in the methods of social control. There has been a marked rise in the sophistication of the instruments of control deployed in the 1970s in Eastern Europe, with the result that show trials and mass terror have vanished. These new methods include the following, not necessarily exhaustive list: 'social isolation', depriving the individual of all legal identity and social contacts, including identity card, work permit, etc. (East Germany, Bulgaria); eviction from one's house (Czechoslovakia, Hungary); dismissal from employment (widespread); military call-up (Poland, Yugoslavia); the establishment of a modern variant of the pillory, whereby petty offenders find their photographs and personal details exhibited on the village notice board (Romania); internal deportation (Romania); daily police supervision (Hungary); repeated arrest and interrogation (Poland, Czechoslovakia); psychiatric asylums (Romania); trial on some non-political charge; assassinations by secret police abroad (Yugoslavia, Bulgaria). All these are backed up by a battery of legislation and a vast network of police, secret police, militia, frontier guards, factory militia, inspectorates, and amateur informers. These informal methods of control have certain advantages. They attract less publicity, they maintain the appearance of a non-political procedure, and they make defence more difficult. To these may be added wholly extra-legal activities, which may or may not be sanctioned from above. The murder of Stanislaw Pyjas in Cracow and the beating-up of Paul Goma in Bucharest by, among others, a deputy Minister of the Interior in

Table 5.1 *Poland, the GDR, and Hungary 1977–80: percentage increases in the budgets of Ministries of the Interior over the preceding year*

		Poland	GDR[a]	Hungary
1977	Total budget	..	..	12.05
	Ministry of Interior budget	..	..	17.01
1978	Total budget	0.94	6.72	7.53
	Ministry of Interior budget	6.48	4.98	8.79
1979	Total budget	21.35	3.51	5.41
	Ministry of Interior budget	9.82	4.89	9.16
1980	Total budget	10.66	6.02	..
	Ministry of Interior budget	14.54	12.62	..

[a] As the Ministry of State Security is not shown separately the relevant figure shows outgoings for 'Public security, the administration of the law and guarding the frontiers'. In other words, this involves a somewhat wider compass than for the other two countries; on the other hand, this does not affect the annual percentage increase and trend towards higher expenditure shown in this table.
.. not available.
Sources: Data taken from *Dziennik Ustaw*, *Gesetzblatt der DDR*, and *Magyar Kozlony*, various dates.

mufti are examples. It may be that well-entrenched police establishments will conclude that the political leadership is unable or unwilling to exercise a high enough level of discipline, and, therefore, that the ministry of the interior must take matters into its own hands. Should this happen, it could again pose serious problems for communist parties in the event of a breakdown of major proportions.

Conclusion
The overall assessment of East European politics at the start of the 1980s must be that these societies are in a form of unstable equilibrium. The crisis in Poland in the summer of 1980 demonstrates vividly how easily the equilibrium can be upset. It does not say much for the stability of the Polish political order that it could be so seriously affected by sporadic strikes and the establishment of a strike committee in Gdansk that was able to validate its authority over the Gdansk area

so easily. Poland was clearly at one end of the spectrum as far as considerations of stability were concerned, but evidently it differed from other East European states only in acuteness of the crisis of authority and legitimacy.

On the other hand, while the kinds of pressures that affected Poland were potentially present throughout the area, there was no inevitability about the eruption of turmoil elsewhere. As long as existing lines of development could be sustained, there was no overwhelming danger of matters going awry. Although it was true that the room for manoeuvre at the disposal of communist leaderships had shrunk appreciably in the late 1970s – declining economic growth rates were the most visible indicator – there was much that favoured the maintenance of the status quo, notably inertia. Where the political leaderships had cause for concern was in a situation where events outside their control could threaten to overturn the equilibrium. It would be foolish to attempt to pin this down with any claim to precision. It might be that nothing short of a major conflagration would trigger off a disequilibrium of this kind and that East European societies would be able to survive well into the 1980s with their existing political systems intact, for all their weaknesses. But the message of the Polish crisis was a serious one, that East European leaders would ignore at their peril.

Notes

1   On modernization and its application to Eastern Europe see Charles Gati, ed., *The Politics of Modernization in Eastern Europe* (London and New York, Praeger, 1975), especially the essay by Vernon V. Aspaturian, 'Marxism and the Meanings of Modernization', pp. 3–21; see also Andrew C. Janos, 'Systemic Models and the Theory of Change in the Comparative Study of Communist Politics', in Janos, ed., *Authoritarian Politics in Communist Europe* (Berkeley, U. of California, 1976) pp. 1–30.

2   On political integration see Zvi Gitelman, 'Power and Authority in Eastern Europe', in Chalmers Johnson, ed., *Change in Communist Systems* (Stanford, Stanford UP, 1970), pp. 235–64. The details of the crisis in Poland are discussed in several studies, including George Schöpflin, *Poland: a Society in Crisis* (London, Institute for the Study of Conflict, 1979; Conflict Study no. 112).

3   The concept of ideological decomposition is taken, above all, from Leszek Kolakowski's work.

4   Marxism and its functions as detailed here are discussed in Milovan Djilas, 'Die versteinerte Ideologie', *Die Zeit*, 28 Sept. 1974.

5   The role of rationality has been widely discussed in this context, notably George Konrad and Ivan Szelenyi, *Intellectuals on the Road to Class Power* (New York,

Harcourt, Brace, 1979); a summary of the DiP (the initials of a Polish organization whose name in full can be translated as Experience and Future) document is in Radio Free Europe Research, *Poland*, 2 Nov. 1979. See also Terez Laky, 'A recentralizalas rejtett mechanizmusai' [the covert mechanisms of recentralisation], *Valosag*, 23/2 (Feb. 1980), pp. 31–41.

6   The nature, quality, and characteristics of opposition are analysed in Rudolf Tokes, ed., *Opposition in Eastern Europe* (London, Macmillan, 1979).

7   Social fragmentation is argued by Ferenc Erdei, 'A magyar tarsadalom a ket haboru kozott' [Hungarian society between the two wars], *Valosag*, 19/4 (Apr. 1976), pp. 25–53, and 19/5 (May 1976), pp. 36–58.

8   This section is derived from the argument in Walter C. Connor, *Socialism, Politics and Equality* (New York, Columbia UP, 1979) and personal discussions with Dr Connor.

9   This point is ultimately based on Istvan Markus, 'Az ismeretlen foszereplo – a szegenyparasztsag' [the unknown principal actor – the poor peasantry], *Valosag*, 23/4 (Apr. 1980), pp. 13–39.

10   On leadership, authority, and stability see Jerzy Wiatr, *Polityka*, 20 Jan. 1979.

11   Corruption in its various forms is discussed in George Schöpflin, 'Where Corruption becomes a Way of Life', *Soviet Analyst*, 8/12 (14 June 1979).

6   Economic Reforms as an Issue in Soviet–East European Relations
by *Wlodzimierz Brus* *

THE purpose of this essay is not to set out the results of specific research but to provide an introduction to the topic. Nor are economic reforms *per se* my subject here. The question addressed is (to put it bluntly): has the USSR opposed economic reforms in the East European countries in the past, and *is this at present or in the near future a likely source of conflict in Soviet – East European relations?* In view of the growing economic difficulties throughout the Soviet bloc and hence the mounting pressures to rationalize the economic system, this question assumes some importance. It goes without saying that any answer given from outside the corridors of power in the USSR and Eastern Europe involves a great deal of guesswork and has to be treated with the utmost caution.

With Yugoslavia left out, the term 'economic reform' used in this essay denotes a move from what I have called the 'centralistic model of a centrally planned economy'[1] (the basic features of which have survived from the beginning of the 1930s up to the present day in the USSR, and which have also been characteristic of all the Soviet-bloc countries of Eastern Europe except Hungary) towards the devolution of current economic decisions to enterprises (or associations of them) and wider use of the market mechanism. There are, of course, several conceivable degrees of such devolution, so we need to draw a boundary: in my own language this boundary may be defined as a 'model of a centrally planned economy with a *regulated* market mechanism' which has its rough equivalent in practice in the Hungarian New Economic Mechanism, particularly as it was designed in 1968. In other words, we disregard an economic reform of the Yugoslav 1965 type, with the enterprises not only autonomous in their current operations but also responsible for the mainstream of investment decisions; this restriction seems perfectly admissible, for such

* The author is grateful to Philip Hanson for constructive comments on an earlier draft of this essay.

a change has not been contemplated as a practical possibility by other East European countries over the period in question.

Within the framework defined above my view is that an economic reform might have become a source of conflict between 'reformist' countries and the USSR (plus other 'conservatives') not basically because of the economic content of the reform, but mainly because (and to the extent which) the economic reform was conceived as part of a broader political blueprint aiming at some sort of democratic pluralism connected with national aspirations and the denunciation of Soviet-type totalitarianism. Otherwise not much proof of Soviet attempts to block economic reforms in the strict sense can be seen, particularly in what I call the 'second wave' of reforms (from the early 1960s), when the initial fears of the inevitably 'subversive' political implications of economic reform subsided, and the ideological reservations against 'market socialism' (especially strident around 1958 in connection with the renewed clash with Yugoslavia and the 'revisionist' Ljubljana programme of the League of Communists of Yugoslavia) lost some of their political urgency. Consequently it would seem that the (generally) unsucessful reform attempts so far can scarcely be regarded as a result of Soviet pressure or the single case of relative success (Hungary) as a hard-won and exceptional concession. This is not to say that there were (or are) no political obstacles to economic reform; the sole point here is that these political (and other) obstacles are in the main not of the 'Soviet-East European conflict' category.

A few historical reminders, which in my opinion corroborate the view expressed above, may be in order. I will not go into the development of official Soviet views on trade, money, the 'law of value' and so on after the 'victory of socialism' which from the early 1930s until Stalin's death (*The Economic Problems of Socialism in the USSR*) constitutes an interesting theoretical and practical trend. What needs to be noted, however, is the fact that the first signs of a tendency towards an economic reform in our sense of the term came from the USSR in 1954–5, and even the first articles by E. Liberman, overshadowed later by his 1962 *Pravda* piece, were published before the XX Congress of the CPSU. In 1955, at an East Berlin conference of economists from socialist countries, a Polish paper with a number of reform ideas received a great deal of sympathetic attention, particularly from the hosts; in the course of the subsequent year and a half relations between

East German and Polish economists developed extremely well, and several quite radically reformist articles were published in leading GDR journals. Contacts with Gyorgy Peter – at the time the pioneer of economic reforms in Hungary – made me believe that prior to the uprising there were no signs of opposition to the idea from the Soviet side.

This attitude changed sharply both within the countries in question and in the USSR when it became clear that an economic reform can also be a component of a broad movement towards political pluralism. Not only the events in Hungary, which have been of the utmost importance from this point of view, but also developments in Poland before and immediately after October 1956, must have alerted Soviet and East European leaderships to the possible implications of economic reform; the marketeers, *inter alios*, were singled out as the prime targets of the anti-revisionist campaign. The main spectre was apparently the link between the economic reform and the independent workers' councils in industrial enterprises. The reform was a factor in the creation of the economic pre-conditions for genuine activity of the councils and stimulated the process of de-stalinization from below, so characteristic of Hungary and Poland in 1956. Hence the strength of the political resistance to economic reforms. I remember well how in early 1957 a conservative member of the Polish Economic Council accused us – the supporters of the workers' council idea – of a plan to create a 'parallel power-network' (*'dvoevlastie'*) ultimately directed against the 'leading role' of the party. It had seemed to us then (and still seems) that the Soviet and local political élite was much more ready to swallow such obvious ideological setbacks as de-collectivization than even tentative threats to the monopoly of power. A contemporary analogy can be found in the apparent absence of any adverse reaction to such phenomena as the revival of private or semi-private activity in several East European countries (small-scale production, trade, services, etc.) or to the widespread circulation of foreign currencies, let alone to the support for individual agricultural plots. The negative attitude to economic reform regarded as an element of fundamental political change has repeated itself – to an appropriately higher degree – in the Czechoslovak case of 1968.

On the other hand, as soon as the threat of a political break-away from the established system (and the bloc) was regarded as past, the idea of economic reform *sensu stricto* was revived and legitimized.

Already in 1958 the conservative Czechoslovak leadership made the first abortive attempt: it was followed by the much more elaborate (and for a while, actually implemented), East German 'New Economic System' in 1963/4. In 1965 the Hungarian Central Committee accepted the blueprint of a comprehensive reform put into practice according to the original timetable (1 January 1968). In the same year the 'Kosygin reform' was announced in the USSR, putting the final seal of legitimacy on formerly revisionist economic ideas; this made an immediate impact on the Bulgarian party leadership which came out with probably the most radical blueprint in 1966. The year 1964 also saw another attempt at a Polish reform. Again, may I mention some personal experiences during this period which in a way illustrate this change of climate: in 1964 I was invited to lecture on problems of economic reform to selected groups of staff-members of Gosplan and Gosekonomkomissya in Moscow and similar audiences in Tashkent, and I found the atmosphere most businesslike; the only ideological question that I can recall concerned the predominance of private agriculture in Poland. In December 1966, at an international conference of economists from socialist countries near Prague, the Soviet delegation (with Gatovsky as its head) almost enthusiastically supported the Czech economic blueprint.

The Czechoslovak events of 1968 obviously contributed again to a change of heart; nevertheless the Hungarian reform went ahead and I could not find any evidence (private contacts included) that the USSR had tried to put pressure on the Hungarians to back-pedal, although it was fairly evident that both in the USSR and in Hungary influential political groups and bureaucratic strata were reluctant to go along with the reform. An alliance between these groups was probably a factor in forcing a partial retreat from the principles of the New Economic Mechanism in 1972/3, and in this sense one could perhaps speak about Soviet involvement. Whether this should be regarded as an indication of a more general and lasting conflict between the USSR and Hungary over the issue of economic reform is doubtful, particularly in view of later developments which point to the intention to deepen rather than to abandon the New Economic Mechanism.

Poland presents another example of a similar nature: in March 1968 accusations of market revisionism were used as a propaganda weapon; but again, when this 'mini-cultural revolution' achieved its objectives, the plans for economic reform surfaced again (while Gomulka was still in office), and afterwards were widened and pursued more energetically in the first few years of the Gierek leadership, without any signs of Soviet displeasure.

Some kinds of inter-country differences, with the USSR assuming a more 'anti-market' position, could be detected at the beginning of the 1970s with regard to the *methods of Comecon integration*. At a conference (formally theoretical but with strong political connotations) held in Budapest in November 1970 the Soviet representatives clearly opposed the Hungarian (and Polish) view of the predominant role of the market-type instruments of integration.[2] It would be fairly easy to explain the rationale of the then Hungarian position in terms both of straightforward economic interests and of the consistency problems of the New Economic Mechanism. Whether the Hungarian position in this respect remains the same today it is difficult to say. I should not be surprised, however, if, in view of developments in world markets for primary commodities, Hungary became less insistent on the 'marketization' of intra-Comecon relations. State economic and political interests play the decisive role here, and it seems hardly appropriate to extrapolate positions taken with regard to the methods of inter-state relations on the general attitude towards domestic economic reforms. Besides, both in practical operation and in the 'Comprehensive Programme' of 1971, some signs of recognition of the need to enhance the role of market instruments appear as well.

As indicated above, none of this means that economic reforms in Eastern Europe (and in the USSR for that matter) no longer face political obstacles. On the contrary: in my view political reasons figure prominently among the causes of failure of the reforms: (i) vested interests of the party and state bureaucracy still interact with fears that, however narrowly the reform may be circumscribed within the economic sphere, an 'overspill' into the political sphere cannot be excluded; (ii) there are political elements in the persistent difficulty faced by the Soviet and East European élites in checking over-expansionist tendencies which result in general market disequilibria highly inimical to market-oriented systemic changes; (iii) the lack of political channels of conflict-resolution aggravates some of the intrinsic difficulties of the reformed economic system which is called upon to solve the formidable problems of combining central planning with a regulated market mechanism: schemes meant to harmonize common and individual goals by attempting to make only *direct* interests coincide, i.e. based on incentives only, without developing the feeling of partnership in the decision-making process both in the work-place and (most important) through democratic political processes on a national scale, are hardly likely to succeed as instruments of integration of autonomous parts into a more cohesive whole. The latter point seems to me particularly relevant for explaining some of the troubles the Hungarian New Economic Mechanism has run into.

The political obstacles listed above are basically common to all countries of the Soviet bloc. If they persist and make the present predominating system essentially unreformable, despite the economic pressures, internal conflicts are bound to grow. As I have tried to show, these conflicts are primarily not of the Soviet-East European or generally inter-country type. They may in some circumstances develop such when, for example, the leadership of a particular country decides under exceptionally strong domestic pressures to surge ahead with an economic reform disregarding political risks that in turn may prove unacceptable for the USSR – which is especially cautious because of superpower considerations. Then we may experience some sort of repetition of the Czechoslovak case, even without any open commitment of the local leadership to a 'deviationist' political line. A more probable scenario, however, would seem to be a further search for solutions carrying at least some promise of improving the system's performance without endangering the political edifice. In my opinion economic reforms will, therefore, remain on the East European agenda – with Moscow's blessing but with slim chances of substantial success.

Notes
1   W. Brus, *The Market in a Socialist Economy* (London, Routledge & Kegan Paul, 1972).
2   The proceedings of the conference were published (in English): *The Market of Socialist Economic Integration. Selected Conference Papers* (Budapest, Akademiai Kiado, 1973).

7 Soviet Trade with Eastern Europe
by Philip Hanson*

OUGHT we to expect a growth in East European[1] economic dependence on the USSR in the early 1980s? That is the question to which this essay is addressed. Addressing a question does not, of course, entail answering it, and I shall adopt the usual academic practice of reformulating the question so that it becomes more answerable and less interesting.

Economic 'dependence' has been defined, for the purpose of foreign-policy analysis, as the percentage reduction in GNP over a specific period of time which can be visited on the 'dependent' nation by deliberate policy action to that end on the part of the government of another nation on which it is dependent.[2] Such dependence can be, and usually is, reciprocal, but there is no reason why the reciprocal dependence of each of two nations should be equal or even of similar scale.

Actually measuring 'dependence', thus defined, is tricky and can seldom be done with great confidence. A country which is the target of such economic pressures will attempt to substitute alternative markets, inputs, or sources of supply for those withheld or reduced by the nation waging economic welfare. The cost of this substitution is very hard to assess in advance. So is the extent to which sanctions can be evaded. There can be little doubt, though, that Eastern Europe is quite heavily dependent on the USSR, and that the degree of dependence of the USSR on Eastern Europe is very much less. In recent years East European trade with the USSR has been about one-third of total East European trade, while the latter has been of the order of one-fifth of estimated total East European GNP. Thus exports to the USSR have been of the order of 6 per cent of total East European output, and imports from the USSR of the order of

* The author is indebted to Mr Frank Bignell, Professor Wlodzimierz Brus, Professor Carl McMillan, Mr Jeremy Russell, Mr Alan H. Smith, and the two Readers of the volume for comments on an earlier draft of this essay.

7 per cent of total final domestic expenditure in Eastern Europe. Since Soviet GNP in 1978 was about 3.3 times that of the whole of Eastern Europe, these same flows loom much less large in Soviet than in East European economic activity.[3] (See Tables 7.1 and 7.2 and Appendix, Table E1.)

The commodity composition of these flows, moreover, reinforces the impression of relatively great East European dependence. Fuel and raw materials have made up around a half of Soviet exports to Eastern Europe in recent years (in current prices), but around a tenth of Soviet imports from Eastern Europe, while machinery has constituted about a half of Soviet imports from these countries (55 per cent in 1978, in fact).[4] Broadly speaking, it is the fuels and raw materials which are more readily exportable to the West and for which there tends to be excess demand at existing prices within CMEA ('hard' goods), while a considerable part of intra-CMEA machinery trade represents an 'exchange of inefficiencies', or 'soft' goods not readily saleable on competitive markets and tending to be in surplus within CMEA.

Unless, therefore, the composition of East European trade or output was to change dramatically, a rise in the ratio of East European-Soviet trade to total East European economic activity is likely to entail an increase in East European 'dependence' on the USSR. The initial question can therefore be re-phrased as follows: should we expect trade with the USSR to rise relatively to other trade and to production in Eastern Europe? Even this question is still too large for a short paper, however, since changes in this ratio will be the outcome of a large number of influences. The discussion that follows will therefore be focused on the two influences that are most interesting from a foreign policy point of view: the influence of East–West relations and the influence of Soviet policy.

The layout of the rest of the paper is as follows. The first section outlines basic issues in Soviet–East European economic relations; the second summarizes some major developments of the 1970s; the third deals with the likely influence of East–West relations; and the last section considers Soviet policy aims.

Issues in Soviet-East European Relations
There is a huge Western literature on intra-CMEA relations, much

Table 7.1   Eastern Europe: trade with the USSR as a percentage of total
trade 1960–78 (selected years: current prices)

	Exports	Imports
1960	36.9	38.1
1965	39.8	38.2
1970	36.4	36.7
1973	34.6	30.9
1975	34.5	31.9
1978	35.4	35.1

Note: The trade values in the source were all expressed in current US dollars, derived
from CMEA trade data converted from national currencies into dollars either
directly through official exchange rates (total trade) or indirectly through
foreign-trade roubles into dollars at official rates. The Soviet-share figures are
distorted by the fact that trade with the USSR is conducted at different prices
from trade with non-CMEA countries, and the distortion will not be constant
in direction or degree.

Source: Derived from CIA, HES 1979, p. 105.

Table 7.2   Eastern Europe and the USSR: 1978 trade and GNP values
(US $ bn at 1978 prices)

	GNP	Total Exports	Total Imports
USSR	1,254	52.4	50.8
Eastern Europe	384	64.2	71.0

Note: The trade value data are composed of transactions at different prices with
different groups of trade partners, as indicated in the Note to Table 7.1. The
GNP data are CIA estimates at US prices which again are not comparable to
the prices underlying the trade values.

Source: CIA, HES 1979, pp. 22, 100, 105.

of it directed to the question of who is doing what to whom. Only
the very broadest issues are reviewed here.

First, it is important to distinguish between long-term and medium-
term gains and losses from Eastern Europe's Moscow connection.
Nearly all the serious economic analysis has of necessity been concentrated on the latter. This should not lead us to omit all reference

to long-term considerations. In the long term (more than 10 years, say) it is likely that the orientation of Eastern Europe's trade towards the USSR, within the framework of CMEA trade arrangements, has been detrimental to the growth of production and income levels in the region. As a matter of history, this (postulated) effect can hardly be separated from the effects of the enforced espousal of adversary or semi-adversary relations with the Western world and of a Soviet-style economic system. There is every reason to believe, however, that exclusion from much of the Western world's technological traffic (through international investment, especially) has been deleterious to East European growth. The imposition of Soviet-style priorities for investment and labour mobilization may have brought more than offsetting growth advantages for the least developed of the East European nations (Romania and Bulgaria), but is unlikely to have done so for those at the top of the development range (GDR, Czechoslovakia). Among the studies providing tentative evidence for this view is the fascinating comparative study of FRG and GDR development by Gregory and Leptin.[5] They conclude that the GDR's relatively low involvement in trade (with all partners) may be the main reason for the GDR's failure to grow more rapidly than the FRG after greater immediate post-war economic losses.

Generally, the East European countries were pressed into an economic mould in which foreign trade activities tended to be lower, relatively to production, than was normal in the West. The evidence of 'systemic undertrading' was strong, at all events, in the 1950s and 1960s, though there is some indication that this phenomenon had ceased to be evident by the early 1970s.[6] Within this systemically circumscribed trade total, their trade was focused, not merely on other CMEA trade partners, but on the USSR in particular, in the famous radial pattern.[7] For the most developed CMEA nations, that meant a focusing on trade with an economy less technologically advanced than themselves. There must be a strong presumption (which many of the Czechoslovak reform economists of the Dubcek era shared) that this operated to retard technical change.

The medium-term consequences of CMEA arrangements for member states have lent themselves to more systematic assessment, however, and here the picture is different. The evidence of East European economic benefits' outweighing those of the USSR in the past two decades is strong. Indeed some studies have suggested that the USSR, far from making the usual gains from trade, makes losses from its trade with the rest of CMEA. In other words, the full resource costs of its exports to its CMEA partners may in at least some periods have been greater than the full resource costs that it would have incurred in providing directly by its own productive efforts the goods which it received in exchange.[8]

Assessments of this kind, indicating absolute Soviet losses from trade with Eastern Europe, are controversial. In particular, apparent East European 'exploitation' of the Soviet Union indicated by relative prices in intra-CMEA trade may be mitigated or even reversed by Soviet success in imposing on CMEA trade partners quantities of imports and exports very different for those which the trade partners would freely choose at the prices in question. Any such imposition is inherently hard to measure. It has at least been firmly demonstrated, however, that (a) changes over time in the net barter terms of trade between the USSR and Eastern Europe have often been to the disadvantage of the former (this was especially so in 1964–6), so that any Soviet gains from this trade have at certain periods been significantly reduced; (b) the USSR has for considerable periods of time traded with the East European countries on terms that imposed on it a considerable opportunity cost in more profitable opportunities forgone on the world markets, so that any Soviet gains from this trade have at least been less than they could have been.[9] This latter relationship means that Poland or Hungary, for example, could obtain oil, iron ore, rolled steel, etc. from the USSR at a lower resource cost (in making the exports to pay for them) than they could from any non-CMEA source.

This is still the case with respect to the average terms, at least, of Soviet-East European transactions. By requiring oil deliveries (for instance) above a stated level to be reciprocated either with hard currency payment or by additional investment in Soviet energy projects, it is true that the USSR in the mid-1970s attempted to move its 'marginal' terms of trade for some products in Eastern Europe closer to world-market relativities. The Orenburg gas pipeline (completed early in 1979) is the major example of the joint project approach. But additional CMEA joint energy projects do not seem to have been initiated in the late 1970s.

It is in this sense that Eastern Europe could be said to have enjoyed an advantageous economic relationship with the USSR in the 1960s and 1970s, at least as far as medium-term consequences are concerned. And it has been natural for Western observers to interpret this as an economic *quid* for a political *quo*: the cost to the USSR of buying an economic dependence that is politically useful for Soviet control of Eastern Europe. Hewett has argued persuasively, however, that the shifts over time in the terms of trade have not simply been manipulated by the USSR, but have to some extent arisen through superior East European skill and knowledge in price negotiations. Soviet policymakers, in other words, have probably not willed the extent of the actual costs incurred. It is rather that political considerations may have led them to accept a commerical beating more readily than they might otherwise have done.

There are two more aspects of Soviet–East European economic relations which merit separate mention: the relationship between 'East–East' and East–West trade, and the forms and methods of CMEA integration.

For reasons of arithmetic, of course, there tends to be an inverse relationship between the percentage shares taken by the West and by other CMEA nations in the trade of a CMEA member-state. (Trade with the Third World and with other socialist countries also comes into the total, but it has remained relatively small for Eastern Europe.) It is far from self-evident, however, that East–East and East–West trade are necessarily and in most respects substitutes for each other, and not complementary. There seem in fact to be a number of actual and potential complementarities between the two categories of trade.[10]

For example, the acquisition of imported Western technology, though often uncoordinated and competitive as between different CMEA economies, has also in many instances worked to strengthen production specialization and co-operation within CMEA. For one thing, the Western seller of technology will generally prefer a deal (e.g. over a turnkey project) that is on the scale of the CMEA market as a whole rather than on the scale of a single member-state's market. Fiat's East European deals are a frequently cited example. Fiat has probably done more than intra-CMEA planning to integrate the East European motor industry.[11]

Similarly, the growth of hard-currency trade with the West may have intensified pressures within CMEA for hard-currency payment for intra-CMEA deliveries which themselves embodied hard-currency settlement within CMEA, and this represents a certain multilateralization of intra-bloc trade, which should facilitate the growth of this trade. And pressures to bring intra-CMEA prices closer to 'world' prices should tend to promote CMEA integration because, to quote McMillan:

> So long as some system of regional preferences is retained, the removal of sharp divergences between regional and world market price relatives ... will reduce pressures to divert goods previously underpriced within the region to extra-regional markets and, by exerting competitive pressures on goods hitherto relatively over-priced, raise their quality as well as their price-attractiveness to regional purchasers.[12]

The nature of CMEA integration methods is obviously important to Soviet–East European economic relations. The Soviet Union has tried, on the whole, to increase the role of plan co-ordination and has pushed on occasions in the direction of unified supranational planning. In doing so, it seems to have been fighting on two fronts: first, against nationalist demands for autonomy in economic development, pressed most conspicuously by Romania; second, against economic reformers' preferences – articulated most conspicuously by Hungarian economists and officials – for economic co-operation on market-economy lines, with intra-CMEA currency convertibility and direct international transactions between enterprises, and without detailed central planning. Recent developments on these fronts have been analysed by Alan Smith, who concludes that developments in the middle-to-late 1970s were mainly on 'Soviet' lines, but that the Soviet approach is still far from being clearly and decisively victorious.[13] It remains the case that the extent of supranational powers within CMEA is minimal. Soviet ability informally to pressure the smaller East European countries to follow Soviet economic dictates is in many ways limited. In the judgement of Professor Brus, the USSR seems to treat informal pressure and formal control as substitutes, relying more on the former under Stalin. Moscow may now once more be better able to use informal pressure; Soviet policymakers may therefore worry less about increasing supranational (formal) authority.[14] The CMEA joint projects (mostly on Soviet territory and mostly in the energy and raw materials sectors) are of some importance but are none the less still quite small in aggregate relatively to total investment and trade.

Developments in the 1970s
In retrospect one can identify three elements in Soviet and East European policies in the late 1960s and early 1970s: a turning away from economic reforms; the adoption of import-led growth strategies (emphasizing the import of Western technology); and intensified efforts to increase CMEA integration.

I am inclined to see rather more complementarity than conflict between these policies. The workings of the unreformed economic system seem to reduce the benefits derivable from technology imports compared with those obtainable in a capitalist market economy[15] but they certainly do not eliminate these benefits altogether; to that extent, the import-led growth strategy was a substitute for domestic economic reform. Such reform, moreover, had tended to conflict with existing modes of CMEA integration.[16] And it has already been suggested that there is considerable complementarity between CMEA integration and an increasing involvement in East–West trade.

Consistency is not to be confused with success, however, and it now looks as though this cluster of policies has failed, at least for the time being. The rapid and sustained growth in exports to the West that would have paid for a sustained growth of technology imports did not materialize; greater openness to the Western world economy meant *inter alia* a greater vulnerability to imported 'Western' inflation, and Western inflation accelerated dramatically; and, for reasons largely unconnected with the Western slowdown, Soviet growth decelerated markedly through the 1970s.

To what extent the failure of the import-led growth strategy can be blamed on the weaknesses of unreconstructed economic systems, and to what extent on Western stagflation, is obscure. My guess is that a really dynamic late-developing economy would have been able to push up its share of OECD imports substantially even amid the uncertain growth and the increasing protectionism of the 1970s: countries like Brazil, Singapore, Hong Kong, and South Korea have done so. These four countries accounted for 1.5 per cent of OECD imports in 1970 and 3.3 per cent in 1978, while the Soviet share rose only from 1.3 to 1.6 per cent.[17] And it may well be that dynamism of that sort, if it is attainable at all through anything so superficial as a set of policy decisions, requires economic reorganization more drastic than that of the Hungarian New Economic Mechanism.

In the late 1970s, therefore, all the CMEA countries strove, with varying degrees of urgency, to curb imports from the West and reduce hard-currency deficits and outstanding debt. In the Soviet case this has been largely successful. New orders for Western machinery were sharply reduced after 1976. It is true that large grain imports recurred in 1977/8, obscuring the underlying improvement, and that the lag between orders and deliveries, in the case of machinery (about a year on average), further complicated things. All the same, the merchandise trade deficit with the West fell between 1978 and 1979 from about $3 billion to about $1.6 billion. And rising hard-currency arms sales and the increase in gold prices probably put the Soviet hard-currency account in the black even in 1978, and enabled outstanding Soviet debt to be reduced.[18]

For the East European countries, apart from Czechoslovakia, the hard-currency position has been much harder to rectify. Not blessed with mineral and fuel reserves on the Soviet scale, nor with a super-power's arms industries, they lack the main ingredients of the Soviet Union's external financial strength (not completely, as the existence of Czechoslovak and Polish arms exports indicates, but East European resources and capabilities of these kinds are of a very much smaller order of magnitude).

It is rash to assume, however, that these circumstances necessarily led to a turning inward towards greater reliance on intra-CMEA trade and investment. Martin Kohn, making this point in a paper written early in 1979, noted that statistical evidence of increasing Soviet–East European trade volume (as distinct from increasing value in current prices) did not show a clear turning inward between 1974 and 1976.[19]

What did happen, however, in the mid-1970s was that the USSR both improved its (net barter) terms of trade with Eastern Europe, and, at the same time, lessened the potential impact of this shift by extending aid to its CMEA partners in the form of annual merchandise trade surpluses that were larger than had generally been tolerated under the usual bilateral balancing régime. This phenomenon was noted by Kohn and elegantly analysed by Hewett.[20] Hewett shows that the USSR's gross barter terms of trade with Eastern Europe did not move in line with its net barter terms of trade in 1974–6. That is to say, the index of Soviet export volume did not fall in relation to the index of import volume as much as the export unit value index rose in relation to the import unit value index. To put it another way: as the purchasing power of a unit of Soviet exports in terms of imports from Eastern Europe increased, the USSR did not extort a corresponding increase in the number of units suppled from Eastern Europe; instead it ameliorated the harshness of the terms-of-trade shift by (in effect) extending credit.

At the same time, as Hewett also shows, the Soviet Union was not raising its export prices, relatively to the prices of its imports from Eastern Europe, by as much as would have been 'justified' by the concurrent changes in world prices – given the commodity-composition of Soviet–East European trade. Far from acting towards Eastern Europe like hard-faced men who had done well out of the oil-price war, the Politburo behaved like the better sort of landlord: raising the rent belatedly and by rather less than the general rate of inflation, and allowing more time to pay. Moscow had taken the opportunity to reverse some of the terms-of-trade losses it suffered *vis-à-vis* Eastern Europe a decade earlier, but was still making implicit subsidies available to its CMEA partners – several of whom have higher average living standards than their patron. This was not being done, we may safely assume, out of the kindness of Mr Brezhnev's heart, but rather out of a combination of *realpolitik* and happenstance.

The movement of Soviet net and gross barter terms of trade in the late 1970s is harder to trace, because of the reduction in the volume (and some value) data published in the Soviet trade returns. It looks as though the same pattern may have been repeated: a period of fairly stable net barter terms of trade being accompanied by a closer approach to bilateral balancing, and then a further gain in Soviet net barter terms of trade towards the end of the decade being accompanied by substantial Soviet trade surpluses. Thus in 1978 Soviet merchandise trade with the six European CMEA partners showed, according to Soviet trade returns, a small overall net surplus of $249 million, which represented the excess of surpluses with Bulgaria and the GDR over deficits with the other four. For 1979, however, the Soviet Union reported merchandise trade surpluses with each of these six partners, totalling $1,623 million.[21]

Meanwhile CMEA integration, as Alan Smith has documented, developed in the 1970s towards greater integration and co-ordination of CMEA nations' investment programmes, compared with the earlier emphasis merely on co-ordination of some current output (as well as trade) decisions. Even the joint projects funded by the Comecon International Investment Bank, and the new international management organization (Interatominstrument, Intertekstilmash, etc.), however, probably amount to a less extensive co-ordination of bloc investment decisions than results in Western Europe from the activities of multinational corporations. The problems stemming from the differences (and rigidities) among national price structures and the absence of a common currency or of currency convertibility are still considerable. Two observations by the Soviet authority O. Rybakov indicate their extent. In early 1979 he observed that the need to reach agreement on the allocation of output from joint investment projects before trying to co-ordinate investment had been neglected 'until recently'. And he pointed out that foreign-trade effectiveness criteria applicable to CMEA as a group had not yet been developed.[22]

The Influence of East–West Relations
East–West relations can affect Soviet–East European economic relations in two main ways: first, through the economic linkages from the state of the Western-world economies through East–West trade: second, through policy changes arising from alterations in East–West political relations. With respect to the former, it has been argued above that a slowdown or reduction in East–West economic exchanges may not have the automatic result of increasing intra-CMEA trade. Indeed there are some linkages which could tend to reduce the latter. This is not surprising. After all, there is no reason for the total trade of an East European or any other nation to be a fixed quantum; and elementary trade theory envisages trade-creating as well as trade-diverting effects of the formation of customs unions (for example).

It might none the less be supposed that there could be some mechanisms tending to substitute one trade partner for another. If Poland, say, can no longer get particular items of advanced machinery from the West for balance-of-payments reasons, will it not be natural to turn to the GDR, perhaps, as an alternative supplier? And if Soviet net barter terms of trade with Eastern Europe have improved, does not that compel the East European nations to deliver more goods than before merely to obtain the same quantity of oil and so on from the USSR? And given the greater external financial strength of the USSR and the tendency of Western bankers to relate the creditworthiness of East European states to the apparent capacity and willingness of Moscow to bail them out, does not the present financial conjuncture enable the USSR to exert especially effective pressure to reorient East European trade in a more Easterly direction?

These are plausible scenarios, but there is no obvious reason *a priori* why factors of this sort should outweigh those which tend to link the destinies of East–East and East–West trade. One can merely say that the former are rather more of a static kind (a reshuffling of given CMEA resources) while the latter are more dynamic in nature, with East–West trade tending to affect – generally after a time-lag – the growth rate of CMEA output and the nature of intra-CMEA relations. The gist of this argument can be put rather more precisely and formally as follows. Assume (oversimplifying somewhat) that European CMEA nations' trade consists solely of trade among themselves and trade with the West. Then total trade in any year consists of 'Eastern' plus 'Western' trade. A fall in the volume of the latter, other things being equal, necessarily entails a rise in the share of 'Eastern' in total trade. Given the ratio of total trade volume to real GNP, however (see the definition of 'dependence' in the introductory section above), this change in itself entails no increase in East European dependence on the USSR. In practice (see the previous paragraph) there will probably be some substitution of 'Eastern' for 'Western' transactions for various traded goods, so some increase in dependence should be expected.

Over time, however, the trade:GNP ratio in real terms for this group of countries (as for most others) has been tending to rise. The factors engendering this increase are various. Both Soviet and Western economists, using somewhat different terminology, attribute a major role to post-Second World War technological change as an influence favouring greater internationalization of production and exchange. The hypothesis that is suggested here is that for CMEA, in addition to such general influences, the volume of East–West trade is a separate factor tending to raise both the total foreign-trade:GNP ratio and the 'Eastern' trade:GNP ratio over time. This proposition has not yet been rigorously tested but it seems to be broadly consistent with the observable development of CMEA trade since 1960.

If this is so, then a reduction in the volume of East–West trade has three consequences (other things equal) for intra-CMEA trade. First, as a matter of arithmetic, it raises the share of 'Eastern' to total CMEA trade. This has no implications at all for East European trade.

Second, it leads to some substitution of 'Eastern' for 'Western' trade. This tends to raise the 'Eastern' trade:GNP ratio and to that extent to increase East European dependence on the USSR. The argument here is that this effect is mainly of a once-for-all kind. Third, a reduction in East–West trade, sustained for an appreciable period, tends to reduce the growth rate of the CMEA nations' trade:GNP ratios by more than just its own immediate arithmetic impact: that is, it tends to reduce the growth rate of the 'Eastern' trade:GNP ratio as well. This effect tends to operate with a time-lag: e.g. imports of Western pipeline technology for the Orenburg project in one period tending to raise intra-CMEA natural gas deliveries in a later period. Whether over a five-year period the second effect or the third effect predominates is an empirical question.

The effects of Western stagflation, then, and of Eastern Europe's need to adjust to it, may well be to reduce the absolute and relative volume of East European exchanges with the West, without necessarily generating an offsetting growth in East–West exchanges over a period of, say, two to five years. The direction of the net effect on East European economic dependence on the USSR cannot be predicted *a priori*.

Changes in the political climate between Moscow and the West raise different issues. In particular, there is the question whether a deterioration in Soviet-Western political relations necessarily spills over into Western-East European trade relations. At present a gloomy picture is easy to draw. The Western response to Afghanistan, such as it has been so far, has been focused on the USSR. But can this virtually exclusive focus be maintained when (for example) technology withheld from the USSR might simply be channelled indirectly to that country through East European intermediaries? Will not the general deterioration of Western relations with the USSR tend – even irrationally – to spill over on to its East European Warsaw Pact allies?

The possibilities are obviously there. On the other hand, they do seem to depend on conscious policy decisions to be taken in the West. There may be good reasons for Western policies to distinguish sharply between Eastern Europe (or at least the goodies in Eastern Europe like Hungary and Poland) and the Soviet Union. US commercial policies (most favoured nation treatment and the extension of Eximbank credits, in particular) have now been differentiated in this way for some time, which was not the case in the classic Cold War

period, so the important influence of inertia favours future differentiation. The news from Kabul may also tend, however illogically, to
strengthen the perception of Eastern Europe as another Soviet 'victim',
and therefore a suitable case for sympathetic treatment. The experience of more extensive East–West trade has tended to suggest,
moreover, that in practice Eastern Europe is a poor conduit for the
channelling of Western technology to the USSR. Instances of East
European proxy purchasing on behalf of the USSR have occurred;
the tightening of US exports controls announced by the US Secretary
of Commerce on 18 March 1980, however, envisages the scrutiny of
licence applications for exports of CoCom list items to Eastern Europe
to check that diversion to the USSR is not likely, but no other tightening of the controls *vis-à-vis* Eastern Europe.[23]

A distinction should be made between the transmission of production
know-how and the transmission of the products of that know-how.
Poland has supplied the USSR with sulphuric acid plants designed
by Polimex-Cekop on the basis of technology bought in the West,
and something similar has happened in the case of ships and ship-
building technology. There may well be a significant number of flows
of this kind. It is possible that the capacity of at least some East
European countries' industrial sectors to assimilate imported Western
Technology is greater than that of Soviet industry. It must also be
remembered that the CMEA area as a whole can almost certainly
receive a larger total extension of the Western credits which facilitate
technology imports than the USSR on its own could expect. Diffusion
of the know-how itself, however, is usually considered more important
than the movement of the products of that know-how (particularly
in operating the strategic embargo), and diffusion in this sense seems
to be relatively sluggish within – let alone between – CMEA
economies. The major hazard for Eastern Europe's trade with the
West that has been created by recent Western policy seems to be an
unintended one: a climate of confusion and some discouragement
among Western business executives about prospects for trade with the
CMEA region as a whole.

In general, it seems to be far from clear that the Western response
to Afghanistan either will or should include a further deliberate
curtailment of Western transaction with Eastern Europe. On the
contrary, the current economic difficulties of countries such as Poland
prompt the question whether Western policymakers might not wish

to increase efforts to assist Eastern Europe. That in turn raises the crucial question of Soviet policies and attitudes. Would the USSR necessarily wish, for foreign-policy reasons, to reduce Polish economic links with the Western World?

The Influence of Soviet Policy

The foreign-policy aspects are best left to others. I shall merely point out that Soviet economic interests in this matter are substantial, and probably point towards continued acquiescence in East European cultivation of economic links with the West.

In the first place, the Soviet desire to maintain a useful minimum degree of East European economic dependence on the USSR can, I think, be taken as given. This sets limits, no doubt, on the extent to which East European commercial reorientation towards the West can be tolerated. But these limits are hardly likely to be tested in the near future. It must be assumed, on the contrary, that the extent of the East European commercial opening to the West in the early and mid-1970s was within these limits, and that subsequent developments have only tended to reduce a previously acceptable level of involvement with the West. If this is so, Soviet objections to a return to greater East European economic involvement – provided it was soundly financed – with the West would seem to be minimal.

In the second place, such shifts might even be welcomed at a time when Soviet economic growth has come down to low rates and the burdens of subsidizing Eastern Europe may be felt more acutely than before. In particular, energy supplies to Eastern Europe may be an especially sensitive issue now that the growth rate of Soviet primary fuel production (oil, gas, and coal in standard 7,000 kilocalory coal-fuel units) has fallen to 3.4 per cent in 1979 and Brezhnev has referred to energy constraints on Soviet output as significant.[24] One does not have to accept the CIA projection of an absolute decline in Soviet oil production to believe that the supply constraints on key Soviet exports to Eastern Europe are severe.[25]

Agricultural trade is another case in point. If, for a time at least, the Soviet Union itself is going to be faced with harsher terms and reduced availabilities in its agricultural trade with the West, then the greater the extent to which Eastern Europe can continue to deal advantageously with the US, Canada, and the EEC the better – from the Kremlin's point of view. It would at least mean that the potential burden on the USSR of the bloc's food supply problems would be reduced. (This argument applies to East European food imports, *e.g.*, Polish imports of US grain. It would, admittedly, go into reverse in the case of East European food exports to the West, so it is presumably not an argument for greater Soviet tolerance of individual East European countries' separate deals with the EEC over Common Agricultural Policy exemptions.)

Financial arguments, on the other hand, are less straightforward. Moscow can hardly be expected to welcome heavy hard-currency indebtedness on the part of any of its CMEA associates if this is such as to create serious debt-servicing problems. Such problems might be seen as rendering Warsaw Pact allies more amenable to influence by Western banks and governments; and they also threaten Soviet liquidity and creditworthiness in so far as Western banks and governments perceive Moscow as a lender of last resort to the rest of CMEA. Once a CMEA country (such as Poland currently) is in such difficulties, Moscow may well be able to exert extra pressure on its trade and other policies precisely by conditional offers of just such last-ditch assistance. This may have occurred in connection with the $1 billion hard currency loan to Poland (if it was really made) that was rumoured and officially denied in April 1980. By the same token though, the USSR cannot wish to be actually forced into financing the whole of Eastern Europe's debt. To that extent, Soviet policy-makers should welcome and foster continued Western lending to Eastern Europe.

Although the *prima facie* indications point mostly in the other direction I have argued that it is by no means clear that recent developments in world trade and East–West relations are pushing Eastern Europe into substantially greater economic dependence on the USSR in the 1980s than was observable in the mid-1970s. In some respects these developments work against increased East European dependence. I recognize that the arguments of the two preceding sections are speculative and often tortuous and that no very strong claims can be made for them. The crude, intuitive feeling that Western stag-flation and deteriorating East–West relations must somehow force

Eastern Europe further into the Bear's embrace should not be too readily abandoned. Reality is under no obligation to be subtle, and the plonkingly obvious often happens.

Notes

1   The considerable and important differences among the East European CMEA countries in their trade with the USSR will be largely ignored here.

2   The concept is developed by F. Müller in A. Shlaim and G. Yannopoulos, eds., *The European Community's Relations with Eastern Europe* (Cambridge, CUP, 1978).

3   The trade:GNP ratios are crude and problematic because of pricing differences. See the tables. They also vary quite widely among East European economies.

4   *Vneshnyaya torgovlya SSSR v 1978 g. Statisticheskii sbornik* (Moscow, 1979). The relative scale and composition of trade with the USSR varies substantially, of course, among East European states.

5   P. Gregory and G. Leptin, 'Similar Societies under Differing Economic Systems: the Case of the Two Germanies', *Soviet Studies*, Oct. 1977, pp. 519–43.

6   Andrzej Brzeski, 'Commerce est-ouest: une estimation des possibilités et des gains', *Revue d'études comparatives est-ouest*, Dec. 1979, pp. 29–51.

7   Paul Marer, 'Intra-Comecon Trade: Patterns of Standardized Trade Dependence', in NATO Economic Directorate, *Comecon: Progress and Prospects* (Brussels, NATO, 1977).

8   e.g. C. H. McMillan, 'Factor Proportions and the Structure of Soviet Foreign Trade', *ACES Bulletin*, Spring 1973, pp. 57–81.

9   E. A. Hewett, *Foreign Trade Prices in the Council for Mutual Economic Assistance* (London, CUP, 1974).

10 See especially C. H. McMillan, 'Some Thoughts on the Relationship between Regional Integration in Eastern Europe and East–West Economic Relations', in F. Levcik, ed., *International Economics – Comparisons and Interdependences* (Vienna, Springer Verlag, 1978), pp. 183–99.

11 See I. Edwards and R. Fraser, 'The Internationalization of the East European Automotive Industries', in USA Congress, Joint Economic Committee, *East European Economies Post-Helsinki* (Washington, 1977), pp. 396–420. Other examples are given in E. Hayden, *Technology Transfer to East Europe: US Corporate Experience* (New York, Praeger, 1976).

12 McMillan, as n. 10 above, p. 190.

13 A. H. Smith, 'Plan Coordination and Joint Planning in CMEA', *Journal of Common Market Studies*, Sept. 1979.

14 Private communication from W. Brus, Mar. 1980.

15 For quantitative evidence see P. Hanson and M. R. Hill, 'Soviet Assimilation of Western Technology: a Survey of UK Exporters' Experience', USA Congress, Joint Economic Committee, *Soviet Economy in a Time of Change*, vol. 2 (Washington, 1979), pp. 582–605.

16 See W. Brus, 'Economic Reform and Comecon Integration in the Decade 1966–1975', in N. Gärtner and J. Kosta, eds., *Wirtschaft und Gesellschaft. Kritik und Alternativen* (Berlin, 1979), pp. 163–77.

17 Data from OECD, *Statistics of Foreign Trade*, Series A. This comparatively weak Soviet performance was assisted, moreover, by terms of trade changes favourable to the USSR. The combined population of these four late-developing countries was about three-fifths of that of the USSR in 1976. Their growth rates of real GDP, 1970–7, ranged from 8.1 to 9.9 per cent a year – much higher than CMEA growth in that period.

18 See P. G. Ericson and R. S. Miller, 'Soviet Foreign Economic Behaviour: a Balance of Payments Perspective', in USA Congress, Joint Economic Committee, as n. 15 above, pp. 208–44. Preliminary calculations for 1979 are by the present author in Economist Intelligence Unit, *Quarterly Economic Review of the USSR*, 1980, no. 2.

19 M. J. Kohn, 'Soviet–Eastern European Economic Relations in 1975–78', in USA Congress, Joint Economic Committee, as n. 15 above, vol. 1 (1979), pp. 246–63.

20 E. A. Hewett, 'The Impact of the World Economic Crisis on Intra-CMEA Trade' (mimeo, 1979).

21 Calculated from the statistical supplement to *Foreign Trade*, 1980, no. 4: US $1 = 0.6841 roubles in 1978 and 0.6558 roubles in 1979 (average of Gosbank monthly rates).

22 O. Rybakov, 'Effektivnost uchastiya SSSR v sotsialisticheskoi integratsii', *Planovoe khozyaistvo*, 1979, no. 1, pp. 17–26, at p. 25.

23 *Times*, 20 Mar. 1980, p. 8. *Business Eastern Europe*, 28 Mar. 1980, pp. 97–8.

24 Calculation from *Narodnoe khozyaistvo SSSR v 1978 g.* (Moscow, Statistica, 1979) and the 1979 plan fulfilment report, *Izvestiya*, 26 Jan. 1980. The reference to Brezhnev is to his speeches at both the 1978 and the 1979 Plenums, *Pravda*, 28 Nov. 1978 and 28 Nov. 1979.

25 See J. P. Stern, 'Soviet Energy Prospects in the 1980s', *The World Today*, May 1980, pp. 188–95.

8 Economic Factors Affecting Soviet–East European Relations in the 1980s
by Alan H. Smith*

Introduction

THE purpose of this essay is to project the pattern of Soviet trade relations with the East European CMEA countries over the next decade and its implications for the pattern of integration in CMEA. This requires some examination of current Soviet–East European trade relations, which inevitably implies some overlap with the preceding essay by Philip Hanson. The major area of differentiation will be that the examination of the impact of energy price increases in Soviet–East European economic relations and of the resource cost of joint energy projects in the late 1970s is principally directed at attempting to see whether there has been any change in the Soviet Union's attitudes to relations in CMEA that would critically affect the terms on which it supplies energy to Eastern Europe over the next decade, which would in turn affect both trade relations and the pattern of integration in CMEA. Furthermore I shall try to indicate the growing cost to the USSR of trade and aid with the less developed, non-European CMEA countries and its possible effect on Soviet–East European relations and finally shall attempt to predict possible trade relations between the USSR and individual East European countries.

A considerable number of common problems have beset the East European members of CMEA at the end of the plan period 1976 to 1980 which have resulted, in the majority of cases, in key economic plan variables' being underfulfilled and have caused each country to project reduced rates of growth of national income, industrial output, investment, and consumption for the period 1981 to 1985.

* I am indebted to Philip Hanson both for suggesting ideas for development in the essay and for comments on an earlier draft and to Professor Marie Lavigne for her comments on an earlier draft. In addition my thinking has been considerably influenced by ideas expressed at meetings of the Chatham House study group.

The primary problem – the price and availability of supplies of energy and raw materials and the consequent worsening of the terms of trade – is, of course, also common to the industrialized countries of the West but the nature and timing of the problem has differed in the two areas for a variety of systemic, institutional, geographic, and political factors, with the consequence that the full impact of the 'energy crisis' on the East European members of CMEA has effectively been delayed to the latter half of the 1970s and may be expected to increase through the 1980s until either accelerated increases in efficiency slow down the rate of growth of consumption of energy and raw materials or prospected, but hitherto undeveloped, sources of energy come on stream, or both.

Geopolitical factors, notably the low proportion of oil in total East European energy supplies in general and the low level of dependence on OPEC oil in particular, reduced the initial impact of the energy crisis while the 1975 agreement to adjust intra-CMEA prices for quota deliveries on the basis of a sliding average of the preceding five years' world market prices created a considerable time lag before the full impact of the first round of increased energy prices was felt in East Europe. Furthermore, as Philip Hanson has demonstrated here, the USSR, as principal energy supplier to the bloc, did not immediately require the East European countries to make the resource transfers that even this change in the terms of trade would have required. In addition, the 1979 world price increases have affected only over-quota deliveries and extra-bloc purchases and have not yet had such a serious impact on Eastern Europe as on Western Europe but they will be a major concern (together with the physical problem of supplies) when both the quantities, and therefore effective prices, of Soviet oil deliveries to Eastern Europe are negotiated for the 1980s.

Further systemic factors also resulted in the East European economies' being able to insulate themselves from the initial effects of world stagflation, but possibly at the expense of longer-run economic efficiency. The separation of domestic from foreign prices, the absence of international money flows, and a relatively straightforward system for controlling money supply, together with effective centralized control over retail prices and wage levels, have meant that increased costs of imported raw materials have not automatically filtered through directly to domestic prices, whilst aggregate demand has been maintained at a high level without direct effects on the price level and (where the foreign trade monopoly has remained in central control) without direct leakages to imports (although some 'export substitution' may have taken place).

It can, however, be argued that the systemic factors have only enabled the East European economies to avoid the multiplier effects of the specific adjustment process that market economies are experiencing and that the adjustment to reduced resource availability consequent upon worsening terms of trade has yet to take place. Indeed, the net transfer of resources from Western economies to Eastern Europe has been partially facilitated both financially (through the development of Eurodollar and Petrodollar markets) and physically (through the search for additional markets by Western manufacturers) by the low absorptive capacity for Western commodities on the part of the OPEC countries.

It may be expected that many of these factors will be of reduced significance in the 1980s or may entail problems of economic efficiency. The isolation of domestic producers from world market price relatives simultaneously reduces the pressure to economize on high-cost imported raw materials and the incentive and ability to seek profitable lines of production on world markets, while, as Holzman has indicated, isolating producers from Western consumers provides them with little incentive to meet Western quality specifications, particularly when unsold commodities scheduled for export can be easily absorbed in domestic markets.[1] However, decentralizing foreign trade decisions to large enterprises or associations may result in a rapid influx of imports (e.g. Poland prior to the recentralization of banking authority over the use of Western credits in 1977–8),[2] while decentralizing only export decisions may lead to difficulties for enterprises in obtaining essential imported components for exports and/or insufficient appreciation of their cost.

Meanwhile, current levels of East European indebtedness, particularly in comparison with potential export earnings, are causing Western banks to evaluate certain countries quite critically, and, although they may remain a more attractive case for credits than many developing countries, it appears unlikely that the rate of expansion of credits in the 1980s will be as rapid as in the 1970s and that such credits as are available may be at top market interest rates.

Consequently each of these factors requires that the East European economies will have to reduce their rates of growth of either consumption or investment in the 1980s. The impact of this will be partially offset by the fact that rates of growth of investment in the 1970s in most countries except the Soviet Union have been faster than the rate of growth of capital stock; consequently, purely maintaining the level of investment would still result in an increase in the supplies of capital and machinery available to those economies in the first half of the decade. This effect would be reinforced by the relatively low proportion of old machinery that would be expected to become obsolete in that period. Furthermore, demographic factors that will also cause a slowdown in the rate of growth of the working population as a whole may make a reduced rate of growth of investment a more desirable policy and will further reduce the growth of demand for energy and raw materials.

Finally, however, per capita consumption levels may still pose a problem. All the East European countries have experienced a decline in the rate of growth of consumption in the current five-year plan period[3] and although there may be an apparent equilibrium with reduced growth rates of capital, labour, and the demand for raw materials and energy, the total population will continue to grow more rapidly than the working population through the 1980s, possibly resulting in demand (at least in the form of consumer aspirations) growing more quickly than supply. Furthermore the rapid growth of personal savings in the 1970s, although not necessarily indicative of repressed inflation, can otherwise be best explained in terms of deferred demand for durables. This does require (even if excess demand is siphoned off by a high level of turnover tax on those commodities which do not enter official retail price indices) that an increased volume of resources may have to be diverted to the production of durables if inflationary pressures or increased dissatisfaction are not to be felt. As noted earlier, however, a high level of domestic demand reduces the pressure on producers to raise quality standards to Western levels.

Soviet–East European Economic Relations in the 1980s

Each of the factors outlined in the previous section may be expected to exercise a considerable influence on the pattern of Soviet-East European economic relations in the next decade, and they are of course interrelated. For purposes of simplification I shall proceed under three headings: the first one concerned with trade patterns in the 1980s, the second with patterns of integration in CMEA, and the third with Soviet economic relations with individual countries.

Trade patterns in the 1980s

In his paper to the study group Philip Hanson provided a cogent argument for not regarding the total trade of the East European countries as a fixed volume and indicated areas where East–West trade should be regarded as complementary to, rather than a substitute for, East–West trade. This argument will probably have considerable force in the next two decades, and, although it may be expected that the *value* of East European imports from the USSR will grow more rapidly than those from the industrialized West in the immediate future and that there may be some short-run substitutability between East European exports of commodities to the West (for payment in convertible currencies) and of similar commodities to other CMEA countries, in the longer run a slow-down in East–West trade may have considerable repercussions on intra-CMEA trade. On the supply side a slow-down in capital investment based on Western technology may have corresponding effects on the growth rates of output and intra-CMEA trade, while on the demand side the presence or absence of economies of scale that could result from sales to Western markets may affect the viability of constructing plants of optimum size for intra-CMEA specialization. Both these factors may also affect the critical problem of Soviet energy supplies to Eastern Europe. The speed with which deep-lying oil deposits in the warmer areas north of the Caspian Sea and in the more hazardous offshore areas of the northeast European sector of the USSR are developed may well depend on imports of Western technology, while it has been further argued that Western markets may be necessary to make the development of additional oil and gas pipelines economic.[4]

In the longer run Soviet economists appear sanguine about their ability to develop and sell large quantities of oil, gas, and raw materials to the West, and East European participation in developing Soviet supplies of these commodities on the basis of joint investments and plan co-ordination (see below) still appears to be the most significant form of intra-CMEA co-operation over the next ten to fifteen years. As a result the radial pattern of trade (which both focuses East European trade on the Soviet Union and also means that the supply of Soviet raw materials in exchange for East European machinery and equipment is the major area of intra-CMEA trade whereby countries do not bilaterally balance the commodity composition of their mutual trade) may be expected to be strengthened in the foreseeable future, as indeed it has been in the 1970s.

In the next five, and possibly ten, years, however, problems concerning both the cost and the size of Soviet oil and gas supplies to Eastern Europe will be critical. In view of the controversy concerning the ability and/or willingness to meet additional CMEA demands for oil, it may be best to proceed on the basis of estimating the increased resource cost to Eastern Europe of meeting current (1980) levels of deliveries (which the USSR has already agreed to supply) before speculating about the possible availability and cost of additional supplies.

Provided no serious changes are made in the current system of intra-CMEA pricing, the East European countries may expect the price of current deliveries (80 million tons of crude oil per annum) approximately to double between 1978 and 1985, purely as a result of world price increases that have already taken place. In addition Czechoslovakia, which will continue to receive 5 million tons of crude oil per annum at the price of 15 roubles a ton[5] (approximately 10 per cent of the 1980 world market price), may incur additional costs of over 1 billion roubles per annum when this agreement runs out in 1984. Therefore the East European countries (excluding Romania, which is effectively outside the CMEA energy supply system) may find themselves paying an additional 6 to 7.5 billion roubles per annum in 1985, purely to cover existing deliveries of oil and gas even under the optimistic assumption that the relative world price of oil should stabilize over the next five years. Consequently, although the sliding world average price system would still effectively represent a considerable Soviet subsidy to Eastern Europe, it would also place considerable additional costs on them.

The critical question for the next decade, therefore, would appear to be whether the USSR will exercise its increased 'claims' on East European resources or whether it will continue effectively to extend credit to Eastern Europe and what the effect of these actions would be on intra-CMEA trade.

Evidence from the 1970s is conflicting, but the existence of considerable difficulties in Soviet–East European economic relations towards

the end of the decade as the effects of world energy price rises worked
their way through the CMEA price system cannot be ruled out. Table
8.1 provides an indication of the major components of Soviet exports
to the East European CMEA nations between 1974 and 1979. Energy
supplies accounted for 54 per cent of the increase in value of Soviet
exports, while the value of oil deliveries increased fivefold and gas
eightfold (in 1979 energy supplies alone accounted for 85 per cent
of the increase in value of exports over the preceding year). Although
Soviet statistics do not provide an indication of the change in volume
of either oil or gas deliveries for the entire period in question,
information on quota deliveries indicates that exports of crude oil
to Eastern Europe were planned to rise by about 36 per cent between
1974 and 1980. Consequently, if we make an optimistic assumption
that the real volume of Soviet oil deliveries actually rose by 50 per
cent between 1974 and 1979, oil price changes alone resulted in the
gradual build-up of a gross gain to the USSR of 3.4 billion roubles
per annum on its deliveries to Eastern Europe. This gain could be
financed by a combination of three possible methods: (i) an increase
in the price paid for Soviet imports from Eastern Europe; (ii) an
increase in the real physical volume of Soviet imports; (iii) an increase
in the Soviet visible trade surplus with Eastern Europe.

*Table 8.1   Value of USSR exports to East European members of CMEA
1974–9 (million transferable roubles)*

	1974	1975	1976	1977	1978	1979
TOTAL	8,705	11,866	13,107	15,266	16,946	18,549
Energy	1,601	3,202	3,707	4,680	5,593	6,951
(of which)						
Oil	1,062	2,143	2,539	3,333	4,156	5,001
Gas	127	267	437	561	684	1,063
Marginal energy						
export propensity[a]	0.19	0.50	0.41	0.45	0.54	0.85

[a] Annual change in exports of energy ÷ annual change in total exports.
Source: Calculated from *Vneshnyaya torgovlya SSSR*, various years (data relating, say,
to 1978 appear in the handbook for both 1978 and 1979).

Table 8.2   Estimated financial and resource transfers from East European
members of CMEA to the USSR 1975–9 (billion transferable roubles)
(All figures indicate estimated change over the preceding year)

	1975	1976	1977	1978	1979
Change in value of					
Soviet exports	3.2	1.2	2.2	1.7	1.6
Soviet imports	2.7	0.9	1.6	2.9	0.7
[1] Change in balance	0.5	0.3	0.6	−1.2	0.9
Estimated change in value caused					
by price changes					
Soviet exports	2.2	2.3	1.3	1.1	1.1
Soviet imports	1.4	1.7	0.6	0.6	0.9
Change in net price gain to USSR	0.8	0.6	0.7	0.5	0.4
Change in USSR oil price gain	1.0	0.4	0.6	0.6	0.7
[2] Estimated change in value caused					
by real volume changes					
Soviet exports	0.9	−1.1	0.9	0.6	0.3
Soviet imports	1.2	−0.8	1.0	2.3	−0.2
[3] Estimated change in net resource					
transfer to the USSR	0.3	0.3	0.1	1.7	−0.5

[1] Change in Soviet balance of trade surplus with East Europe over the preceding year.
   Negative sign indicates a fall in Soviet surplus.
[2] Negative sign indicates that the real volume of Soviet imports/exports was below that
   of the previous year.
[3] Change in real volume of Soviet exports minus change in real volume of Soviet imports.
   Negative sign indicates a loss in resource transfers to the USSR over the preceding year.
Source: Calculated from *Vneshnyaya torgovlya SSSR*, various years (data relating, say,
   to 1978 appear in the handbook for both 1978 and 1979).

The vital question for the 1980s therefore can be reduced to
estimating the combination of these techniques that will be used to
finance the corresponding gross gain. Table 8.2 provides a crude
attempt to answer this question for the period 1975 to 1979 with the
intention of trying to discern any pattern that may be applicable in
the 1980s. The estimates are subject to a number of statistical
limitations (which have been described in an appendix that is available from the author on request). The technique employed has been
to divide the annual change in value of Soviet exports to and imports
from East European CMEA nations into price and volume components on the basis of calculations from the Soviet physical volume

index for intra-CMEA trade after making allowances for trade with the non-European CMEA states. The change in the annual rate of Soviet visible trade surpluses with Eastern Europe (row 3) and estimates of the net price gain to the USSR (reflecting the changes in net barter terms of trade referred to by Hanson) over the preceding year (row 6) and of the increase in the transfer of real resources (reflecting the changes in gross barter terms of trade referred to by Hanson) over the preceding year (row 10) are also indicated. The slightly cumbersome technique of estimating price and quantity changes over the preceding year rather than over a base of 1974 has been chosen partly for statistical reasons and partly to give a better impression of the gradual impact of the sliding five-year average and if possible to reveal any change in pattern. Although the technique employed may under-estimate real volume changes and over-estimate price changes, this problem is not so significant when the *net* figures are considered. Consequently it may be argued that, although the absolute size of the figures may be questioned, the broad pattern indicated is reasonably accurate.

Rows 6 and 7 in Table 8.2 indicate the general pattern that in each year from 1975 to 1979 the USSR benefited from a net price gain over the preceding year in its trade with Eastern Europe and that over the period the net gain was slightly less than that arising from oil prices alone (implying therefore that price increases in Soviet deliveries of other commodities, including raw materials and gas, were more than compensated for by increased prices for East European deliveries to the USSR). From 1975 to 1977 the difference between the real volume of Soviet imports over the real volume of exports was insufficient to cover the price gain to the USSR, confirming the hypothesis referred to by Hanson that over this period the price gain was only partially financed by a net transfer of resources and substantially by an annual increase in the Soviet balance of trade surplus with Eastern Europe, (rising from 100 million roubles in 1974 to 1.4 billion in 1977).

The figures for 1978 and 1979 indicate the possibility of a change in pattern and provide considerable problems of interpretation. Soviet statistics for 1978 show an exceptionally high increase in the real volume of Soviet imports (2.3 billion roubles) which not only compensated for improved Soviet terms of trade for that year but restored the Soviet visible trade surplus to its modest 1974 level. In 1979 the

real volume of Soviet imports fell below the 1978 level and the visible
trade surplus re-opened but remained below its 1977 level, while a
substantial increase in Soviet import prices partially offset export price
gains. Even if the figures for 1978 are disregarded, the net gain in
resource transfer to the USSR in 1979 compared with 1977 is still
about 1.3 billion roubles (composed of an increase in the real volume
of imports of 2.1 billion roubles against a real increase in exports of
0.8 billion roubles), a rate of increase substantially higher than that
carried out in the middle of the decade. Tables 8.3 and 8.4 permit
a more detailed analysis of the country distribution and commodity
structure of the increase in value of Soviet imports from Eastern
Europe between 1977 and 1979. Imports of machinery and equipment
comprise 89 per cent and 76 per cent of the increased value of imports
in 1978 and 1979 respectively over the level recorded in 1977, while
Table 8.4 indicates that a considerable proportion of the increase in
both years is comprised of categories for which no further breakdown
is indicated in Soviet statistics ('the unspecified machinery residual').
Indeed the growth of the unspecified machinery residual over the 1977
level in both 1978 (1.8 billion roubles) and 1979 (1.2 billion roubles)
is very similar to the growth in the net transfer of resources to the
USSR for the corresponding periods.

*Table 8.3   Value of Soviet imports from East European members of CMEA
1974–9 (million transferable roubles)*

	1974	1975	1976	1977	1978	1979
TOTAL	8,600	11,312	12,226	13,852	16,776	17,473
(of which)						
Machinery and equipment	4,004	5,182	5,718	6,573	9,161	9,332
Percentage of machinery and						
equipment	46.6	45.8	46.8	47.5	54.6	53.4

Source: *Vneshnyaya torgovlya SSSR*, various years (data relating, say, to 1978 appear
in the handbook for both 1978 and 1979).

This poses a major problem for establishing a more detailed analysis
of both the price/volume breakdown of the increase in imports and
of a change in structure of Soviet imports that might be expected
to continue in the 1980s. It is generally accepted that unspecified
residuals in Soviet foreign trade statistics are not solely the result of
under-reporting but are frequently used to conceal items that the

Table 8.4   Soviet imports of machinery and equipment from East European members of CMEA 1977–9 (million transferable roubles)

	Soviet imports of machinery			Unspecified machinery residual			Change in unspecified machinery residual over 1977	
	1977	1978	1979	1977	1978	1979	1978	1979
From:								
Bulgaria	1,101	1,569	1,639	383	769	710	386	327
Hungary	896	1,379	1,207	195	595	381	400	186
GDR	1,991	2,590	2,708	238	566	496	328	258
Poland	1,071	1,515	1,701	184	452	409	268	225
Romania	225	237	290	50	45	50	− 5	0
Czechoslovakia	1,289	1,871	1,787	258	668	441	410	183
TOTAL	6,573	9,161	9,332	1,308	3,095	2,487	1,787	1,179

Note: Where the provision of commodity categories for machinery and equipment differs for any given year, from one statistical handbook to another, the lowest possible 'unspecified residual' has been calculated.

Source: Calculated from *Vneshnyaya torgovlya SSSR*, various years (data relating, say, to 1978 appear in the handbook for both 1978 and 1979).

USSR does not wish to reveal in detail, but which would be conspicuous by their absence if not included in the broad aggregate figures. A recent US Department of Commerce study[6] identified a major component of the unspecified residual in Soviet machinery and equipment imports from Eastern Europe as being communications equipment.

It would appear unlikely that the substantial increases recorded in 1978 and 1979 can be attributed purely to this and my own calculations indicate that the composition of unspecified residuals in Soviet trade statistics has been altered in recent years to include a larger number of non-strategic items.

The similarity of the distribution of the increases between all East European countries (with the exception of Romania) does not appear to indicate a spontaneous move by those countries to eliminate trade deficits but suggests either a CMEA or Soviet initiative. A most likely explanation of the residuals would appear to be that they include deliveries of machinery and equipment for CMEA joint investment projects that have not been included in the appropriate commodity categories.

It is also possible that the residuals may be narrowed down more specifically to deliveries in connection with the Orenburg gas pipeline which was scheduled to be completed in 1978 with deliveries phased over the preceding three and a half years.

Explanations for the delay in recording could range from the entirely plausible hypothesis that for purely accountancy reasons such deliveries are not recorded until the project is completed to rumours that disagreements over the price of gas repayments caused the USSR to annul the joint venture aspects of the project and instead credit the participating countries with the export value of their contribution. Another explanation could be that delays in accounting were largely a reflection of the inability of many East European countries to meet their commitments from domestic resources – which resulted in the shortfall having to be obtained from Western sources. This explanation would also be consistent with the fact that the Polish residuals first increase in 1977 rather than 1978, and that Bulgaria, which made a larger original contribution in the form of labour provision, has a higher residual than all the other countries after an initial sharp increase in 1976. Whatever reason is advanced for the delay in recording, if it is assumed that the 'unspecified machinery residuals' are explained by deliveries to Orenburg (and/or other joint projects) the implication is that at the beginning of the five-year plan period from 1976 to 1980 the USSR *planned* to import a greater volume of machinery from Eastern Europe than is shown in official statistics, in which case the planned volume of Soviet imports would have resulted in a more even growth of net resource transfers of about 0.5 billion roubles per year. Almost any other explanation indicates a tightening of Soviet economic pressures *vis-à-vis* Eastern Europe.

What do these figures imply for the 1980s? The problem of financing the development of Soviet energy and raw material resources in the interests of the bloc as a whole has been a critical area of discussion and dispute within CMEA over the past two decades. In the early years of the Brezhnev/Kosygin era, following Khrushchev's abortive attempts to balance the supply and demand for raw materials by means of a joint planning organ, Soviet grievances within CMEA were largely directed at the perceived unfairness to the USSR of a price system based on world average prices when, as a result of the location of Soviet raw material, the USSR was a high-cost producer. In the 1970s greater emphasis was placed on the physical participation of East European countries in developing Soviet resources and their transportation to Eastern Europe, culminating in the Agreed Plan of Multilateral Integration Measures for 1976 to 1980. The economic justification for these proposals was that the optimum distribution of bloc investment required a concentration of capital resources in the eastern sector of the USSR, involving in the short run a transfer of resources from Eastern Europe to the USSR. The device of joint ventures involving deliveries of machinery and equipment in exchange for repayment in products at a later date was largely intended to overcome any suggestion of ownership of capital on another member's territory. World oil price changes accelerated this process by giving the East European countries a greater interest in co-operation in joint investment projects but simultaneously gave the USSR the where-withal to alter prices to effect resource transfers without destroying East Europe's economic interest in the projects. Indeed the resource cost to Eastern Europe of fully implementing world market prices would have caused serious problems; therefore in the initial stages the USSR relieved the pressure, firstly by applying the sliding world average price system and secondly by not demanding the full resource transfers that this would have required. The figures for the end of the decade appear to indicate that the level of resource transfer the USSR planned to receive from Eastern Europe in the mid-1970s was greater than the actual level, probably as a result of the inability of the East European countries to meet plan commitments, and con-sequently the increased price of Soviet oil supplies was largely met through an increase in the level of East European indebtedness to the USSR. Given, however, the considerable difficulties the East European economies will have to face in the 1980s there is little reason to believe that a similar state of affairs will not prevail in the 1980s, with the Soviet Union seeking the best arrangements possible on its dealings with Eastern Europe but being forced to ameliorate some of the pressures.

It is also possible that the windfall effects of the oil price rise brought some embarrassment to the USSR in the shape of renewed pressure

from the less developed countries in CMEA to implement the commitment to 'levelling up' the economic levels of member countries largely
through aiding domestic investment programmes, a commitment
which had been initially established in the Basic Principles (1962),
when Mongolia joined CMEA, and was later ratified in the Complex
Programme of 1971. The resource cost of investing in Mongolia in
the 1960s with a population of just over a million people had been
comparatively low and almost entirely borne by the USSR.

In 1972 the extension of CMEA to Cuba, with a population of
9.5 million, considerably increased the potential cost of the levelling-
up process and was followed in the mid-1970s by complaints from
Mongolia, repeated in Soviet journals, that although her rate of
growth was faster than that of the industrialized CMEA countries
the *absolute* gap between them was widening not narrowing.[7] A series
of measures was approved at the 30th (1976) CMEA Session to improve the levelling-up process, including joint CMEA investment
projects for the development and processing of raw materials in Cuba
and Mongolia, and, more significantly as far as Cuba was concerned,
the establishment of favourable prices for the export of staple commodities to CMEA member countries. A fairly rough estimate
indicates that Soviet aid to Mongolia trebled between 1974 and
1978 to around 450 million roubles per annum[8] (approximately 300
roubles per head). In addition to a 300 million rouble credit granted
for 25 years at 2.5 per cent interest[9], the principal form of aid granted
to Cuba was the favourable price for its sugar exports. World sugar
prices have changed sharply since 1976 and moreover prices on the
world sugar market, which is essentially a market for residual sales,
diverge considerably from prices involved in many long-term supply
arrangements. It is therefore difficult to estimate the cost the USSR
actually expected to bear as a result of this agreement when it was
signed, but if a comparison is made with the price the USSR actually
pays for supplementary sugar imports (largely in hard currency) the
cost to the USSR has risen from 0.8 billion roubles in 1976 to 1.2
billion in 1977 and 1.6 billion in 1978, a sum equivalent to 75 per
cent of Cuban exports to the USSR, and meaning that the value
of the agreement was over 160 roubles per head of the Cuban
population in 1978.

Consequently the cost to the USSR of 'levelling up' Cuba and
Mongolia has increased by at least 0.5 billion roubles per year since

1975 and accounts for a substantial proportion of its price gains. The critical problem for CMEA and Soviet–East European economic relations in the 1980s may well be the extent to which the levelling-up process will be continued. The admission of Vietnam to CMEA in 1978 (believed to have been opposed by Czechoslovakia) would appear to extend the cost of levelling-up beyond the capacity of the USSR alone. With a population of around 40 million (four times Cuba and Mongolia combined) each 100 rouble per capita of aid would cost 4 billion roubles. Although the level of aid has not reached that figure the USSR would have had to bear considerable aid costs to Vietnam whether or not that country was admitted to CMEA. It is therefore highly possible that the granting of CMEA membership to Vietnam may serve to bring some of those costs under the CMEA umbrella and help the USSR to pass some of the burden on to Eastern Europe. Any further extension of membership (particularly to Vietnam's neighbours) would lead to a severe escalation of costs and could limit the degree to which the USSR will find it in its power to alleviate the impact of energy price increases to Eastern Europe.

The additional problem of the price and availability in the medium and long run of Soviet oil supplies over and above current levels remains. Western estimates of Soviet production and availability range from the pessimistic CIA projections which envisage Soviet oil production declining from current levels of around 600 million tons per annum to 400–500 million tons by 1985, and the USSR as a net importer by 1982, to the optimistic Swedish Petrostudies report which estimates that the USSR will be capable of supplying 25 per cent of Western needs in 1985.[10] Similarly, estimates of prospected reserves range from 30–40 billion barrels to 150 billion. The question of the availability of additional supplies to Eastern Europe depends quite critically therefore on small changes in assumptions about the rates of growth of supply and demand in the USSR and the necessity to maintain deliveries to the West. With exports to the West currently running at about 70 million tons per annum, a 3 per cent rate of growth of Soviet demand with production constant would quickly eat at this amount without affecting the existing level of deliveries to other CMEA countries. If, however, existing major fields have already reached peak production and their output declines before major new fields can be brought into production (which may not be before 1985), the Soviet oil balance will depend critically on increasing output from existing marginal fields. It is difficult therefore to be optimistic about further Soviet oil deliveries to socialist countries in the first half of the 1980s without a considerable reduction in the volume of deliveries to the West. In the immediate future the prospects of nuclear power making a substantial contribution to the East European energy balance are slight. Czechoslovakia, the major bloc supplier of nuclear reactors, plans to operate two new nuclear plants in the first half of the decade but still plans to increase energy imports, while previous experience of construction delays indicates that this schedule may be optimistic.[11] Given the existing low proportion of oil in East Europe's primary energy consumption the major prospects for domestic substitution lie in the intensive development of low quality sources. This may be partially offset by the fact that the majority of East European countries are high consumers of energy per unit of GNP[12] and could at least in theory cut back consumption without an equivalent effect on output, while other equilibrating factors, such as the slow rate of growth of the industrial labour force and reductions in planned levels of output, will further slow down the rate of growth of demand. On balance, in the next five years, Eastern Europe will be heavily dependent on Soviet supplies of gas and whatever oil the USSR can make available to meet its primary energy needs.

The crucial questions of how willing the USSR will be to reduce oil sales to the West, which in 1977 accounted for 37 per cent of its total exports to non-socialist countries, and the price it will ask for deliveries to Eastern Europe remain. On the positive side, the USSR could accommodate a fall of 30–40 per cent of volume sales to the West without effect on its 1977 level of earnings purely as a result of 1979 world price rises, while it has also benefited substantially from world price rises for gold and other precious metals. Although in the longer run these price increases will affect the prices of commodities the USSR imports, its terms of trade with the West can be expected to improve over the next five years. Consequently the most likely formula will be that the USSR will initially demand payment in hard currencies for above-quota deliveries of oil charged at current world market prices, but will in all probability choose some method of offsetting the impact in bilateral negotiations with individual East European countries in order to preserve good relations. A major method of such offsetting may be to accept imports of East European consumer goods in lieu of hard currency. This may be of mutual advantage where the quality factors that lead to difficulties in sales in Western markets are largely a function of fashion and technical obsolescence.

Patterns of integration in CMEA

I have argued elsewhere[13] that the major integration measures adopted in CMEA in the 1970s (i.e. the establishment of the CMEA Committee for Co-operation in Planning Activity, the Agreed Plan of Multilateral Integration Measures 1976–80, and the Long-Term Target Programme for Integration Measures 1975–90) and the actual operation of the International Investment Bank indicated that patterns of integration in CMEA were proceeding along the lines of improved methods of plan co-ordination and joint investment projects, rather than through the increased use of money and market levers. Furthermore, it was also argued that these proposals largely reflected proposals emanating from the USSR Gosplan and in certain instances bore strong similarities to Khrushchev's 1962 proposals with the important exception that they carefully avoid any implication of supra-national authority by emphasizing the 'interested party principle'. It also appears that the USSR has remained opposed to any activity that indicated commodity convertibility in intra-CMEA relations (i.e. the ability of an enterprise to purchase inputs directly from an enterprise in another country while bypassing the central planning authorities or foreign trade organizations of the countries concerned) at the same time as the concept of commodity convertibility was receiving a fairly enthusiastic reception from Hungarian, Polish, and Czechoslovak economists.

The energy crisis initially increased the impetus towards solutions based on joint-planning activity, partly by increasing the East European interest in developing Soviet energy reserves and partly because many of the problems involved appeared particularly amenable to planned solutions. On the supply side energy outputs can be more easily reduced to common denominators in physical than in money units and the scale of investment involved frequently meant that projects could at least in theory, be divided into identical physical components for the participants (viz the Orenburg gas pipeline), which reduced much of the distributional need for accurate value comparisons or decentralized them to bilateral negotiations. Similarly on the demand side, restricting bloc investments in the production of energy-intensive outputs is also particularly suited to physical planning techniques, while the foreign trade monopoly and central control over the supply of consumer goods makes it easier to control consumer demand for oil-based products (but reduces the pressure on producers to develop low-cost alternatives) without recourse to rationing by price.

Towards the end of the 1970s, however, some Hungarian and even Czechoslovak economists were beginning to propose an increased role for market levers, extending as far as commodity convertibility, which, combined with Romanian hostility to joint-planning proposals *per se*, aroused speculation that Romanian intransigence might again be used to impede progress within CMEA. The Romanian dimension to the problem will probably not be so large in the 1980s as it was in the 1960s. Firstly Romania is effectively outside the bloc energy balance and is unlikely to be able to re-enter it on her own terms, while the interested-party principle enables bloc countries to pursue joint projects without securing the agreement of those countries which do not wish to participate. The question remains, however, whether the progress of joint-planning activity would be affected by Soviet unwillingness or inability to provide additional oil supplies for anything other than hard currencies and in particular whether the East European economies would be capable of generating sufficient hard currency earnings to pay for these (or Middle Eastern supplies) without domestic reform that could in turn lead to renewed pressure for the use of market levers in CMEA.

Holzman's argument[14] that East European hard currency deficits are chronic and are systemically induced by the separation of domestic producers from foreign markets, which leads to a 'saleability illusion' whereby quality gaps remain unclosed and planned export targets unfulfilled, implies that in the longer run domestic reform extending as far as commodity convertibility is a prerequisite for a hard currency surplus. However, his argument that the socialist countries are 'a high cost, low variety, low quality region relative to the rest of the world'[15] and that 'any relaxation of controls or mutual reduction of East–West barriers will lead to a tendency towards more imports by East than West'[16] makes it by no means certain that such reforms would act sufficiently quickly in an impending short-run crisis.

Consequently, although the East European countries may attempt to bring domestic producers closer to foreign markets and may even permit them to retain a greater proportion of their foreign currency earnings in order to buy imported inputs, a radical decentralization on the import side would appear unlikely in the immediate future. Furthermore, as Zielinski has indicated,[17] a period of economic crisis is not the most suitable period for launching far-reaching economic reforms, and a period of balance of payments pressures combined with rising import prices would appear to be an inauspicious moment to dispense with the benefits of the '*Preisausgleich*' and to rely on the control of domestic demand and price levers to contain the volume of imports. The benefits of the planned approach to rationing imports and directing them to the areas of the greatest perceived importance and linking enterprise success indicators more closely to the successful fulfilment of planned export targets are likely to appear attractive to East European central authorities over the next few years. Indeed something on the lines of Soviet *Vstrechnii* or counterpart planning (enabling enterprises to pay bonuses for increasing output from fixed quantities of inputs) may also appear attractive in the short run to East European economies. Paradoxically, if and when energy supplies improve, the sub-optimalities that may have been generated may lead to renewed pressure for market-type solutions in the non-energy sectors.

It is probable that several of the East European countries are now starting to question the benefits of the 'import-led growth' strategy pursued in the 1970s and may voluntarily stabilize or curtail their imports of machinery and equipment from the West and concentrate more on diffusing technology already acquired. Although this would ease some of their hard currency problems Holzman's strictures about their inability to export (particularly in a time of Western recession) have considerable validity and lead one to doubt whether their hard currency earnings will be sufficient both to pay off existing loans and to make increased hard currency payments for raw materials. If our predictions about trade patterns are correct, the early 1980s will see a period in which the USSR will accumulate additional surpluses in its trade in 'hard goods' with Eastern Europe over and above those negotiated in the initial five-year agreements.

The tendency towards Soviet surpluses in trade with each East European nation is likely to reduce the pressure towards monetary solutions in intra-CMEA relations. The interest of East European nations in commodity convertibility is likely to be reduced as it would weaken their power to restrict the export of key commodities in the face of deficits, while the USSR would probably find the political consequences of exercising the economic benefits of purely financial convertibility unacceptable. (Could the USSR export oil to Czechoslovakia, say, and then use the surplus to buy commodities from the GDR while simultaneously withholding oil exports from that country?)

Under these circumstances the most probable solution is that the USSR will pursue bilateral approaches to the individual East European countries to secure the most acceptable solution (to both partners) in each case. In general, such solutions could range from increased Soviet imports of agricultural commodities and consumer goods to the extension of Soviet credits in hard currencies, but it would not be surprising if the solutions involved political as well as economic compromises, with the degree of hardness of terms involving judgements about both the political stability of East European régimes and their amenability to Soviet policy objectives.

Soviet economic relations with individual countries

Political factors may be predominant in relations with Bulgaria and the GDR. *Bulgaria*, whose principal visible exports to the USSR (other than machinery and equipment) are cigarettes, tobacco, and food products whose output cannot be drastically increased in the short run, already faces severe balance of payments problems with the West and may be expected to receive Soviet credits as a result of its continued compliance with Soviet objectives in CMEA and elsewhere (not, as Philip Windsor observes in the final chapter of this volume, a total compliance, but still a considerable degree of conformity with Soviet policies).

The Soviet trade agreement with the *GDR* for 1981 to 1985 specifies that quota deliveries of major raw materials will be around the same levels as for 1976 to 1980.[18] Additional deliveries may be expected to be contingent on increased deliveries of East German machinery and equipment, which is generally of a higher quality than the CMEA average, and for increased assistance in providing military and other aid to the Third World, particularly the Horn of Africa and the Middle East. Such assistance may also make it easier for the GDR to obtain raw material supplies from the Third World.

The expiry of the oil agreement in 1984 will probably lead to Czechoslovakia's experiencing a greater increase in its import costs from the USSR than any other East European country. While Czechoslovakia itself will play a vital role on the energy supply side through the provision of nuclear reactors to other CMEA countries, and increased imports of Czech machinery and equipment and consumer goods in particular may be desirable to the USSR, a considerable increase in hard currency payments is highly probable. Under these circumstances Czechoslovakia's low level of indebtedness to the West may prove to have been a prudent policy.

Similarly, *Hungary*, which has established a hard currency surplus in its intra-CMEA trade, will probably find this reversed and may also have to increase its exports of machinery and equipment and consumer goods.

Poland posed problems to the forecaster even before the strikes of summer 1980. Faced with a high level of indebtedness to the West ($20 billion) and a growing cost for servicing this debt, Poland had indicated its intention approximately to double its volume of exports to the West by 1985 while roughly maintaining its volume of imports. Given the problems concerning the rapid increase of exports of consumer durables referred to earlier, such an expansion would appear to be dependent on increased exports of coal and meat products. As total trade in agricultural products was planned only 'to be brought into balance in 1985' this implied a continued deficit in trade in agricultural products with socialist countries, involving possibly the import of fodder crops and lower quality foodstuffs. Although in the longer run cut-backs in investment and improvements in efficiency (particularly in the distribution of foods and basic consumer durables) could make a significant contribution to improved living standards, in the shorter run such an improvement may require at least a postponement of the planned export expansion – which in turn would require increased borrowing whether from the East or the West, or both. It has been reported that the East European countries will increase agricultural exports to Poland (despite in certain cases food supply problems of their own) and that the USSR will provide loans. The extent to which the other East European countries (particularly those that have made efforts to curtail their imports from the West) may perceive that Poland is receiving more favourable treatment than themselves, and the extent to which their populations may feel that they are subsidizing concessions not available to themselves (which in turn would appear to diminish the economic cost to the population of arousing Soviet hostility), could place severe constraints on the concessions that the USSR can grant to Poland alone among its East European partners. Consequently the level to which the USSR can offset price changes in its terms of trade with Poland by credits and continue to supply agricultural commodities will become a question of fine political judgement with ramifications far beyond Poland itself.

Finally *Romania*, a country with substantially lower living standards than Poland and a leadership of uncertain popularity in Moscow could be affected by the demonstration effect of any concessions granted to Polish workers, particularly as there have been indications of domestic unrest. Romania suffered from miners' strikes in 1977 and the communiqué on plan fulfilment for 1979 referred ambiguously to the 'unjustified discontinued operation of installations'. A major feature of the reforms launched in 1978 was to increase the powers of workers' councils in enterprises, a development which is officially referred to as workers' control. The function of the councils, however, appears to be primarily to act as a transmission belt for centrally determined decisions. The extent to which Ceausescu may be able to limit the autonomy of workers' councils by making full use of the need to avoid arousing Soviet hostility may be considerably limited if enduring concessions are granted in Poland. Consequently Ceausescu may have to find a political balance between making economic concessions to the population and not antagonizing the Soviet leadership, which in turn may be reluctant to offer him much assistance. Ironically, with a comparative advantage in oil prospecting, Romania would appear to be peculiarly suited to CMEA projects that would enable it to receive crude oil for use in its petrochemical industry in exchange for oil-drilling equipment. Similarly, co-operation and specialization agreements which would limit its development of energy-intensive industries and concentrate its industrial development in those areas where it is reasonably well endowed with raw materials could permit a level of industrialization without the attendant balance of payments problems, while the guaranteed markets involved in CMEA trade agreements appear peculiarly suited to Romania's large-scale plants. Its centralized economy (despite the apparent reforms of 1978) and its attitudes to the Third World appear consistent with Soviet policy objectives. On balance it could be argued on economic grounds that a pliant Romania could be one of the principal beneficiaries of the current organizational structure in CMEA.

However, Romania currently does not participate in several joint investment projects, and, despite recent agreements to import small quantities of oil from the USSR, effectively remains outside the bloc energy balance and conducts only 40 per cent of its trade with the bloc, while its trade per capita inside the bloc is less than one-third that of other East European countries. Although Romania is careful not to challenge the USSR directly, one is forced to speculate whether Romania's membership of CMEA is *de facto* (as opposed to *de jure*) any stronger than that of Yugoslavia, particularly as it can now be bypassed by the interested-country principle. Romania's case illustrates the supremacy of political over economic considerations and indicates the limitations of any analysis based purely on the latter. On balance it would appear that the best policy for Romania would be to seek a greater economic and political rapprochement with the USSR and CMEA. How enduring any such rapprochement would be is a moot point.

The limitations of economic analysis would appear to have equal force in speculations on the relations between the USSR and Yugoslavia. It would appear that current relations between CMEA and Yugoslavia allow them to embrace most activities that could be considered (economically) mutually beneficial. Any tightening of Yugoslavia's relations with CMEA would appear to involve a zero-sum game, with gains to one partner involving losses to another. Furthermore the USSR might have to bear the political burden of increased pressure for market solutions in CMEA. As the major economic concession it could offer would appear to be cheaper and more plentiful oil supplies, it would seem unlikely on purely economic grounds that the USSR would welcome a closer relationship between Yugoslavia and CMEA for some years. This conclusion could, however, be completely invalidated by political considerations, particularly after membership of the European Community is extended to Greece.

Conclusions

The problem of the interrelationship between economic and political factors makes prediction difficult, but if the CMEA bloc is taken as a whole the following patterns and problems of development seem likely to be observed during the 1980s.

To begin with, the rate of growth of resources at the bloc's disposal will grow less rapidly than in the 1970s, although this will be partially offset by the sustained growth of capital stock resulting from investment undertaken in the 1970s. The change in the rate of growth of resources available for Soviet and East European development will be largely determined by three factors. First, a slow-down in the growth of (or a possible fall in) domestic energy supplies will make it necessary to divert investment to areas with a high incremental capital : output ratio, and will reduce the ability to command resources from outside the bloc. Second, there will be a slow-down in the rate of growth of the industrial labour force. Third, there will be the pressure of the increased liabilities undertaken by the bloc in the shape of the admission of Vietnam, together with the expected increase in the cost of military and development aid extended to non-bloc members.

The distribution of income between bloc members may be the most critical policy issue. How it is resolved will depend heavily on political judgements, but two points may be noted. First, under existing CMEA pricing policies the major beneficiary will be the USSR, at the expense of the East European countries. Second, the 'levelling-up' commitment implies an obligation to use the resources of the industrial member-states to maintain a higher rate of growth of investment in the less developed than in the more developed CMEA countries. To the extent that this investment is primarily concentrated on the supply of raw materials, this investment could be beneficial to the bloc as a whole in the long run.

Evidence from the late 1970s indicates that the USSR is pursuing a policy of passing on a greater share of the burden resulting from price increases for raw materials to East European countries in the form of resource transfers than was apparent in the mid-1970s, while simultaneously increasing its aid to the less-developed non-European countries in CMEA. The USSR still delivers raw materials to the East European countries more cheaply, however, than the latter can obtain them from outside. This policy will probably be continued through the 1980s. In particular, the East European countries may have to pay the full world market price for deliveries of fuel and raw materials (particularly oil) above 1980 levels; but at the same time the USSR may seek to ameliorate the impact of this on a bilateral basis, through the provision of credits and by accepting consumer goods in exchange. The balancing of these policies may require fine political judgement.

Altogether, this implies that a considerable proportion of the reduction in the rate of growth of available bloc resources will be borne by the East European countries. Any reduction in the rate of growth of consumer goods supply could have a more serious impact on living standards in Eastern Europe than it would have in Western Europe, where even a cut-back in absolute income levels could be largely reflected in a slow-down in the rate of accumulation of consumer durables rather than in an absolute cut in living standards for many consumers. Such a 'West European' pattern of adjustment is less likely to be feasible, the nearer incomes are to subsistence levels.

As far as trade patterns are concerned, the radial pattern whereby the exchange of Soviet fuel and raw materials for East European machinery and equipment predominates in intra-CMEA trade will probably be strengthened over the next decade.

As far as bloc economic organization is concerned, planning-type solutions, including joint planning activity and investment projects involving pay-back in raw materials, will be likely to predominate over market-type solutions. Policies in most fields of long-term activity in CMEA will be aimed at increasing the supply of, and reducing the demand for, energy and raw materials.

Notes

1   F. D. Holzman, 'Some Systemic Factors contributing to the Convertible Currency Shortages of CPEs', *American Economic Review*, May 1979.

2   D. W. Green, 'The Role of Banking and Finance in East European Reforms', a paper presented to the NATO colloquium 'Economic Reforms in Eastern Europe and Prospects for the 1980s', held in Brussels 16–18 Apr. 1980. The proceedings of the conference are to be published under the same title by Pergamon Press.

3   C. Hudson, 'The Consumer in Eastern Europe', a paper presented to the NATO colloquium referred to in n. 2 above.

4   *The Guardian*, 3 Dec. 1979.

5   F.-L. Altmann, 'Prospects for the Czechoslovak Economy in the 1980s', a paper presented to the NATO colloquium referred to in n. 2 above.

6   USA, Department of Commerce, *Description and Analysis of Soviet Foreign Trade Statistics*, 1974.

7   P. Lufsandorsh, *Planovoe khozyaistvo*, 1978, no. 9.

8 Calculated from discrepancies between three sets of figures: those published in an article by E. Ochir in *Ekonomicheskoe sotrudnichestvo stran-chlenov SEV*, 1977, no. 3; those in the annual editions of *Statisticheskii yezhegodnik stran-chlenov SEV* for the years 1974–9; and those in the annual editions of *Vneshnyaya torgovlya SSSR* for the years 1974–9. A more detailed study is in preparation.

9 *Vneshnyaya torgovlya*, 1979, no. 12, p. 15.

10 See e.g. *The Guardian*, 30 Nov. and 3 Dec. 1979.

11 Altmann, as n. 5 above.

12 F. L. Pryor, *Economic Journal*, Sept. 1979.

13 A. H. Smith, 'Plan Co-ordination and Joint Planning in CMEA', *Journal of Common Market Studies*, Sept. 1979.

14 Holzman.

15 Ibid.

16 Ibid.

17 J. G. Zielinski, 'On System remodelling in Poland'. *Soviet Studies*, Jan. 1978.

18 H. Haase, 'Prospects for the GDR Economy in the 1980s', a paper presented to the NATO colloquium referred to in n. 2 above.

9 Military Considerations in Soviet–East European Relations
by Malcolm Mackintosh

THE aim of this essay is to consider some of the military factors in the Soviet Union's relationships with the countries of Eastern Europe, to try to see how Soviet military control over the area is carried out, and to discuss the attitudes of the East European countries to the military requirements and aims of the Soviet Union in this part of Europe. First we look briefly at the Soviet attitude to military power and the use of force in external relations with particular reference to Eastern Europe. Then we discuss the Soviet establishment of its military 'buffer zone' in Eastern Europe during and after the Second World War, and the nature, organization, and role of the Warsaw Pact which provides the machinery for the Soviet military control of the area. Finally we consider some of the 'permanent factors' (to use a Soviet phrase) in the military relationship between the Soviet Union and its East European allies and neighbours, including issues of national identity and history, which may affect the Soviet–East European relationship in the military and strategic field in the years ahead.

The Soviet Attitude to Military Power
Some appreciation of the long-standing and traditional Russian as well as Soviet concept of the importance and role of military power may be helpful in the attempt to understand Soviet aims and motives in establishing permanent military control over the countries of Eastern Europe. Russia has always felt vulnerable to military pressure ever since its people tried to set up a national state in the vast plains of the northern parts of the Eurasian land mass. Lacking natural defences, the Russians found their territory overrun by Tartars and Mongols from the east, by Turks from the south, and attacked by Poles, Swedes, French, and Germans from the west. This experience

fostered in the Russians a deep sense of the need to amass military power and to entrust their survival exclusively to their own military effort. It also led them to feel an overriding suspicion of the aims, ambitions, and superiorities of other nations, at first militarily, and later in economic and technological terms. The Russians feel therefore that they and they alone have to take the necessary measures to preserve their state and its power, avoiding, in particular, too much trust in political or diplomatic arrangements with potentially 'hostile' countries on defence issues.

These historical and traditional attitudes to military power and defence combine today with more recent political and ideological trends to form the current Soviet attitude to military power. The preservation of the Soviet system wherever it exists as well as the defence of the homeland and its client states are the first priorities of the Soviet armed forces. Defence issues have also played an important part in Soviet attempts to protect the frontiers of the USSR by establishing pro-Soviet régimes in neighbouring states close to the Soviet border, in other words, the long-standing Soviet tradition of the buffer zone. The most important of these zones, which was set up after the Second World War, is, of course, Eastern Europe. But the pattern exists in Soviet minds today in Mongolia and Afghanistan, and was also tried out in Iran, Sinkiang, and in post-war Soviet territorial claims against Turkey and Finland.

Military power is also essential to the Russians in the maintenance of the status of the Soviet Union as a superpower. And it must be available to support or carry out tasks overseas, on an opportunistic basis, to expand Soviet influence, and to encourage, where appropriate, additional countries and régimes to become friendly and then obedient to the Soviet Union. This policy summarizes, in effect, the role of Soviet communist ideology in Moscow's foreign policy towards the Third World, much of which in any case relies on powerful backing provided by the large and sophisticated armed forces which the Soviet Union has built up, particularly in the last two decades.

Soviet Military Control over Eastern Europe

The military and strategic factors involved in the Soviet control of Eastern Europe can be seen, in realistic terms, against this general background. In the last year of the Second World War the victorious Soviet army occupied both Allied and Axis countries of East and Central Europe up to the lines in Germany and Austria agreed with the Western Allies at the wartime conferences of Teheran and Yalta. At the same time, collaboration with Communist-led resistance movements in Yugoslavia and Albania (to which Britain and the United States gave a great deal of aid and support) brought two additional countries into the Soviet camp at the end of the war. The final composition of this camp was not decided until 1948, with the incorporation of Czechoslovakia, the defection of Yugoslavia, and the Soviet agreement to allow Finland a form of neutrality acceptable to the Soviet Union. But by 1945 the countries of East and Central Europe which had been reached by the Soviet Army during the war had acquired the status – in military and political terms – of a buffer zone which has, with a few exceptions, remained in being until the present day.

The role of a buffer zone in Soviet political and military thinking is on the whole a fairly straightforward one. Politically the zone in Eastern Europe protects the Soviet Union from direct territorial contact with foreign countries (except for Berlin, northern Norway, and Turkey) and helps to fulfil the ideological requirements of the Soviet Communist Party in its relationship with neighbouring states. It also enables the Party in Moscow to ensure that Soviet standards and Soviet practices in administration, accountability, and authority (including the superior status automatically given to Soviet citizens and officials in most East European countries) are followed and obeyed in the countries concerned. Control of the buffer zone allows the Soviet security services to operate freely throughout the area, providing the KGB, among other things, with the authority to overrule its East European opposite numbers in defining and handling security issues. Economically and technologically, access to the resources of the buffer zone countries in manpower, skills, and material is available to the Soviet Union; methods have ranged from outright seizure in the Stalin era to the more sophisticated arrangements of recent years through bi-lateral contracts or the CMEA.

In the military field the buffer zone performs two functions for the Soviet Union. Defensively it provides the Soviet armed forces with space for deployment and manoeuvre in depth well forward of the Soviet frontier. In particular, it gives adequate space for the location and training of the large ground and air forces on which Russian military tradition insists for defensive purposes. Soviet control of the buffer zone enables the Russians to choose the strength and concentration areas for their forces, e.g. the twenty Soviet divisions in East Germany cover the main axis of operations in the North German Plain while the forces on the southern flanks, in Hungary and Czechoslovakia (four and five divisions, respectively), are much smaller. Romania and Bulgaria have no Soviet forces deployed on their territory.

In terms of planning for offensive operations against Western Europe, the possession of the zone enables the Soviet Union to concentrate, if possible in conditions of the strictest secrecy, the forces considered necessary by the Soviet General Staff for an attack on NATO, well to the west of Soviet territory. This includes the advance preparation of lines of communication and reinforcement routes from the Soviet Union, the dispersal of air and naval forces, and the pre-positioning of the arms, ammunition, and supplies necessary for such a campaign in the event of a general war in Europe.

The control of Eastern Europe also enables the Russians to make use of the military manpower and skills of the East European countries. The machinery set up to achieve this goal is, of course, the Warsaw Pact. Now the Russians recognize, especially in the light of their own suspiciousness and mistrust of other nations, however politically close to the Soviet Union they may be, that East European nationalism and pride could create problems for a Soviet High Command expecting absolute obedience and military efficiency from its East European allies in all possible situations in the event of war. The organization and role of the Warsaw Pact shows how the Soviet Union has tried, among the other priorities of its military relationship with Eastern Europe, to solve some of those problems, while retaining absolute authority over the military power of Eastern Europe.

The Warsaw Pact

The Soviet Union and its East European allies, Poland, East Germany, Czechoslovakia, Hungary, Romania, and Bulgaria have been organized for political and military purposes in the Warsaw Pact since 1955 (Albania having 'defected' in 1961). Under Stalin's rule, and for a brief period after his death, Soviet military control over the East European armies had been carried out by direct rule from Moscow, often through Soviet officers such as Marshal Rokossovski in Poland and General Panchevski in Bulgaria. But in 1955 the Soviet Union's relations with these countries had reached a stage when a new organization was needed to co-ordinate the Soviet–East European military effort along more effective and up-to-date lines. This task has been carried out since then by the Warsaw Pact.

Politically, the Warsaw Pact was in some respects modelled on NATO. It has a Political Consultative Committee with a civilian Secretary-General, a military Commander-in-Chief drawn from the strongest power, and a Combined Staff. The Consultative Committee is supposed to meet at regular intervals to discuss foreign and military policy and formulate political initiatives in East–West relations in Europe. But here any similarity with NATO ends. The Consultative Committee is largely a transmission belt for Soviet instructions and recommendations; some debate certainly takes place, but no basic divergence is permitted on the foreign policy line to be followed as far as the public communiqués are concerned. There is good evidence, however, that in recent years disagreements within the Pact have occurred: for example, on Romania's insistence on following an independent foreign policy, on her refusal to commit her troops to Warsaw Pact exercises on other members' territory, and (in 1978) to increase her defence budget. The Warsaw Pact still maintains the political position that it would dissolve itself in return for the dissolution of NATO, although, of course, the Soviet Union has bilateral political and military treaties with all its East European allies, which would continue to exist after the end of the Warsaw Pact.

In military terms the Warsaw Pact HQ has grown from a directorate in the Soviet General Staff (in 1955) to a large, multinational staff attached to the Soviet Ministry of Defence. Its High Command at present consists of the following: the Soviet Commander-in-Chief, Marshal Kulikov, advised by two consultative bodies – a Committee of National Defence Ministers of all member countries, and a Military Council. The Military Council, which includes a senior officer from each country plus the Soviet Chief of Staff and a Soviet Political Officer, appears to meet regularly, and does give the East European forces a greater say in military matters than before the Czechoslovak crisis. The Pact also has a Soviet Inspector-General, General Pastushenko, who also appears to be a member of the Military

Council, and a Soviet head of the Pact's Military–Technical Committee, General Fabrikov.

Subordinate to the Commander-in-Chief is the Combined Staff of the Pact, headed by General Gribkov, and Deputy Chiefs of Staff drawn from each member country, as well as a Soviet Political Officer. The Headquarters also administers the Soviet Military Missions in each of the East European capitals. These missions are normally located within the Ministries of Defence of member countries, and have considerable powers over training programmes and weapons utilization in the forces concerned.

The most important feature of the Warsaw Pact's military organization, as far as we can tell, is that the Headquarters has no operational capability in peacetime. It has for example no logistic branch, and no transportation or supply services organizations. All these are provided by the Soviet Ministry of Defence. Moreover, the air defence of the buffer zone is the responsibility of the Soviet Homeland Air Defence Command. Each of the NSWP countries is the equivalent of a Soviet Air Defence District, and the national air defence forces are linked directly to headquarters, Homeland Air Defence Command in Moscow.

My suggestion is, therefore, that the Warsaw Pact's military headquarters, as constituted at present, is a peacetime organization only. In wartime the Soviet High Command, supported by the Soviet General Staff, would take command of whatever East European forces were available, properly trained, and considered politically reliable for the task in hand. Such evidence as we have suggests that in military terms most of the East European forces are effectively trained and armed (with the possible exception of Romania), and that, at least in the initial phase of a successful campaign, most would probably fight well in the professional sense. We do not know if, or which, specific East European formations are 'earmarked' for integration with the Soviet army in the event of war, although geographical factors would play a part in deciding how some of the forces might be used, for example, Polish forces in the Baltic area, and Bulgarian troops in the Balkans.

Soviet military policy in Europe seems to be concerned with the best way to wage a European campaign in the event of general war, at any level of weapons employment. In such a war Soviet forces would attempt to seize the initiative, take the offensive, and try to defeat

NATO forces and occupy the whole of Western Europe as quickly as possible. They would, if necessary, rely upon their forces-in-being; but as a general principle the Russians would hope to be able to introduce reinforcements from the Soviet Union before launching an offensive. As for the campaign itself, it could be waged at the non-nuclear, tactical nuclear, or nuclear level, according to current Soviet military doctrine, although it seems unlikely that nuclear weapons would be entrusted to any of the East European armed forces in a European campaign.

As far as force levels and deployments are concerned, in Soviet terms the numerical superiority and the widely diversified nature of the forces available represent what the Soviet military leaders think they need to wage a European campaign in general war. During 1980 in particular the Soviet Union has been particularly concerned with NATO's decision to modernize its Theatre Nuclear Forces (TNF), in response to the deployment of the SS-20 and the Backfire bomber against targets in Europe. In a co-ordinated campaign to weaken NATO's determination to introduce new medium-range systems the Russians have used political, diplomatic, and propaganda means, including the withdrawal of elements of a Soviet division from East Germany. But it seems unlikely that the Soviet leaders will expect NATO to change its TNF policy, and with tension rising between East and West over Afghanistan, there may be little progress on this force reduction issue.

The Soviet Union is, however, taking part in the MBFR talks on force reductions in Vienna. In these talks the Russians have refused to accept the concept of *balanced* force reductions, and deny any degree of military superiority to the Warsaw Pact, claiming that on a global basis NATO is superior. They have, however, made some concessions to the West on force ceilings, the timing of reductions, and force-level data. What the Russians are offering at Vienna (in oversimplified terms) is a fixed cut in manpower by the two alliances in stages over a period of two to three years. They offer to disband the formations concerned on their withdrawal to their homeland, but steadfastly refuse to consider any form of international verification, which the West regards as vital to an agreement. These Soviet proposals seem, in fact, to aim at retaining local Soviet military superiority in Europe, at reducing the strength of American and West German forces there, and perhaps actually increasing the Soviet military advantage in the European theatre, at a lower level of forces – which would be more damaging to the West than to the Soviet Union.

The Military Reliability of the East European Countries

Let us now look at the individual countries of the Warsaw Pact, with particular reference to their reliability in peace or war. First of all I believe we should consider the historical background and traditions of the member states and the long-standing attitudes to Russia and the Soviet Union. Sometimes we tend to think of Eastern Europe solely as a unified Soviet-controlled bloc of communist states, ruled by men trained in the Soviet Union and all dedicated to the success of Soviet policies at home and abroad. To some extent this is true. But the Russians have also ample experience of the historical, cultural, and political differences between them and their East European allies, some going back centuries; almost all of them are still relevant today.

Poland is the largest and perhaps the most controversial of these countries. The Poles are a Slavic people whose flat and open country historically posed serious problems which led, at the height of Polish national power, to expansionist policies in search of security and military strength. At one time (as Poles of all political persuasions tell you), Poland included most of the Ukraine and the Baltic states, and a Polish army once occupied Moscow. Polish power collapsed, however, in the eighteenth century and the country was divided between her main neighbours. Poland, meanwhile, had made her mark on European civilization, culture, literature, and music, and her people were and still are devout Catholics, as the visit of the Polish Pope to his homeland in 1979 showed so vividly. Polish soldiers won enviable reputations during the risings in 1831 and 1863, the war of 1920, and the Second World War for courage and endurance in adversity.

To the Russians, therefore, Poland is a formidable nation with an unrivalled sense of pride in its own nationhood and history. Poland is, however, the vital country astride the main route and axis from Russia to Western Europe. The Soviet Union therefore has to work to achieve the dominance of Poland – which it needs – while warily taking account of traditional Polish pride, independence, and unanimous suspicion and even contempt for the Russians. It was partly for this reason that the Russians recoiled from using force against the Poles in October 1956, and again after the riots of December 1970; and it is a curious fact that alone of all the Warsaw Pact armies the Poles still wear a copy of their pre-war uniform instead of a Soviet version. Control of Poland is, however, vital to the Soviet Union, and the Polish government under Edward Gierek seemed to combine obedience to Moscow with a respect for Polish nationalism understood by the Polish people. Soviet control, therefore, has to be exercised with due respect for Polish–Russian history and the fierce independence of Polish national traditions.

For this reason there must be considerable doubts in Soviet minds on the reliability of Poland as an ally, or of the Polish army in a war in Europe. The Russians would probably be reluctant to leave the Polish army at home astride the Warsaw Pact's communications from the USSR to the front line in a European campaign. Their plan may be to use Polish forces in flank operations, for example against Denmark or in the Baltic area generally. But however Polish forces were used, if the Warsaw Pact advance into Western Europe was checked or defeated Polish reliability in the Soviet cause would be seriously in doubt. In the event of a major setback or defeat of a Soviet attack, the Poles would, I believe, try to keep their forces in being to handle any situation that might develop on a national basis.

Soviet attitudes to Czechoslovakia are rather different from those towards Poland. Czechoslovakia, a new state formed in 1918 out of the Austro-Hungarian Empire, had none of Poland's military or nationalist traditions, but prided herself more on cultural and political consciousness and her absorption of West European civilization and its social and political concepts. Let down by the West in 1938, the Czechoslovaks played little part in the Second World War, apart from small-scale contributions to the armies of East and West. They accepted the Soviet ultimatum in favour of total communist power in 1948, and offered no military resistance to the Warsaw Pact invasion of 1968. Nevertheless, their great strength is their basic political-intellectual maturity, especially in the production of rival ideas and concepts to Soviet communism: it is no accident that the 'Spring' of 1968 developed in Prague, or that 'Charter 77' is a Czechoslovak document. Czechoslovakia is, in Soviet terms, basically a stable society governed by a group of extreme adherents of obedience to the Soviet Union. They are unlikely to cause the Soviet Union political or security problems. Czechoslovak opposition is intellectual and political; their military efficiency or reliability in war is uncertain, partly because of their armed forces' lack of experience. But I believe that they would take part loyally in the early phases of an offensive, with their future conduct depending on the outcome of the Soviet attack.

Hungary, too, has proved to be a difficult country to master and to keep within the Soviet orbit. The suddenness and ferocity of the Hungarian rising in 1956 took everyone, especially the Russians, by surprise; and when the rising was over, the Soviet Union's initially harsh discipline and methods eventually gave way to a more flexible attitude to Hungarian nationalism, particularly in the economic and commercial field: today, Hungary's economic and trade policies under Janos Kadar seem to be the most liberal of the East European countries. Hungarians and Russians are deeply suspicious of each other for national reasons: the language barrier is almost insurmountable, and, like the Czechs, Hungarians feel links with Western Europe through their history within the Austro-Hungarian Empire.

Like Czechoslovakia, Hungary is at present a stable member of the Soviet bloc and unlikely to repeat the 1956 rising. But memories of that rising are vivid in Soviet as well as Hungarian minds and play a part in maintaining a cautious, suspicious, and to some extent cool Soviet-Hungarian relationship. In the event of war, if the Hungarian army was employed on the southern flank, or against Yugoslavia, it would probably fight loyally and well. If it operated more directly against NATO, its reliability too would depend on the success of the Warsaw Pact offensive and on the importance, in strategic terms, of the front on which it was engaged.

In the Balkans, Romania provides serious difficulties for the Russians. Romanians are of mixed race: part Latin (like their language), part Slav, and part Turkish, with elements of long-forgotten Asiatic tribes which settled in the Danube valley in early medieval times. Romanians have always regarded themselves as West Europeans, close to France and Italy, but in fact their political character is bound up with their centuries of Balkan history. Romania's present leader, Nicolae Ceausescu, is ruthless and authoritarian among his own people, and his communist régime in Romania is disciplined and rigid. He is hard-headed and tough in dealing with opposition and skilled at assessing how to handle a powerful overlord such as the Soviet Union. Romania under Ceausescu is in many senses, and through its own national character, a 'rebel' against Soviet rule;

but Ceausescu is a skilful rebel, and has avoided giving the Soviet Union an excuse to expel or overthrow him, even on issues of defence expenditure – though I am sure the Soviet leaders would dearly like to do this. The Romanian armed forces are not regarded as well armed or highly trained. The Soviet leaders probably consider them to be fundamentally unreliable and would not employ them directly in a war with NATO – except, perhaps, with Staff representation or in defence of their own country.

Almost alone of the East European countries Bulgaria has never given the Soviet Union any real trouble. Once again, a mixed race of Slavs and Tartar tribes, speaking a language older than, but close to, Russian, the Bulgarians have traditionally accepted foreign rule without opposition; they were ruled by the Ottoman Empire for five hundred years, accepted German domination from the 1880s to 1944, and since then have been docile and subservient to the Russians, to whom the ordinary Bulgarian feels, unlike the Poles or the Romanians, a sense of respect and even friendship. The Bulgarians are hard workers and by tradition disciplined and responsive to authority. I expect them to continue their allegiance indefinitely under their present long-standing ruler, Todor Zhivkov, as long as the Russians remain in control in Eastern Europe. Their armed forces are disciplined, and well armed and trained. They would be likely to participate actively in operations against Turkey and Greece in an all-out war against NATO, though not on their own, or in a small-scale 'probe' operation in the Balkans. Their reliability would probably be good, and they would fight alongside the Russians whatever the outcome of the war.

Finally within the Soviet bloc we have the East Germans. As we have seen, as soon as the war was over and the initial years of hostility and 'punishment' came to an end the Soviet Union set about establishing a separate communist state in their zone of Germany. After the brief workers' rising in June 1953 East Germany moved into a phase of economic and industrial development which was not only efficient but also of considerable value to the Soviet economy. The growing national crisis based on emigration to the Federal Republic was solved in ruthless fashion by the building of the Berlin Wall in 1961. But, in spite of having twenty Soviet divisions on East German soil, a six-division army of their own, and a highly complex situation in Berlin, part of which they use as their capital, the East

Germans have created the most industrialized, orderly, and efficiently administered of all the Soviet bloc countries. Its efficiency is, I suspect, in some ways a matter of envy to the Russians. East German leaders show no visible tendencies to question Soviet domination; if anything, on local, German matters they seem to support a hard line – sometimes more extreme than that of the Soviet Union. But they too have the potential, through their economic and industrial strength and their discipline, to cause problems for the Russians, who are very careful to keep the East German party and government under close observation and control.

The East German forces are also well trained and disciplined. They would certainly play a key role in the opening phase of a Warsaw Pact offensive across the North German Plain in a major war against NATO. It is hard to asses how reliable they would be in the event of a serious setback; but I believe their leaders would try to hold them together as a power base in support of any policies that they decided to follow.

Yugoslavia and Albania

These are some of the main problems and issues which the Soviet Union faces today in its buffer zone in Eastern Europe and is likely to face in the years ahead. In addition, there remains the problem of the two former members of the Soviet bloc – Yugoslavia and Albania – who 'defected' in 1948 and 1961 respectively. Soviet leaders have neither forgotten nor forgiven these countries' 'desertion', and in political and ideological terms there can be no doubt that ultimately the Soviet Union will try to secure their return to the bloc. The problem is particularly topical in the present phase because of the death of President Tito in June 1980. Tito's long illness enabled the Yugoslav Party and government leaderships to prepare for the succession. The post-Tito régime has functioned well, although there are clearly anxieties and suspicions in Belgrade as to future Soviet (and perhaps Bulgarian) policies towards Yugoslavia.

In all probability the Russians will decide that any early attempt to use force against a post-Tito Yugoslavia would be unsuccessful and indeed counter-productive. An attack of that kind would arouse Yugoslav patriotic feelings and perhaps lead to Soviet involvement in a long drawn-out guerrilla war in the Yugoslav mountains in which the Yugoslavs might receive some Western military aid. The Soviet Union is much more likely to adopt a position of formal acceptance of the Yugoslav Federal State in its present non-aligned role, while engaging in less formal support for regional or national groups anxious to change the régime in Belgrade – such as the pro-Soviet so-called 'Cominformists' – most of whom are at present either in prison in Yugoslavia or living in exile in the Soviet Union.

If such contacts flourished, and if internal Yugoslav tension grew, for example between Serbs and Croats, the Russians will hope that skilful Soviet political moves would lead either to the establishment of a pro-Soviet government in Belgrade or perhaps to some form of break-up of the country's Federal system and an end to Yugoslavia's role as a leader of the Third World and an effective opponent of Soviet orthodoxy and authoritarianism in Eastern Europe. The Soviet Union might consider revising support for long-standing Bulgarian claims to Macedonia in such a situation. In either case, the fate of Albania would be sealed. With Soviet influence re-established along Albania's borders, it would only be a matter of time before Albania too was brought back into the Soviet bloc through some form of intervention or external pressure.

This assessment of likely Soviet policies towards a post-Tito Yugoslavia and its Albanian neighbour is based on predictions which are somewhat favourable to the Soviet point of view. It is equally possible that Yugoslavia will not only avoid internal regional disputes, but with economic aid from abroad and a continuation of its important role in the non-aligned movement – which could act as a deterrent to direct military action by the Soviet Union against Yugoslavia – the country could also remain, as we hope it will, a stable member of the European comity of nations.

Conclusions

The picture of military relationships and considerations between the Soviet Union and Eastern Europe offered in this paper suggests that the 'permanent factor' in Soviet thinking is the retention of military control over the communist countries of Eastern Europe in order to support the existing Soviet political domination of the area. Military control also satisfies traditional Russian and Soviet concepts of a buffer zone protecting the Soviet frontier and providing in the event of a general war in Europe a concentration area for troops intended for an offensive against Western Europe. The organization of the military forces of the Soviet Union and the East European countries is in the hands of the Warsaw Pact, whose most senior officers all come from the Soviet armed forces. The Pact is responsible for the peace-time training, co-ordination, and administration of the East European and Soviet forces; all the evidence we have suggests that, in the event of war or the direct use of military force in Europe, command and control would be exercised by the Soviet High Command.

In professional military terms the Warsaw Pact appears to have made use of East European military manpower, resources, and skills in a reasonably effective way. Such evidence as is available suggests that most of the East European forces are well armed and trained, and that military service seems to be generally an acceptable commitment of young men in these countries. How these forces would perform in war is impossible to predict; but it is probably true to say that in the initial phase of a successful war in Europe, most of the East European armies, navies, and air forces which were used in action by the Soviet Union would obey the orders of the Soviet High Command.

Clearly, however, there are stresses and strains within the Warsaw Pact on political, economic, and military issues, but apart from the evidence of disagreements between the Pact and Romania – and, in the past, an occasional item from Poland and Czechoslovakia – it is hard to identify their main causes or results. So far the Russians have been able to keep dissatisfaction, however severe, under control. It would certainly be unwise for any existing or future East European leadership to underestimate the Soviet Union's power to control, dominate, and, in the last resort, overcome any serious resistance from the East European countries. But each of them is a nation in its own right. Each has a history and a tradition of relations with Russia and of dealing with a large and dominating power; each has a national language, a culture, and a political attitude which have been, and can be again, of great importance to the future of Eastern Europe. The Soviet Union cannot ignore these distinctions and differences, and in both the short and the long term East European nationalism will be one of the Russians' fundamental problems in maintaining their military posture within their European sphere and in pursuing their general aims in Europe as a whole.

10 The Warsaw Pact – the Shape of Things to Come?
by John Erickson

THERE are many reasons for the low opinion, not to say the denigration, of the Warsaw Pact Organization over the past two decades. One of the most obvious features has been (and is still, to some degree) the absence of any comprehensive study of the Warsaw Pact, though a special place must be accorded to Professor Robin Remington's pioneer work *The Warsaw Pact*, published in 1971.[1] The problem is compounded by that supposed shortage of information on the separate non-Soviet national military establishments, a situation which could be easily remedied without too much effort on the part of military analysts – for example, the Polish army has compiled its own interesting autobiography in *Ludowe Wojsko Polskie 1943–1973*.[2] As for the argument that these non-Soviet military elements are somehow a ramshackle, second-rate, indifferently equipped motley force, the parade in East Berlin in November 1979 of the East German army (NVA) gave the immediate lie to that assumption, with T-72 main battle tanks, Mil Mi-24 'gunship helicopters', and 122-mm self-propelled guns on parade, while in Budapest for the May Day parade the Hungarian air force put its latest MiG-23 aircraft on display. Even if this was just filling the shop-window, it was not unimpressive.

The Warsaw Pact is not going to vanish from the scene and all the talk about 'the dissolution of the blocs' – a favourite Romanian theme – was, is, and will continue to be just talk. Quite the reverse, in fact, for from the Soviet point of view (and that of the East European nations also) the military scene in Europe appears to be darkening and will remain the source of considerable tensions throughout the present decade. If the Warsaw Pact is not on the point of fading away, similarly NATO is far from drifting into disintegration or impotence and a new arms race is clearly in the making. It might be useful, therefore, to consider the present form and possible evolution of the Warsaw Pact under four main headings, which correspond to the priorities of Soviet security policies at large: the overall strategic picture and the general position of the Warsaw Pact within it; the political and military utility of the Pact (non-Soviet organization and effectiveness); the military-industrial effort; and internal politics and policing.

The Strategic Environment and the Pact

We can make some general assumptions about the course of Soviet military policy in the coming decade. The trend (established in the early 1960s) to increase the Soviet 'margin of advantage' over the USA and/or NATO will continue, with the development of the capability to wage nuclear war with the United States and any given 'coalition' of powers, accompanied by greater emphasis on strategic defence, while what is commonly called 'power projection' – air and naval resources – will be expanded steadily, if not in overly dramatic style. Equally, effective battle management techniques at the strategic and operational-strategic (general purpose) level will require substantial resources, signs of which are already apparent.

Already the Soviet Ground Forces (the Soviet army) are the most 'equipment-intensive' of any military establishment, so that we should see a slower pace in the expansion of actual inventories but with qualitative improvement – the new T-80 main battle tank (MBT), already under test, more combat engineer support, the introduction of advanced munitions, further electronic warfare capability and, above all, command, control, and communications (C_3) improvement and innovation. NATO's eventual introduction of the cruise missile will almost certainly mean the reinforcement of Ground Forces PVO (Air Defence) troops with improved surface-to-air missiles, and Theatre Nuclear Force (TNF) modernization on the part of NATO could be countered, at least in principle, by the introduction of a 'tactical anti-missile system' (a field Anti-Ballistic Missile system (ABM) in essence). All within the 'combined arms' concept, the Soviet Ground Forces will continue to develop that capability to wage and to win any theatre campaign whatever the level of weapons (nuclear or conventional, plus chemical warfare) and also to develop something akin to an independent 'theatre option', with provision for *both* European and Far Eastern operations in a 'two-front' war configuration.

Under these conditions of 'active defence' at the strategic and theatre level it is unlikely that the Warsaw Pact and Soviet interest in manipulating the European 'balance' in the Soviet Union's own favour will slip within the Soviet order of priorities. While I have never subscribed to the notion of unassailable and 'overwhelming' (*sic*) – 'massive' is another synonym – Soviet superiority in the European theatre, there can be no doubt that the Soviet command is intensely interested in maintaining a 'correlation of forces' relatively adjusted in its own favour (which may seem to be something of a contradiction in terms, in addition to being one that discomfits the East European alliance as well as NATO; the Poles, for example, being concerned in no small degree at the manner in which the Soviet command 'counts' Polish troops). The forward deployment area of the Warsaw Pact still counts for something in Soviet planning, not least in early warning/air defence, though it has less importance as a staging area now that Soviet forces with improved lift and mobility can 'leap-frog': for example, tactical air no longer needs to be marshalled on forward fields as in previous days and tank crews can be flown in with some speed to prepositioned tank parks.

I am inclined to the view that we have to look for some more intricate explanation of Soviet intentions and requirements with respect to the Pact, other than the clichés about a defensive *glacis* and so on. There is also the question of Soviet commitments beyond the confines of the European theatre and the geographical delineation of the Warsaw Pact as such: it is unlikely that the Pact will be formally extended or expanded to cover, say, Soviet or 'socialist' commitments to Vietnam. Here Romanian resistance spelled out what was essentially mute but firm objection to any extra commitment on the part of other East European states, but it is conceivable that if Spain joins NATO the Warsaw Pact will respond on a tit-for-tat basis by admitting Cuba as a full member of the WTO. (It might also be noted that East European states may lend assistance outside the Pact area on a strictly bilateral basis, spelled out in the several separate agreements with the Soviet Union.)[3] Already a form of 'division of labour' has appeared in the application of non-Soviet resources and manpower to extra-European commitments, though once again these appear to be separately arranged and negotiated undertakings, including the steadily intrusive East German 'Afrika Korps'.[4]

We can assume, therefore, that the Pact will remain stabilized, or constrained, within its present limitations as prescribed by formal treaty stipulation, though it may stray off 'at the edges' by special commitment and agreement. It will remain central to the Soviet Union's European security programme, pushed at times in the 'Pan-European' direction and at other moments fitted into the European confrontation scene. At the moment and in the foreseeable future a Soviet 'security policy' for Europe is inconceivable without the Warsaw Pact, buttressed as it is by a long-standing and very complex network of bilateral mutual assistance pacts and a system – reduced to its essentials – which relies upon the loyalty of the several national leaders, the Party links of the military, and the pervasiveness of the intelligence/security net. That this works (and may be presumed to continue working) is shown by the fact that the non-Soviet military élites have remained consistently loyal to Moscow, whatever the general political turbulence. This is not to say that what might be called 'indigenous East European' defence requirements have been met and solved, but the internal development of the Pact has slowly and steadily erased many of the worst distortions: for example, it was widely assumed that the 'reforms' of March 1969 were the result of the Czechoslovak crisis of 1968 but the groundswell for reform had preceded Soviet military action and earlier preparation made to accommodate quite insistent demands (even prescribed as a 'commitment' and cunningly leaked by the Romanians).

The case I am propounding *vis-à-vis* the Warsaw Pact is that 'fings ain't wot they used to be', and, even more important, were scarcely ever what they were perceived to be by Western commentators. This is to say that we should pay some closer attention to the *internal evolution* of the Pact as it is construed by Pact members themselves – ranging from the inevitable internal rivalries (such as the Czechs poking fun at the Poles giving themselves military airs and graces) to serious issues of building up (or blocking) an *integrated standing force*, the prime Soviet objective.

The Utility of the Warsaw Pact

While the Soviet Union remains and will remain the strongest member of the Pact, it is worth asking what is gained by the USSR for an expenditure on common armament which is between five and ten times as much as other non-Soviet contributions, not to mention the preponderance of Soviet divisions (four-fifths of the Pact forces are

Soviet, as is the majority of battle-ready divisions in forward deployed positions in East-Central Europe). The nominal order of battle of the Pact is superficially very impressive, but the hard core of military capability is sustained by the Soviet 'Groups of Forces' – Group Soviet Forces/Germany (GSFG) consisting of 19 divisions in East Germany (with one division, 6th Guards Tank, now withdrawn from the previous 20 divisions); 2–3 in Northern Group in Poland, the equivalent of 5–6 divisions in Central Group in Czechoslovakia; and the 4 divisions in Southern Group in Hungary.[5] What Marshal Kulikov, Warsaw Pact C-in-C, actually 'commands' consists only of elements of these Groups of Forces and the 6 divisions of the East German army,[6] which can be increased to 8 divisions by bringing the East German Border Troops up to full strength. In this respect, Marshal Kulikov has less latitude than NATO's Supreme Allied Commander in Europe (SACEUR), who can call upon a larger integrated force should the need arise: the point has doubtless *not* escaped the attention of the ambitious, hard-driving Kulikov.

Nominal order of battle means very little in this context. In the 'northern tier' (East Germany, Poland, and Czechoslovakia) the non-Soviet establishments should provide at least 30 divisions (6, 13, and 10 respectively, plus a Polish airborne division, the 6th) though it is unlikely that these forces can be fielded (or would be fielded in such strength): in the 'southern tier' (Hungary, Bulgaria, and Romania) the tally of divisions – 6, 8, and 10 respectively (with Bulgarian armour brigaded) – hardly represents operational capability in view of the outmoded equipment and the indifferent training in many formations. Thus, the grand total of divisions, 31 Soviet, 54 non-Soviet (85 in all), cannot really be reckoned as Warsaw Pact (operational strength) and the Soviet command knows this. To mobilize this force *in toto* would be a major undertaking and with all the paraphernalia of call-up, movement, and assembly such a process must obviously run counter to the *surprise factor* which is a primary element of Soviet military doctrine and practice: equally, mass mobilization throughout the Pact would not be consistent with the 'in-place, unreinforced' Soviet offensive which does not require mass mobilization but rather the 'topping up' of select attack formations with specialists and logistics personnel, or by flying in extra crews (tank crews, for example) to man the prepositioned vehicles. Of course, general mobilization could be declared within the Pact as a deliberate, even precautionary political act, or yet again, as a measure of premeditated intimidation with division piling up against division in order to display overwhelming Soviet–East European strength *vis-à-vis* Western Europe.

Table 10.1   Armament levels: Soviet/non-Soviet Warsaw Pact area 1980

GSFG (Group Soviet Forces/Germany)	Five Army HQs (2nd Guards Tank Army; 20th Guards Army; 3rd Shock Army; 8th Guards Army; 1st Guards Tank Army) 19 divisions; 1 artillery division 16th Air Army (848 aircraft, total war strength 1,700) Tank holdings: 4,020 T-64/T-72; 2,030 T-62; 2,040 T-54/T-55 (older models being withdrawn). *Only GSFG* deploys the T-64 battle tank.
NVA (East Germany)	Two Army HQs (3rd and 5th) 2 tank, 4 motor-rifle divisions (can be made up to 8 divisions, war strength)^a[a] Air strength: 340 aircraft (including MiG-23) Tank holdings: 50 + T-72; 2,500 T-54/T-55 (T-34s in storage) 1,500 BMP (infantry combat vehicles) Guns/mortars: 330
NORTHERN GROUP	
Soviet: Poland	Nominally 2 tank divisions (20th Tank, 38th Tank Division) could be augmented to 3–4 divisions Tank holdings: 650 + T-62 Air strength: 37th Air Army, 350 combat aircraft
Polish Army	Three Army HQs (Warsaw, Pomorze, Silesia) 5 tank divisions; 8 motor-rifle divisions; 1 airborne division (6th Airborne); 1 sea landing division Air strength: 675 aircraft (35 SU-20 semi-VG) Tank holdings: 50 T-72 (production beginning Katowice tank works, 500 tanks per year); 3,430 T-54/T-55 Guns/mortars: 1,250 (including 122-mm SP guns)
CENTRAL GROUP	
Soviet: Czechoslovakia	6 divisions (10th, 13th, 51st Tank Division, 16th, 55th, 66th Motor-Rifle Division) Tank holdings: deploying T-72; 1,150 T-62; 180 T-54/T-55 Air strength: 2 air divisions, 100–150 aircraft

[a] By assigning 20,000 men of Grenztruppen (Border Guards) to 2 motorized infantry divisions.

Czechoslovak Army	Two Army HQs
	5 tank divisions; 5 motor-rifle divisions; 1 airborne regiment (22nd Airborne)
	Air strength: 460 aircraft (including MiG-23); organized 7th and 10th Air Armies
	Tank holdings: 100+ T-72 (production beginning); 3,600 T-54/T-55
	400 BMP (infantry combat vehicles)
SOUTHERN GROUP	Guns/mortars: 950 (deploying 122-mm SP guns)
Soviet: Hungary	4–5 divisions (strength recently increased)
	Air strength: 275 aircraft
	Tank holdings: deploying T-72; 1,140 T-62; 170 T-54/T-55
Hungarian Army	1 tank division, 5 motor-rifle divisions
	Air strength: 150 aircraft (deploying MiG-23)
	Tank holdings: 50+ T-72; 1,490 T-54/T-55
	Guns/mortars: 300
BULGARIAN ARMY	Three Army HQs (Sofia, Plovdiv, Plevna)
	8 motor-rifle divisions; brigaded armour (5 tank brigades, equivalent to 2 tank divisions); 1 mountain warfare brigade
	Air strength: 165 operational aircraft (3 air regiments)
	Tank holdings: 100+ t-62; 2,000–2,100 T-54/T-55; (T-72 under test in small numbers)
	Guns/mortars: 700 guns, 350 mortars

No Soviet forces permanently deployed, but Soviet 'operational group' 50 officers for planning/command Balkan/Southern theatre.

ROMANIAN ARMY	Two Army HQs (Bucharest and Cluj)
	2 tank divisions; 8 motor-rifle divisions; 3 mountain warfare brigades
	Air strength: 300–330 aircraft
	Tank holdings: 30 T-72; 30 T-62; 1,670 T-54/T-55 (T-55 modified)
	Guns/mortars: 980+ guns, 1,000+ mortars

No Soviet forces deployed in Romania.

Source: A compilation from the author's files.

Since the Soviet command has no wish to commit its forces against a well-prepared and fully deployed NATO defence, intending rather to pre-empt NATO mobilization and rush these same defences with a number of powerful ground thrusts (as well as inhibiting NATO's air capability by a major pre-emptive air strike), it is unlikely that the cumbersome process of total mobilization will be adopted in this context. In any event, it is worth noting that the Warsaw Pact, as

such, lacks any specific mobilization mechanism and logistical support
for military operations and would (as Malcolm Mackintosh has noted)
be heavily dependent on the Soviet system. Here we have to look
at the Pact, not so much in terms of the sum of its several national
establishments but rather in relation to the Soviet General Staff
operational concept of the TVD (*teatr voennykh deistv*, literally, theatre
of military operations) – or several TVDs for the whole European
theatre (TV) (*teatr voiny*, literally, theatre of war), the TV being the
major strategic entity and split into several TVDs (plus the associated
'maritime theatres of operations' – MTVDs).

We can infer with some assurance that the area covered by forward-
deployed Soviet forces and Pact East European troops is divided into
several TVDs – the Northern (covering the Leningrad Military
District and possibly elements of the Baltic Military District), the
Western (Soviet troops in East Germany and NVA divisions), and
the South-Western (comprising the Soviet Kiev Military District[7] and
possibly elements of the Odessa Military District). Each of these TVDs
is further divided into special operational zones with prescribed axes
of advance and set operational tasks: it might be argued quite
plausibly that there are, in fact, two Western TVDs, comprising both
Soviet forces in East Germany (and the NVA) as well as a second
TVD incorporating the Carpathian Military District and the Soviet
Central Group of Forces in Czechoslovakia, with flank cover for the
Soviet Southern Group of Forces in Hungary.[8]

Under conditions of rapid pre-emptive thrusts, select non-Soviet
forces could be used within these TVDs as part of the initial attacks,
while general mobilization proceeded apace in the wake of these
operations. For example, reinforcement from the Odessa Military
District (within the South-Western TVD) could be supplied to
Bulgarian forces committed to a limited operation designed to secure
the European shore of the Sea of Marmara (with some three days
assigned to complete the whole seizure of the Dardanelles passage).[9]
Any combined Soviet–East German attack could be reinforced
steadily by Polish divisions brought forward, possibly some 7 divisions,
while Soviet losses could be replaced by divisions from Northern
Group (in Poland) or yet again from Central Group in Czechoslovakia
(with the Carpathian Military District charged with the task of 'filling
up' these positions vacated by Central Group, again in a three-day
cycle). Under these conditions it might be argued that some 6

Czechoslovak divisions would be available also to act as reinforcement. Over a ten-day period the Soviet command could move up at least 20 divisions to form a fresh reserve or an exploitation echelon.

Operational control under these circumstances would pass inevitably to the Soviet General Staff, with the several TVD commanders – Ivanovskii (GSFG), Gersimov (Kiev), Mayorov (Baltic), to date – acting as the immediate operational commanders: East European commanders would be directly subordinated to these Soviet echelons even where technically 'commanding' joint task forces (say, Soviet–Polish). Co-ordination at this point and on this scale would not be too difficult, for only select non-Soviet formations would have fitted into Soviet TVD operations. Presumably political problems could well arise as Soviet operations unfold in time and space, both in the event of success or failure and here the political dimension must assert itself in forceful manner – war aims, negotiations, settlements. . . .

The integration of the air effort within the Pact seems to be well advanced and it appears to be the intention of the Soviet command to ensure that modernization within the non-Soviet air forces generally keeps pace with the Soviet Air Force (VVS). Air defence is fully integrated as part of the overall Soviet early warning and air defence command system (PVO Strany) with a Soviet Deputy Commander/PVO Strany assigned to supervise East European operations. The bulk of the East European air forces are committed to an air defence role, that is, air defence of their own air space, though some specialized squadrons (Polish ground-attack, for example) are possibly earmarked for operations with first-echelon air units, coming under the control of the Soviet 37th Air Army in Northern Group (Poland): the same might be said for units of the Polish naval air arm which would operate under the aegis of the 'joint' Baltic naval-air command. It is safe to assume, therefore, that a certain number of non-Soviet aircraft could be used against high priority NATO targets in independent air operations, though the non-Soviet force would be small and very specialized. The Soviet command can reckon on some 2,644 aircraft available for immediate operational use, a figure which includes all fixed-wing aircraft in East Germany with Soviet Frontal Aviation, Poland, Czechoslovakia, and Hungary as well as the Leningrad Military District, together with Naval Aviation and Long-Range Aviation elements. Apart from the Soviet Union itself, Poland could supply the largest tactical reserve, with over 800 aircraft (including the 60 fixed-wing aircraft of Polish naval aviation), though the Czechoslovak and East German air forces can also contribute multi-role support since they are being equipped with the MiG-23 BM (NATO code-name Flogger-F) and the MiG-23 MF (NATO code-name Flogger-B) respectively.

Recently non-Soviet naval forces – supplied largely in the northern tier by East Germany and Poland – appear to have undergone their own form of integration, with a mixed (Soviet and non-Soviet) force exercising in the North Sea: a Soviet and Polish missile destroyer combined with the East German frigate *Rostock*, two tankers, and a support ship transited the Baltic into the North Sea, carrying out firing exercises and anti-submarine procedures, passing the German Bight and cruising off Terschelling. Language barriers and signals have presumably been mastered for this type of undertaking. In the southern tier, Bulgaria and Romania can deploy only light coastal forces and pack no significant naval 'punch'. Integration has obvious significance for the northern tier only, with Soviet–Polish–East German combined forces engaged in forcing the Baltic approaches and, if possible, securing the southern flank of the Soviet Northern Fleet, or at least participating in the crucial Soviet effort to obtain domination of European coastal waters.

Against this background it is worth noting the scope of key appointments in the Pact held by *Soviet* officers: in addition to the high command appointments held by Marshal Kulikov as C-in-C and Army General A. I. Gribkov (First Deputy C-in-C and Chief of the Joint Staff), the air defence command comes under Air Marshal A. I. Koldunov (chief of the Soviet PVO Strany), Colonel-General (Air) A. N. Katrich commands the Pact air forces, Soviet Admiral Mikhailin the combined naval forces, while Colonel-General I. A. Fabrikov heads the Military-Technical Committee (dealing with weapons procurement and standardization). Recently Lieutenant-General M. N. Tereschenko joined the Pact as Deputy Chief/Joint Staff from his previous post as Chief of Staff/Belorussian Military District, with Lieutenant-General Merezhko adding to this range of talent: quite significantly Lieutenant-General G. Khoreshko is now identified as 'Assistant to the C-in-C for Rear Services/Logistics'.[10]

If Soviet commanders have been so emplaced, then it is reasonable to suppose that they know what they will be 'commanding' – when, where, and how. In the first place, NVA divisions are fully integrated with Soviet forces (GSFG), though it is open to debate whether these East German divisions would be used in a forward, first-echelon attack role: the Border Guards elements, committed as divisions, could hold the forward zone and secure lines of communication and the transmission of prisoners of war, but the bulk of the NVA might be held back in expectation of the 'anticipated' West German counter-attack aimed at Berlin. While the Polish forces would furnish units for the joint task force operating in the Baltic (under local Polish command) – 6th Airborne, plus the Polish amphibious brigade with its 7,000 men, landing craft and supporting units – the Polish Army is largely equipped for and trained in defensive tactics. The exception may well be one or two of the tank divisions, which the Soviet command judges at present to be well trained and well maintained. (Polish divisions are also taking special 'air landing brigades' into their establishment, which can improve their usefulness in war operations, especially if 'bonded' with Soviet troops.) The Czechoslovak army could probably provide at least 4 divisions for first-echelon operations, in addition to special air transport squadrons and refurbished ground-attack elements now that the newer aircraft are coming into service, though significantly Czechoslovak 'special services' airborne units have been reduced in strength.

If this is the case, that the Pact system depends largely on 'earmarked' formations rather than mass mobilization, then a mobilization administration is not necessary, if the Soviet command can call on particular non-Soviet formations, possibly through the device of 'deployment by manoeuvre'. I have talked to Pact officers who cite the procedure of a five-hour 'alert status' and starting orders, with divisions rolling out of barracks under 'joint' Soviet/non-Soviet operational supervision (Soviet and non-Soviet duty officers initiating the 'alert'). It also means that hand-picked non-Soviet commanders must be privy to these plans and have been trained in Soviet operational procedures (as indeed they have been, with a considerable body of non-Soviet officers having passed through the Frunze and General Staff Academy courses, the latter being particularly important). I also understand that all operational orders are uttered in Russian, being thereafter translated, transmuted, and transposed into the local language (though unofficially in joint exercises German can be the common 'command language').

Some illustration of this principle can be seen in the expanding pattern of multi-national exercises,[11] though perhaps the most important Pact tests are secret – staff exercises putting the *command and control system* through its paces at a very high state of alert (as in July 1979) with thorough preparations for the use of nuclear weapons and chemical weapons, right down to the readiness of medical units. Other complex field exercises such as Druzhba-79, no longer involved standardized manoeuvres but rather a form of a military division of labour with amphibious operations in the Baltic, winter warfare in the Carpathians, and mobile operations in Hungary.

Perhaps it is useful to outline, briefly, one such exercise— Druzhba-79 in Czechoslovakia: nominally (and in conformity with the Helsinki agreements), 26,000 men took part but the actual number could have been as high as 45,000. (Note also that the 'regionalization' of exercises enables the Soviet command to conform to the 25,000 man rule but also carry through via *multiple, synchronized manoeuvres* larger troop exercises.) Central Group's Soviet 51st Tank and 10th Tank Divisions conducted an offensive armoured thrust, supported by elements of the 5th Motor-Rifle Division and 66th Motor-Rifle Division, while Czechoslovak army units provided *rear* support, and the Soviet divisions staged operations in mountainous terrain with armoured thrusts through narrow valleys and night-fighting in heavily wooded country; Soviet units also deployed to cover the right flank of exercises unfolding in Hungary.

Of course, these extensive multi-national exercises can be seen also as a channel of Soviet supervision and Soviet influence: the exchange of military delegations and the training of select East European officers in Soviet military academies does promote some pro-Soviet cohesion, while there does seem to be close contact between the East European political officers, Party functionaries, and their Soviet counterparts. All this represents something of an uneasy compromise between the objective of an integrated standing force and the vicissitudes of the separate national military establishments, though it is seemingly the best that can be managed and will presumably continue as the *modus operandi* into the 1980s.

The intensification of this quasi-integration, if it can be called that, has been accompanied by a dramatic increase over the past decade in the military and political consultation within the Pact – after the 1969 Political Consultative Committee (PCC) meeting in Budapest three new consultative bodies were brought into existence, the Committee of Defence Ministers, the Military Council, and the Committee for the Co-ordination of Military Technology (Military-Technical Committee). The PCC is the senior body, with the Committee of Defence Ministers acting as a link of liaison agency with the PCC and the Joint Staff, as well as the Military Council: policy co-ordination is also managed through a parallel committee of foreign ministers and a 'joint secretariat' under the jurisdiction of Firyubin, a Soviet Deputy Foreign Minister. Since the formal promulgation of the Committee of Foreign Ministers in 1976, consultative sessions have been held twice a year and such occasions have been used to launch major policy initiatives, a pattern that will no doubt persist into the 1980s.

However, this is not to say that all has been sweetness and light. Soviet policy priorities remain paramount, but differences do emerge, for example, over East German misgivings about the pact and the implications of the Pact's own *Westpolitik* vis-à-vis Europe in general and the Bundesrepublik in particular, Romanian resistance to Soviet insistence on closer Pact command integration (hence tighter Soviet supervision) in 1974, and, even more dramatic, the open split in the 'socialist alliance' in November 1978 when Romania again resisted a dual Soviet demand – increased defence expenditure and greater military integration. (In that instance, the Poles were allowed to freeze their defence budget out of consideration for their domestic difficulties though the Polish authorities agreed to a programme involving modernization of command and control systems.)

Mention of modernization raises interesting questions about the further development and future evolution of the Pact: to what degree has the expansion of the *political* role of the Pact outpaced actual *military modernization* and where might present priorities and future commitments lie? It can be argued that the political machinery of the Pact has been duly 'modernized' over the past decade or so, while military modernization tended to lag, understandably so because modernization on any appreciable scale is an expensive business. It would appear that the Soviet leadership has taken a decision to work towards *increased* military effectiveness on the part of the Pact, not only in terms of closer and more effective command integration but equally in actual hardware, 'beefing up' the key non-Soviet forces of the Pact in the first instance and sustaining at least *rough comparability* in firepower and mobility between Soviet and non-Soviet forces. This programme, now showing its early results, inevitably brings some discussion of the military economics of the Pact and the defence effort of the Pact members very much to the fore, a position they are likely to maintain throughout the coming decade.

Standardization, Modernization, and the 'Defence Burden'

Few will dispute the assertion that the military burden is felt very keenly in Eastern Europe, not merely in terms of money expended but also in the opportunity cost of displaced skilled manpower and displaced resources (see the 'defence burden' GNP percentages given by Edwina Moreton on p. 187 below). While the several officer corps have been steadily professionalized, with the Poles in particular emphasizing their national military tradition, the military as a group is not universally popular or even much respected – and the general programmes for the inculcation of 'defence knowledge', modelled on Soviet lines,[12] may not run too deep, especially with its larding of 'friendship for the Soviet Union', most pronounced in East Germany. Nevertheless, it is instructive to watch the process of competition within the 'pecking order' of non-Soviet members, with East Germany now rapidly overhauling Poland as 'chief ally', a situation which at once gives rise to some wry amusement yet concern among the Czechoslovaks, for example. Yet even the Czechoslovaks have put their military house into better order and their forces have moved back into the Pact order of battle. Thanks to difficulties of their own making, the Romanian forces have been deprived of more modern Soviet equipment, though alone of the Pact members Romania has gone outside the socialist orbit for military items, including French helicopters, British aircraft, and a joint Romanian-Yugoslav fighter project (lagging lamentably, it would seem).

In general terms, manpower strengths seem to have levelled off or stabilized over the past decade and it might be assumed that no great changes in military manpower will occur in the next few years.[13] But it is the machines rather than the men – a Polish conscript is paid 120 zloty per month, about 35 new pence on the black market – which cost the money and drain resources. At the November 1978 Pact 'summit' the Soviet leadership demanded of Pact members an increase in defence expenditures in response to NATO's increase of 3 per cent over inflation, a requirement which roused little enthusiasm in Eastern Europe. Over the past decade modernization of elements of the non-Soviet forces has taken place, though the process seemed to be rather indeterminate and selective, assigning specific weapons mixes to the several establishments (a process also governed by what each nation could afford, for example, the Polish air force obtained the semi-variable geometry SU-17/20 but Poland maintained a tank park predominated by the older T-55 tank). So we come to that term 'standardization' within the Warsaw Pact, an oft-quoted Pact advantage which is seriously misunderstood. It is true that the Soviet Union dominates the East European arms market, dominating both research and development (R & D) and production, and thereby inducing a degree of standardization coupled with uniformity of tactical performance (but at the price of persistent East European complaint that little of this meets indigenous defence requirements – recall, if you will, the important memorandum of the Czechoslovak officers of the Klement Gottwald Academy in 1968, the text of which was obtained by Professor Robin Remington).[14]

The structure and ramification of the East European defence industries is a subject in itself, one woefully ignored by Western academics and analysts. The result has been drastic over-simplification of discussions of 'standardization' and related issues in the pact. Czechoslovakia maintains a major production capacity for a wide variety of weapons and equipment (producing, for example, an excellent rocket-launcher with rapid reload capability, purchased by East Germany); Poland has a sizeable defence industry with advanced shipyards though it has a small R & D base forcing heavier reliance on Soviet designs, save in light aircraft and specialized small helicopters; East Germany has major industrial capacity but presumably for political reasons specific military capability has been checked and aircraft production was closed down at an early stage, though East Germany produces excellent computer equipment, good chemical warfare items and logistics vehicles. Hungarian industry is well organized and diversified, relying also on Soviet designs though turning out light military vehicles (armoured personnel carriers, scout cars) and advanced computer equipment, even if tank production is so far banned. Romania, for its part, has worked to develop a native production capacity, though still dependent on

Soviet designs and supplies: foreign help has been enlisted and some bizarre evidence was exhibited recently in the shape of the modified Romanian T-55s, which now have a British Centurion-type skirt protecting the running gear (which is of the Vickers pattern and has an extra roller), a hybrid tank which seems to owe a great deal to Israeli influence (and deliveries of parts). Romanian aircraft plants now turn out British-designed aircraft and the product is reportedly of a very high standard.

Meanwhile the modernization issue is compounded with the standardization aspect. The Pact at large currently maintains *five* types of battle tank, ranging from the T-34/85s to the modern T-72, with the T-64, a variant of the T-72, serving exclusively with Soviet divisions in East Germany: there are appreciable differences in gun calibres, hence ammunition problems – from 100-m to 125-m. The newer battle tanks have major changes in power plants (and the latest Soviet T-80 may have a gas-turbine engine, at present under test); both Poland and Czechoslovakia seemed to 'skip' the T-62 tank and have jumped from the T-54/55 to the T-72, which is now in licence production in both countries. At a quick count, the Warsaw Pact armies use *eight* different types of personnel carrier, including four-wheeled and triple tracked models, and even one half-tracked model. Thus, *four* different track systems and *seven* different types of engine need varying maintenance, while the three basic scout car types have *three* different types of engine and *two* differing tyre sizes. The earlier rather primitive uniformity in trucks and prime movers has now vanished, leading to a bewildering array of vehicles and specialized equipment,[15] such as the Czechoslovak metal-road-laying vehicle, the Tatra 813 8 × 8 heavy-duty truck with its platform for two cassettes holding 40 linked steel plates. For combat engineering equipment, the Soviet army produces its own excellent assault bridging, but East German and Czechoslovak hydraulic cranes and engineer tractors are superior to Soviet items and are in service with other Pact armies.

While the Soviet Union does exercise major control over R & D and production processes, thereby inducing some standardization, there are dissatisfactions and discrepancies. Under the costly licence production there is customer grievance at late deliveries and inferior quality, earlier exemplified in Polish and Czechoslovak complaints at the quality of their Soviet-produced Urals T-55s: not least, metal shavings in the crankcases after only 25 hours of running. Meanwhile, the Soviet command makes heavy calls on East European high technology, notably Hungarian high-speed computer printers and Czechoslovak electronics (for advanced air defence work). But what I have earlier called 'weapons packaging' suited to the tactical tasking of particular non-Soviet units, air and ground, seems now to have given way to overall modernization, bringing the new self-propelled guns 122-mm and 152-mm) into the 'northern tier' armies (Poland having received the 122-mm piece first) and general standardization on the T-72 tanks, which seems to have been forced on the reluctant Hungarians and Romanians. (The spring exercises in Hungary in 1979 may well have been designed among other things to test the new T-72 in this environment.)

The pace of modernization in tactical air has increased markedly and this momentum will certainly be maintained through the 1980s, whatever the cost. Both Czechoslovakia and East Germany have received the MiG-23 which is an advanced warplane; the Pact currently maintains 2,800 combat aircraft in the 'northern tier', and there are 1,100 aircraft available to Soviet Frontal Aviation in the western districts of the USSR: of these, 1,800 aircraft are tasked with offensive ground-support roles and 1,200 with a primary air defence role coupled with limited ground support, and 900 are on an exclusive air defence assignment. Though older types (even the MiG-17) still abound, a growing number of aircraft have been in service for less than five years and have not only all-weather capability but also advanced weapons delivery systems. By way of projection, it has been estimated that the Pact members will take at least 25 per cent of new Soviet aircraft production in the 1980s, a vastly expensive undertaking but there seems to be no slackening in the relentless drive to improve the air capability – offensive and defensive – of the major Pact air forces, right across the board.

Suffice it to say that earlier Western predictions about the shortfall, or the gap, in Pact modernization, producing a major discrepancy between Soviet and non-Soviet capabilities (in training, tactical handling, and widely divergent power-to-weight ratios between old and new vehicles) have not materialized. On the contrary, 'across the board' modernization seems to be generally afoot, and, under conditions of depressed détente and NATO's own modernization, it does not appear that the Soviet leadership is prepared to countenance any slackening or back-sliding.

Problems and Perspectives

In general terms, the Warsaw Pact has lost none of its significance. If anything, this has increased, both from the military point of view with the present importance which attaches to conventional capability in an age of rough strategic parity and from the political vantage point which enables the Soviet Union to attempt accommodation with its allies and at the same time to develop a common negotiating 'front' with NATO and the West.[16] Whatever the turbulence and misgivings, the national leaderships and the bulk of the military élites have accepted Soviet military and political preponderance and conduct business on that basis, though with persistent pressure to enlarge the decision-making process wherever possible and to ameliorate the impact of the 'defence burden', or to rationalize burden-sharing. This method will no doubt endure, coupled with the counterpoint of Romanian resistance to further 'integration' – and Romanian hindrance to this objective has general significance for the whole of Eastern Europe. (One aspect which should be investigated in this context is the nature and scope of Romanian–Chinese military contacts and collaboration, not to mention Romanian military contacts *in toto*.)

To take the military aspect for a moment, though the Pact lacks an *operational command structure* (and in the absence of an integrated standing force, this may well never materialize) the Soviet military, through the Joint Staff, can supervise Pact preparation and training in Soviet interests, with select non-Soviet commanders being involved or alerted for specific operational tasks and deploying select Pact elements in suitable 'battle group' configurations without waiting on cumbersome national mobilization. 'Joint forces' has something of a hollow ring to it, though it may well apply to specific segments of the non-Soviet forces (air defence, specialist units, individual divisions under Soviet-trained officers), all of which is to say that *military bilateralism* may well be more significant than the conglomerate of the Pact as such.

One of the more interesting aspects of the modernization programme is its possible impact on the professional instincts of the non-Soviet officer corps, whose skills will certainly be needed to implement effective command and control programmes and improved tactical effectiveness: this could mean pushing for greater professional parity with their Soviet counterparts as well as intensifying that earlier dispute between Soviet and non-Soviet military specialists about the relationship between national East European military doctrines and the Soviet-imposed 'unified' Pact doctrine. It could easily be that a well-trodden path will be even more heavily tramped, namely, accepting the need to contribute to the 'unified' doctrine but also stressing the role of national doctrines for particular arrangements and supplementary requirements – a good example is the Polish concept of 'territorial defence' and the role of the Territorial Army.[17] What will also engage the attention of all parties, and, once again, that of the Poles in particular, will be the implications of tactical nuclear warfare in Europe and the surety of Soviet 'nuclear defence' in the event of limited conflict – indeed, that seems to be the predominant East European fear, less one of general war but rather a 'spillover' situation, even superpower miscalculation, which forces the activation of Pact military measures to the point of a 'limited' but offensively directed Soviet response. Nor do East European officers and officials look upon increased combat readiness on both sides – NATO and the Pact – with unalloyed satisfaction.

There is something of a paradox here, with the increased role of East European military assets working to Soviet advantage but, at the same time, posing problems of accommodating 'national' interests engaging the professionalism of the military élites: above all, there is the crucial difficulty, or dilemma, of the patent irrelevance of the Pact as a whole to *Soviet operational planning*. This, to my mind, is a much more pertinent question than woolly speculation (and some wishful thinking) about the reliability, or the unreliability, of non-Soviet Warsaw Pact troops – and what, for that matter, might be reliability under dire battle conditions of NATO's conscript troops, all without battle experience and many not half as well trained as an East German division? Thanks to its supervision and training techniques, the Soviet command can have a good picture of the potential performance of most, if not all, non-Soviet units while the very 'management system' in the Pact, with its admixture of strict segregation on the one hand and 'bonding' select units into battle groups on the other, can only add to this perception. There can be no doubt that the framework of the Pact does facilitate the orginization of *battle groups* at Soviet behest and related almost exclusively to Soviet requirements.

Under such circumstances it is unlikely that the pursuit of an 'indigenous' (non-Soviet) military doctrine within the Pact will enjoy much success, while at the same time the form and pace of modernization, particularly in the air forces, will be largely consonant with Soviet operational designs. Such equipment in-flows will, in turn, dominate training programmes, and, even more important, the command and control systems will subsume and even submerge pure 'doctrinal' questions. It is possible that certain national 'styles' will emerge, probably along the lines of further divisions of labour within the Pact, but any upsurge of 'national' doctrines must be scouted for the present. On the contrary, it would appear that national programmes will become increasingly involved in the *technical* construction and modernization of the Pact, which could actually reduce scope for deploying 'national' doctrinal requirements. One of the interesting questions is the degree to which non-Soviet officers and specialists have an entrée to *Soviet* doctrinal discussions: it is readily apparent that the Soviet command will be continuously preoccupied with the requirements for a high-speed offensive which can forestall enemy deployment, so that Pact modernization will follow this general policy – indeed, that much is now apparent with new equipment moving into ground forces while the Pact air element is clearly being updated to provide close air support to supplement (even supplant) conventional artillery.

And there is always the nuclear nettle, which must be grasped gingerly. The nuclear doctrine of the Pact is *ipso facto* Soviet nuclear doctrine, though there is very probably a tacit and joint assumption among all parties that the only way to win decisive success with the necessary rapidity is via the use of tactical nuclear weapons to blast open the necessary passages, an emphasis that could become more pronounced as NATO modernizes its own nuclear armoury and its conventional capabilities, above all, its anti-tank capability. While it is impossible to predict change with any certainty, there is some likelihood either that tactical doctrine will stand in need of revision or that the efficiency of *tactical handling* – command and control, particularly at regiment and battalion level – will require urgent attention, with added urgency furnished by the less-than-successful Soviet operations in Afghanistan at the *small unit level*. It will not have escaped the attention of non-Soviet officers that the Soviet military press has been openly critical of performance at the battalion level, with the battalion commander failing to use his mix of weapons properly and relying too often and too much on his supposed 'superiority'. Thus, we might better look out for changes in the tactical handling/command and control aspects as indicators of change, rather than abrupt shifts in doctrine – and that tactical handling will provide important clues to the development of an effective offensive capability on the part of both Soviet and non-Soviet forces, whatever the mix. So far it appears that Marshal Kulikov has tackled the question 'from the top', that is, greater command and control integration with large units, but the battalion-sized battle groups remain the key to effective battlefield perform-ance – and here an important Soviet asset derived from the Pact could be nullified without close attention to improved training and command effectiveness.

The position of the Pact in relation to Soviet military policy must also be seen in the context of some recent Soviet developments at large, namely, the organization of Soviet forces into a European TV and an Asian TV: current changes in force levels and command and control for the Asian TV do indicate heightened Soviet interest in an Asian war theatre, with improved war-fighting capability facing China, but the European TV and the possibility of a military collision with NATO seem to enjoy a somewhat higher sense of commitment. This division into two main TVs – Europe and Asia – would allow the Soviet General Staff to control a two-front war, or even to control a single TV effectively, which would otherwise be cumbersome and complicated by trying to manage this simply through a system of TVDs (theatres of military operations). Should this be the case, and there is evidence to suggest that such an arrangement is now operational, then the closer integration of the Pact into the European TV (and sequentially non-Soviet forces into the TVD operational frameworks) will be a Soviet objective.

In terms of deployment, therefore, the Pact does at least confer the benefit of some rationalization on the Soviet Union. Yet it is an advantage for which the Soviet Union must pay heavily: in a very unusual article on CMEA and the military effort, Oldrich Behounek points out that the Soviet Union carries 'over 80 per cent of this [defence] burden within the framework of the Warsaw Pact'. Without this Soviet effort, other CMEA countries could not provide 'an economic safeguard' for their defences. However, military management is not above criticism: pressing new claims is 'inappropriate', as is minimizing defence requirements.[18] The management of Pact resources, therefore, bids fair to become a pressing issue in the coming decade.

Nor is it possible to ignore the enduring reality of the Soviet internal policing role in Eastern Europe, what Professor Kennan has called the 'psychological shadow' cast over the whole region. Two aspects present themselves here: the first, wholly obvious, is the presence of a large body of Soviet troops in East-Central Europe; the second, more subtle, is described as the means to prevent the emergence of autonomous Communist régimes through control and manipulation of the national military establishments.[19] While it is true that the multilateralism of the Pact can and does serve wider political purposes, such as arms control and disarmament processes, which can be used to adjust the 'correlation of forces' in Europe as a whole, the fundamental of the military structure rests on *bilateralism*, strictly enforced and assiduously nurtured by the Soviet Union, whatever the talk of a 'socialist military alliance'. It can be argued that the existence of the Warsaw Pact does afford some advantage to the East European states, not least in affording them the protection of the Soviet 'nuclear umbrella' and it does provide some hedge against overweening Soviet military pressures, but the Warsaw Pact is not committed *directly* to the business of waging war, which remains the prerogative of the Soviet leadership, the Soviet high command, and the Soviet General Staff. Ironically enough, while the Pact may not be geared directly to war-waging, it could be used to engineer peace, that is, in the course of, or in the aftermath of military operations it might well be used as the 'peace-making' instrument on a bloc-to-bloc basis (NATO and the Pact). For the moment, it can earn part of its keep by acting as a co-ordinating body for the bloc negotiations on arms control and disarmament programmes, but co-ordination is a long way from enactment and implementation. Power within the Warsaw Pact lies and will continue to lie with the Union of Soviet Socialist Republics.

Notes

1   Robin Alison Remington, *The Warsaw Pact: Case Studies in Communist Conflict Resolution* (Cambridge, Mass., and London, MIT Press, 1971).

2   *Ludowe Wojsko Polskie 1943–1973* (collective authorship) (Warsaw, MON, 1974). For other aspects, see Jozef Graczyk, *Problemy socjologiczne Ludowego Wojska Polskiego* (Warsaw, MON, 1972). An important recent study is R. Herspring Dale and Ivan Volgyes, eds., *Civil-Military Relations in Communist Systems* (Boulder, Colo., Westview Press, 1978). Also the excellent handbooks by F. Wiener, *Die Armeen der Ostblockstaaten* (Munich, Lehmanns, 1977): translation F. Wiener and William J. Lewis, *The Warsaw Pact Armies* (Vienna, 1977).

3   See Marian Jurek and Edward Skrzypowski, *Uklad Warszawski* (Warsaw, MON, 1970), p. 73. In this context it is worth noting specific East European statements that Pact obligations do not automatically apply in the event of a Sino–Soviet conflict, though *bilateral* assistance is not excluded.

4   In addition to general economic aid, the East German army has sent 'advisers' to Angola, Mozambique (assault pioneers), Libya, Yemen, Ethopia (more combat engineers), and Namibia (assigned to SWAPO).

5   There is evidence to suggest that the strength of the Soviet Southern Group (Hungary) has been increased, bringing it up to 70,000–80,000 men (though this additional strength may have been moved in for large-scale exercises and manoeuvre.

6   See 'Mot Schützentrappe der NVA (Nationale Volksarmee)', *Soldat und Technik*, Mar. 1979, pp. 126–7. The NVA fields two commands: 5 Army and 3 Army, each with two motor-rifle divisions (1st and 8th, 4th and 11th respectively): the remaining 4 divisions are tank divisions.

7   There are a number of valid interpretations of the various 'strategic axes' (as we might freely translate TVDs): e.g. the Kiev Military District could operate with the Carpathian Military District in a 'South-Western' TVD, while a 'Near Eastern' axis would be covered by the TransCaucasus and Turkestan Military Districts, the 'Central Asian' axis by the Central Asian District and the Far Eastern TVD by TransBaikal District/Outer Mongolia and the Far Eastern Military District.

8   In the Pact war-games Druzhba-79, units from Central Group (Czechoslovakia) were involved in the *right flank* of the exercises starting in Southern Group (Hungary).

9   I presented two studies on Soviet TVDs: *Northern/North-Western TVD* for Exercise 'Viking Shield', 1976, and the Southern TVD '*Soviet Options and the Southern Flank*' for CINCSOUTH/Naples, 1978.

10 See Lieutenant-General G. Khoreshko, 'Nadezhnyi strazh bezopasnosti narodov', *Tyl i snabzhenie* (Moscow), May 1980, pp. 9–13.

11 See table (pp. 152–3) in Paul Wollina, 'Die Festigung der Warshauer Militärbündnisses – ein Ausdruck des gesetzmässigen Annäherungs – prozesses sozialistischer Staaten und Nationen'. *Militär Geschichte* (East Berlin), 1980, no. 2, pp. 144–56.

12 See F. Rubin, 'The Collective Treatment of Defence in the Warsaw Pact States', *RUSI Journal* (London), Dec. 1978, pp. 43–9.

13 One element I have not discussed is the strong paramilitary force held in each country. Here it should be noted that Border Guards and Internal Security Troops belong to the military establishment and are *not* 'paramilitary forces' at all: workers militia units are paramilitary. See Peter Gosztony, *Paramilitärische Organisationen im Sowjetblock* (Hohwacht, Bonn, 1977).

14 See Remington, pp. 101–3. See also J. Erickson, 'International and Strategic Implications of the Czechoslovak Reform Movement', in V. V. Kusin, ed., *The Czechoslovak Reform Movement 1968* (London, IRD, 1973), pp. 31–54 (with a highly penetrating and illuminating commentary by Professor Snejdarek on the 'independent Czechoslovak military concept').

15 See Lawrence L. Whetten and James L. Waddell, 'Motor Vehicle Standardisation in the Warsaw Pact: Problems and Limitations', *RUSI Journal*, Mar. 1979. pp. 55–60

16 See a recent Soviet study by S. Vladimirov and L. Teplov, *Varshavskii dogovor i NATO: dva kursa, dve politiki* (Moscow, Mezh. otnosheniya, 1979), pp. 62 ff.

17 See e.g. Boleslaw Chocha, *Obrona terytorium kraju* (Warsaw, MON, 1974). Romania, for obvious reasons, has also developed its own 'territorial defence' concepts.

18 Oldrich Behounek, 'RVHP a obranyschopnost Socialismu', *Historie a Vojenstvi* (Prague), 1980, no. 1.

19 This aspect has been thoroughly investigated in Christopher D. Jones, 'The Dynamics of Political Autonomy and Military Intervention', *World Politics*, vol. XXLX, Jan. 1977, pp. 216–41.

11   Foreign Policy Perspectives in Eastern Europe
by Edwina Moreton

JUDGED by their public expression, the foreign policies of the War-saw Pact states, with the notable exception of Romania, have always shown a remarkable degree of similarity. This tradition of alliance solidarity in public, and the inaccessible nature of domestic decision processes, has in the past sharply reduced the scope for investigation of foreign policy perspectives in Eastern Europe. Indeed, despite private East European expressions of concern about the impact on détente of the Soviet invasion of Afghanistan, the general assumption has been that, since the invasion of Czechoslovakia in 1968 and the enunciation of the Brezhnev Doctrine, the East European régimes (again with the exception of Romania) have been forced to abide so closely by Soviet dictates that it is simply not worth the effort of trying to differentiate between East European and Soviet foreign policy goals. Press reports that a number of East European officials cancelled contacts with their Western counterparts under Soviet orders in the months immediately following the Soviet Union's Afghan adventure, precisely to prevent a wedge being driven between the post-Afghanistan foreign policies of the Warsaw Pact states, would seem to confirm the impression.

Indeed officially the member states of the Warsaw alliance are now said to be moving forward to a qualitatively new phrase in their mutual relations. Described somewhat vaguely as a process of 'integration', this new era has been marked by the beginning of a new round of bilateral treaties.[1] As it is said to apply to 'all areas of life' the implication of this qualitative change in mutual relations in the foreign policy sphere is presumably that the principle of 'proletarian internationalism' – the doctrinal basis for the Soviet Union's physical and political influence in Eastern Europe – is being further refined. Must we consequently expect even closer co-ordination of foreign policy within the Warsaw alliance? The short answer is probably 'yes'. With some quibbling over the fine print, it is very likely that for the foreseeable future the broad outlines of the Soviet Union's foreign policy are unlikely to be seriously challenged publicly by any of its East European allies, again with the exception of Romania. Since major foreign policy decisions are 'co-ordinated' under the protective umbrella of the Warsaw Pact, hard evidence of foreign policy divergence in Eastern Europe is likely to remain – traditionally – scant.

Yet a discerning glance behind this public façade would reveal a parallel, by no means contradictory, and possibly more important conclusion: namely, that each of the East European states *without exception* has autonomously defined foreign policy interests based on nationally determined priorities and preoccupations which may or may not coincide with those of its allies in Moscow, or for that matter the other capitals in Eastern Europe. What has distinguished the different régimes from one another at different points in their post-war history has been the ability or inclination to pursue such interests, and the degree of success achieved. Despite appearances to the contrary, there are good grounds for assuming that, although public foreign policy statements will continue to show a remarkable degree of co-ordination, national East European policy preferences and needs will in the future play an increasingly important part in the process of joint foreign policy formulation within the Warsaw alliance.

An Argument for a Different Approach

There is no shadow of doubt that the Soviet Union's military, economic, and political power far outweigh that of the rest of Eastern Europe. Yet a glance at the political development of the alliance over the past decade would suggest that the Soviet Union has found itself far from able to translate this military and economic advantage directly into corresponding political influence and control. It is precisely this ambiguous relationship between Soviet power and influence on the one hand and the developing interests and capabilities of the various East European régimes on the other which holds the key to an understanding of Soviet–East European relations in the 1980s.

The assumption of many analysts in the decade or so since the invasion of Czechoslovakia in 1968 has been that, faced with the choice between 'cohesion' and 'viability' of the bloc, the Soviet Union will always opt for cohesion and control, and that consequently the last decade has witnessed a 'counter-reformation' in Eastern Europe, designed to reinforce apparently shaky Soviet control.[2] Following this line of argument, the present emphasis on integration represents what might be termed the 'highest stage' in this process. On the other hand, such exclusive focus on Soviet power reveals little either of the root causes behind the challenge which has provoked this Soviet reaction or of the complexity of the Soviet–East European foreign policy environment which conditions Moscow's reponse.

The most obvious barrier to grasping the underlying complexity of the problem is the habit of equating 'national' with 'anti-Soviet' in Eastern Europe. The two are by no means synonymous. But nor are individual East European states above allowing 'subjective factors' to enter into their relations with each other or the Soviet Union. From the earliest days, diversity in domestic political cultures and historical experience have helped to shape the divergent foreign policy perspectives of the East European states.

Cultural patterns play a direct role in the case of cross-border tensions resulting from irredentist claims on the territory or national minorities of neighbouring states. Eastern Europe is certainly not without evidence to support this argument: despite many 'objective factors' and shared interests, several states have long-standing border disputes which periodically cloud their bilateral relations (e.g., Romania's dispute with the Soviet Union over Bessarabia, the problem of the Hungarian minority in Romania, Bulgaria's dispute with Yugoslavia over Macedonia). Indeed, in the case of Yugoslavia nationality problems have become security problems and pose a particularly grave threat to the stability of south-east Europe. Socio-economic and political divisions within the country reinforce national boundaries within the Yugoslav federation. But internal tensions are magnified by cross-border rivalries for the allegiance of some of the smaller Yugoslav national groupings. In recent months Yugoslavia has shown particular concern over its Moslem minority. The standard of living of the one million ethnic Albanians in Kosovo province is the lowest in the federation. Their cousins in Albania itself fare even worse, but this does not necessarily lessen the force of national feeling.

In the case of the other East European régimes, the suspicion has always been that inter-state tensions of this nature often act as a barometer of inter-party relations in other spheres, rather than as contentious issues in their own right. At the same time, however, as the Yugoslav example suggests, the degree of national cohesion must affect the ability of individual East European régimes to pursue their own foreign policy interests within the bloc. More specifically, the exclusive focus on Soviet power as an arbiter of the foreign policy process blocks consideration of a number of otherwise interesting avenues: firstly, it makes obvious foreign policy deviancy and its corollary, Soviet inability to control divergence from its prescribed policy, the sole yardstick of foreign policy autonomy in Eastern Europe. Not only does this ignore the possibility of large areas of foreign policy where the interests of the Soviet Union and its allies might naturally converge, it also excludes by definition any chance that the individual East European states might be relatively successful in legitimately defending their own interests in the bargaining process within the alliance. Conflict is always assumed to be 'resolved' on Soviet terms. Yet the recent history of both the Warsaw Pact and the CMEA would suggest that foreign policy and particularly co-ordinated alliance policy is of necessity the result of some form of compromise, rather than simple Soviet fiat. And there may be at least a hint of suspicion that what appears to be short-term concerted action may in fact be based on differing long-term policy objectives. Or indeed, conversely, different policies or foreign policy orientations may reflect either differing national priorities or an agreed division of labour within a broadly acceptable political framework. Such considerations should at least be entertained.

A second and related problem is that the traditional focus on Soviet power not only understates the complexity of Soviet–East European relations on a broad scale, it also excludes the possibility that events and policy concerns in Eastern Europe might have a reciprocal modifying impact on Soviet policy. Yet the argument is a compelling one that it is precisely Moscow's insistence on a close and inter-dependent relationship between the East European régimes and the Soviet Union that helps forge a close link in Eastern Europe between domestic and foreign policy. Unless the Soviet Union is prepared on occasion to modify its own peculiarly national foreign policy perspectives, it may well be that over the coming decade this close interrelationship between domestic and foreign policy will ultimately reinforce the potential for conflict over a wide range of issues within the alliance.

One of the fundamental concerns at stake is that of security. Over the years, as the external threat from the West has receded, attention in Eastern Europe has been focused on maintaining the ideological security and stability of the régimes placed in power by the Red Army after the Second World War. But whereas Soviet power was sufficient (and largely appreciated at the time by the régimes in question) in the early years as the guarantor of territorial and physical security, over the past two decades or more justifiable doubt has arisen as to whether Soviet military, economic, and political power is an equally reliable guarantor of régime security. Indeed the events of 1968 would suggest that Soviet doctrine and Soviet military power have replaced the threat from the West in challenging the very security and stability of the East European régimes.

But an equally challenging and perhaps more potent threat to régime security in Eastern Europe has arisen from changes in the domestic political system. There is potentially greater conflict inherent in the relationship between the security needs of the political élites of Eastern Europe and the aspirations of their respective populations.[3] Yet should the Soviet Union, by accident or design, adopt policies likely to exacerbate such domestic political tensions, it is uniquely placed to upset the underlying balance of interests to its own disadvantage in Soviet–East European relations. At times the East European régimes may be uncertain of the support of major segments of their population. Yet in dealings with the Soviet Union the interests of those régimes, in different combinations on different issues, are a vital element in the pattern of relations within the Warsaw alliance.

In sum, the major problem facing all the East European régimes during the 1960s and 1970s in the transition to 'developed socialism' has not been the world outside as such, but the adaptation of political structures and the maintenance of party authority and control in the face of increasingly complex economic tasks and in the light of the Soviet Union's self-appointed role as arbiter of bloc orthodoxy.[4] It is precisely this aspect of régime security – caught between domestic pressures and externally imposed constraints – that provides the most fruitful avenue for analysing the foreign policy perspectives of Eastern Europe.

From this broader viewpoint three underlying principles emerge to shape the foreign policy perspectives of the East European states: first, the communist régimes as at present constituted in Eastern Europe will oppose any development – internal or external – which in their view threatens to jeopardize the leading role of the party. Second, decisions taken at the domestic level, attempting to resolve the pressures of modernization and adaptation, must at the same time not be allowed to threaten the continued existence of the wider ideological community, however loosely defined, of Warsaw Pact states. It is from this source that the present political élites claim to derive their authority to govern. Finally, any foreign policy decisions by other states, including the Soviet Union, which threaten to undermine the pillars of régime security as defined by the indigenous régimes will be resisted.

Soviet Influence in Foreign Policy Formulation

However logical the argument that the individual East European régimes can – and indeed must in the interests of their own political survival – establish autonomous foreign policy priorities and goals, it is, to put it simply, impossible to ignore the Soviet Union's role both in shaping the external environment and in resolving the internal debate. The East European states are not the first or the only ones to discover that the direction and nature of their relations with the outside world are largely dictated by the foreign policy shifts of 'great powers'. The pervasive influence of Soviet power within the Warsaw Pact and CMEA – leaving aside any less formal channels of influence – is as much a domestic as a foreign policy issue in Eastern Europe. Add to this the ideological dimension of common adherence to Marxist–Leninist principles, however loosely defined, and clearly any foreign policy debate in Eastern Europe is likely to be conducted within a relatively highly structured political and ideological framework.

What is more, from a Soviet point of view, the stake in the continued adhesion of Eastern Europe to Soviet policy guidelines has grown, not diminished, in the decades since the Second World War. Initially regarded as a physical buffer and widely assumed to be a potential springboard for Soviet expansion, Eastern Europe has since emerged not only as the power base for the Soviet Union's transition from regional to global superpower, but also as an ideological security zone, directed as much against Chinese and Eurocommunist influences as against iniquitous Western capitalism. In short, it represents a much-needed legitimation of the Soviet model of political and economic development. Thus, despite the partial settlement of many of the specific issues outstanding in East–West relations since the war, from a Soviet point of view Eastern Europe remains an integral component of Soviet foreign and security policy. Faced with the threat that the 'loss' of Eastern Europe would pose to the Soviet Union's ideological and material position in the world, the East European states are likely to remain the Soviet Union's primary sphere of influence.

At the same time, however, it has evidently dawned on successive Soviet leaders since Stalin that an alliance held together solely by Soviet military power can be more of a liability than an asset.[5] Yet in aiming at the twin goals of cohesion and viability in its relations with Eastern Europe, in the past the Soviet leadership has found its definition of cohesion in practice incompatible with, and hence frustrated by, pressures for a more mature and – in their definition – viable relationship with its fraternal allies. As was demonstrated by Czechoslovakia in 1968, indigenous communist parties can often have more confidence in the process of managed change in both domestic and foreign policy than their protective Soviet ally. (Although the GDR and Poland in this instance seem to have sided firmly with the Soviet Union.) Seen in its best light, this dilemma stems largely from the problems of confidence and compromise: i.e. confidence that the ideological alliance of Warsaw Pact states guided by the Soviet Union can withstand the pressure of political compromise. Largely although not exclusively as a result of this dilemma, since the role of physical buffer remains important, successive Soviet leaderships have evidently never been entirely clear in their own mind whether Eastern Europe represents a socialist commonwealth to defend or a Russian empire to garrison.[6] It is perhaps hardly surprising that the picture has seldom been clear to the outside world either.

If one looks at this aspect of the relationship from a vantage point in Eastern Europe, the focus is different but the picture is still blurred. Although each of the East European régimes would claim to be pursuing the same long-term ideological goals – creating international conditions favourable to the development of socialism, and strengthening the socialist alliance – there is far less inclination to agree, either among themselves or with the Soviet Union, when it comes to the specific short- and medium-term objectives or the strategies designed to secure them.

This is not a recent phenomenon. The picture of a Soviet-inspired monolith in Eastern Europe has always lacked credibility – and probably most of all in Moscow. Stalin had been obliged to expel Tito in 1948 in order to preserve his own authority in Eastern Europe. Khrushchev, in his turn, whether by accident or design presided not only over the partial de-stalinization of the domestic political systems in Eastern Europe, but also the separate if related process of de-satellization of the East European régimes. Even before the upheavals in Poland and Hungary in 1956 several of the East European states had already begun the uncertain and potentially hazardous transition from obedient satellite to junior ally.[7]

The German Problem

Far harder to trace, but of greater importance for the conduct of alliance politics, are those issues directly affecting a particular régime's perceptions of its own security and stability. Here a number of general concerns can be identified, including the continued threat to the security of individual East European régimes created by the failure to find a solution to the German problem. For East European governments their membership of the Eastern bloc, and since 1955 of the Warsaw alliance, increased and reinforced the threat from the West. Yet clearly the credibility of this threat has declined over the years and its impact on foreign policy has varied from state to state.

In the early post-war years few of the East European states could be accused of having a foreign policy. For roughly the first decade, until the mid-1950s, common ideology was consistently, and for the most part effectively, invoked and manipulated by Moscow as a means of co-ordinating bloc foreign policy under the Soviet aegis. Since the major foreign policy issues of concern to the East European régimes – territorial integrity, definition of post-war borders – were effectively the monopoly of the major powers, there was little to do in the way of autonomous foreign policy initiative. East Germany and Poland in particular had vital interests to defend: respectively continued existence, and international recognition of the Oder-Neisse border as Poland's western frontier. Yet, whatever the shortcomings of their fraternal Soviet allies – and the East Germans were particularly nervous on this score – there was simply no alternative source of support available.

From the point of view of the alliance as a whole, despite the declining credibility of the West German threat in particular, the issues involved in the German problem were sufficiently important in principle to hamper relations between East and West until 1969. West German modifications to its own Ostpolitik proved conducive to the GDR's allies, Poland and the Soviet Union, if not the GDR itself. For those East European states not directly threatened by an unresolved German problem, frustration at being forced to decline West German offers of improved trade relations in the interests of alliance solidarity had already become increasingly apparent. Romania had already broken ranks in 1967 and exchanged diplomatic recognition with the Federal Republic; Hungary and Czechoslovakia were apparently ready to follow suit but were obliged, in the event, to await a settlement of the central issues. As soon as West Germany and the Soviet Union had settled the framework of a new relationship in the Moscow treaty of 1970, the others lost little time in falling into line.

For the GDR the issue was more complex and the ideological threat from a socially acceptable West Germany loomed large. For much of its thirty-year history the prime concern of GDR foreign policy was to ensure that West Germany gained no political influence in Moscow or Eastern Europe at the expense of the GDR. Consequently, GDR foreign policy, such as it was, aimed at maintaining alliance discipline in support of GDR national policy. However, by the end of the 1960s the political barometer in Europe was set for rapid change. Once again the role of the Soviet Union was crucial in determining the outcome but the process was far from smooth.

As long as Moscow saw its immediate interests in the German problem as coinciding with those of East Berlin, the GDR leadership appeared to wield considerable political influence in Eastern Europe. Once Soviet policy began to respond to a change in signals from Bonn, the GDR could only block Soviet initiatives. Much to Soviet annoyance the GDR did so repeatedly during the course of 1970 and early 1971. Although ultimately GDR actions were unable to deflect

Moscow from its chosen course, clearly the German problem was an area where the GDR leadership had clearly defined interests, considered vital to the security of the state. It had been prepared to defend these interests prior to the conclusion of the treaties between East and West in the early 1970s; it has consistently done so since.[8]

The German problem has now been partially resolved both in Eastern Europe and between East and West. However, the GDR has shown over the past decade that it will remain sensitive to any move on the part of its allies towards acceptance of West Germany's definition of a special relationship with the GDR or Berlin. At the same time, to the extent that the unresolved German problem gave Moscow additional leverage over the foreign policy of its allies, the future may conceivably see an increased potential for autonomous foreign policy activity, particularly on the part of the GDR and Poland.[9] In the nature of things, however, willingness to make use of any greater room for manoeuvre will depend on numerous other considerations.

Romania's Defiance

Membership in any political or economic alliance is likely to generate conflict between primarily national concerns and the wider interests of the alliance as a whole. Where an alliance comprises states at widely divergent levels of socio-economic development such conflicts can become acute. This has been the case in Romania's relations with the Soviet Union in the CMEA. What started as a difference in policy perspective on economic issues has tended to spill over and sour relations in many other areas too.

It was in attempting to avoid becoming the market garden and raw materials supplier to the more developed CMEA economies that Romania first embarked on its occasionally spectacular course of foreign policy autonomy. Alliance with the Soviet Union had enabled the Romanian Communist Party (RCP) to gain power initially, but the party leadership in the late 1950s and early 1960s under Dej was then obliged to break with the Soviet Union on important economic and foreign policy issues precisely to retain that power.

There is evidence to suggest that from the very early stages, in 1956–8, Romania successfully exploited the limited leverage afforded by the slowly emerging Sino–Soviet dispute to induce Khrushchev to water down dramatically his 1958 proposals for the supranational integration of the CMEA.[10] Having taken advantage of Khrushchev's new mood to obtain the withdrawal of Soviet troops from Romanian territory, the RCP first sought to bolster national autonomy by mediating in the Sino–Soviet dispute. The attempt failed, leaving the RCP out on a limb in the Eastern bloc. It was largely in order to defend this exposed position and maintain Romanian policy autonomy that in 1964 Ceausescu enunciated the Romanian party's 'declaration of independence', emphasizing national autonomy and party sovereignty. These principles have since consistently guided Romanian policy both within the alliance and beyond. In 1968, although the RCP had little sympathy for the reform programme being contemplated by Dubcek in Czechoslovakia, Ceausescu went to considerable lengths publicly to defend the Czechoslovak party's right to determine its own internal course. On a wider plane the RCP's insistence on foreign policy autonomy has led to differences with Moscow over policy towards West Germany, the Middle East, arms control, and so on. This independent stance within the alliance has been given practical assistance by strenuous efforts on the part of the régime to diversify Romania's foreign economic ties outside the CMEA: e.g. contacts with the EEC and membership of GATT, the IMF, and the Group of 77.

In all these respects Romania has been relatively successful. Economic considerations and the consequent need to defend national integrity as defined by the leadership of the RCP were the original catalysts to Romania's subsequent pursuit of an autonomous foreign policy. On the other hand, is it simply the fortuitous absence of Soviet troops, Romania's geographical location in the strategically less important southern tier of the Warsaw Pact, and a favourable international climate that have enabled her to evade the deadening paw of Soviet domination? Must it be assumed, for example, that a degree of rapprochement in Soviet–Romanian relations *ipso facto* represents a loss of cherished autonomy on the part of the Romanian régime and a corresponding boost to Soviet hegemony?

The answers to these questions are important but by no means obvious. The international climate in the latter part of the 1970s was far less suited to Romania's support for its autonomous foreign policy. Western interest in a maverick East European state tended to decline as relations with Moscow improved. Clearly, too, in recent years the limits of Romania's semi-autarkic industrial development policy have become increasingly apparent. There has consequently been a need for an external policy better suited to Romania's new economic needs. Both political and economic developments have led to the elaboration of a policy of selective economic co-operation both in the socialist (CMEA) and world capitalist economies.[11] On the other hand, both policy shifts – initially away from entanglement in CMEA integration, and then the more recent moves towards selective economic co-operation with Romania's East European and Soviet allies – have been inspired by domestically determined priorities. Thus far these remain the cornerstone of Rumanian foreign policy.

The China Factor
The prolongation of the Sino–Soviet dispute has served to enhance still further the political, ideological, and even military value of Eastern Europe to the Soviet Union. Yet the very seriousness of the dispute has diminished the ability of the East European states to use the conflict as a lever in their relations with Moscow.[12] Thus, all the East European states, including Romania which is thought to have attempted to gain most from its mediation attempts, have for one reason or another sided firmly with the Soviet Union against the Chinese. Indeed, on occasion the Chinese Communist Party (CCP) has proved more of an irritant than an ally to the East Europeans.

However, although China provides no practical or ideological alternative to alliance with the Soviet Union, the 1980s are also likely to see continued debate within the Warsaw alliance over the issue of the correct relationship to China. None of the East European states has ever wavered from a position of support for the Soviet Union in its ideological dispute with the CCP. However, there are other issues at stake. Since 1969 and the much-publicized clashes on the Ussuri River the Soviet Union has evidently put considerable pressure on its allies, not only to join in an attempt to excommunicate China from the world communist movement, but also and more significantly to extend the commitments of the Warsaw alliance to the defence of the borders of socialism outside Europe – namely, to defence of the Sino–Soviet border. Although all the East European states have bilateral treaties with the Soviet Union committing them in one form or another to mutual defence without specific territorial restriction all, including the GDR as the most actively loyal to the Soviet foreign policy line, have declined to support the Soviet position. In the circumstances the refusal has only symbolic importance, but with the invasion of Afghanistan and the Soviet Union's recent reinterpretation of the Brezhnev Doctrine in mind, its importance should not be under-rated. However, the clearly unhelpful response by Romania, Poland, and Hungary to the Soviet Union's Afghan adventure would seem to suggest that if the Soviet leadership is to press this issue further, the struggle in the 1980s will be uphill all the way.

Régime Security

Régime security, that is, the ideological and political survival of the East European régimes themselves, has become perhaps the most sensitive area of foreign policy concern in the Warsaw alliance. By 1968 it must have seemed to several East European régimes, but notably the Czechoslovak, Romanian, and possibly the Hungarian, that the direct threat to both their physical and their political security came more from the east than from the west. It does not take an event as disastrous as the Soviet invasion of Czechoslovakia to high-light the connection between domestic and external constraints in Eastern Europe. But clearly the Czech case represents the most recent dramatic example of how an individual East European régime's per-ceptions of its own sources of political stability and ideological security can differ totally from those of the Soviet Union.

When it comes to the acutely necessary political exercise of meeting the social and economic needs of modernizing societies, the constraint imposed both by the adoption of the Soviet model in the first place and insistence – whether on the part of the Soviet Union or on the part of indigenous élite groups – that it be maintained largely intact, represents the most significant problem facing all the East European régimes. Here the connection between foreign and domestic policy is made in two ways: (1) to the extent that the Soviet model of political and economic development does hamper the flexibility of political and economic management, this enforced inability to deal with problems created by modernization adds fuel to the flames of the potentially most dangerous threat to political stability in Eastern Europe, namely economic discontent; (2) owing to the very instability caused by inflexible and inappropriate management, particularly of the more advanced East European economies, the Soviet Union has the capacity in its own policies towards Eastern Europe of switching the points for disaster. Especially in those East European societies already seriously flawed by the challenge of alternative sources of political authority, such as Poland, it should be obvious to all concerned that the East European régimes operate on a much shorter fuse than their Soviet counterparts. Soviet action, using loans and other preferential arrangements in order to alleviate the most immediate detrimental impact of the post-1975 oil price rises in the CMEA, indicates at least some appreciation of the close connection here, as does the flow of funds rather than guns into Poland after the riots of 1970 and 1976.

What this suggests is that the growing interdependence of the Soviet Union with its East European allies in economic, but also military and political terms, may conceivably give the East Europeans a greater say in policy formulation in the future, precisely because of to shared concern over régime security. Where the issues at stake are considered vital to a particular régime the bargaining process in bloc councils is likely to be heated and the reciprocal impact on Soviet policy more direct.

Paradoxically, shared interests can be as important as competing ones. After the Helsinki agreements and the wave of dissent throughout Eastern Europe which followed, concern for régime security resulted in considerable policy co-ordination both domestically and with respect to the outside world. Even Romania, the most resolute in defending national autonomy and rejecting Soviet overtures for enhanced ideological and political co-ordination, actively participated in formulating joint strategies – including the arrest and possible deportation of dissidents – aimed at ideological co-operation in order to stamp out the growing tensions.

In this respect the Helsinki accords have probably proved disappointing to Western governments. East European participation in East–West relations has certainly been institutionalized; it is not clear that it has been significantly expanded.

Divergence within CMEA and WTO

It has already been noted that economic issues are likely to loom large on the foreign policy horizon in the 1980s, and Romania's autonomous policy concerns have been discussed. Chapters 7 and 8 above, by Philip Hanson and Alan Smith, highlight the important undercurrents of CMEA development in this sphere. These various analyses point to the general conclusion that in the 1980s, perhaps more than was the case in the 1970s, foreign economic policy and above all the intricacies of CMEA energy policy will have a direct impact on the political stability of the East European states and hence on the security concerns of the Soviet régime also. While there undoubtedly may be circumstances where the Soviet Union will hope to rely on its oil exports to Eastern Europe as a potential lever to concentrate minds, the serious political repercussions of any drastic Soviet interference with the flow of oil to its allies at the same time limits Soviet ability to use the oil weapon in a blunt but effective manner.

The pressing need for economic co-operation in many areas gives the East European régimes a greater opportunity and incentive to make their own voice heard in the formulation of joint CMEA strategy. Their inclination to press autonomous policy concerns and make use of any additional room for manoeuvre is also likely to be reinforced by the undiminished seriousness of the threat posed by the prospect of economic discontent throughout the region. For many sound economic and technical reasons, states with more highly developed economies, such as the GDR, Czechoslovakia, and Poland, are likely to be increasingly attracted by the 'international socialist division of labour' within the CMEA. At the same time, however, each of these states may legitimately have reservations on a number of economic issues in its dealings with the Soviet Union. These are likely to be at least articulated, and perhaps listened to.

But aside from their direct implications for bloc policy, economic issues also play an indirect but major role in other spheres of foreign policy. One recent example has been the East European reaction to Soviet pressure for increased defence commitments on the part of its allies in the Warsaw Pact. Over the past decade, but most notably since the November 1978 Political Consultative Committee meeting in Moscow, the Soviet Union, understandably from its point of view, has been pressuring its allies on a number of issues. As shown in the essays by Malcolm Mackintosh and John Erickson, debates have focused on the familiar issues of 'burden sharing', the integration of military establishments within the Warsaw Pact, and the modernization of national armed forces. The debate has intensified recently as the Soviet Union has been pressing its allies to respond directly to recent NATO decisions concerning increased national defence budgets and the deployment of new weaponry. The financial commitment of the individual East European states in any case varies considerably, as Table 11.1 shows.

Table 11.1   Comparisons of Warsaw Pact states' defence expenditure 1979

	$ per head[a]	% of GNP[b]
Bulgaria	81	2.1
Czechoslovakia	159	2.8
GDR	285	6.3
Hungary	84	2.1
Poland	99	2.4
Romania	57	1.4
Soviet Union[c]	574[d]	11–13

[a] The difficulty of calculating suitable exchange rates makes conversion to dollars imprecise.
[b] Based on local currency. GNP estimated where official figures unavailable.
[c] Figures for the Soviet Union are taken from (US) Central Intelligence Agency estimates. The percentage range is based on CIA rouble estimates of GNP and defence spending. See *The Military Balance 1980–1981*, pp. 12–13.
[d] Figure for the year 1978.
Source: Adapted from *The Military Balance 1980–1981* (London, International Institute for Strategic Studies, 1980), Table 4, p. 96.

At the meeting of the Political Consultative Committee (PCC) in November 1978 the Soviet Union called for a 5 per cent increase across the board in military expenditure by the smaller Warsaw Pact states. Yet whatever the internal logic of the Soviet argument, the deteriorating economic situation throughout Eastern Europe makes it both politically and economically difficult for the East Europeans to undertake such increased commitments, even were they inclined to do so. Undoubtedly in such circumstances military co-ordination and integration probably make economic sense. But with the exception of the GDR, whose entire armed forces are anyway subject to Warsaw Pact (i.e. Soviet) command, there has been little enthusiasm for such a move. Romania may be the only public opponent of Soviet policy in these two areas, but the suspicion is that the RCP enjoys at least tacit support from some of its less vocal allies. Romania effectively walked out of the November 1978 PCC meeting. On his return home, Ceausescu explicitly rejected Soviet policy both with respect to multilateral integration within a Soviet-dominated command structure and the need for increased budget allocations for defence. In rejecting the latter, he drew public attention to a problem much discussed in Warsaw Pact capitals in private (and already demonstrated in practice in Poland in 1970 and 1976), namely that in Eastern Europe popular contentment, or at least the absence of unrest, is a primary strategic resource.

It is clear from the current drift of Soviet policy and East–West relations in general that the 1980s are likely to see increasing focus on these organizational aspects of the Warsaw alliance. Yet it is equally clear from present form that if it is to be successful Soviet pressure for greater co-ordination, integration, and commitment on the part of its allies is going to entail also greater need for effective consultation, reasoned argument, and flexibility, precisely in the interests of the greater efficiency and co-ordination the Soviet Union desires.

Policy Divergence in the Outside World

If we now consider policies towards the non-socialist world we find that foreign policy conflict may be submerged for public consumption, but potential problems are not far from the surface. Polish, Hungarian, and indeed East German nervousness over the health of *East–West détente* in the post-Afghanistan era is obvious. In the case of Poland and Hungary the causes are not far to seek. Both states have allowed their economies in one way or another to become increasingly outward-oriented and intertwined with those of the capitalist West. Both would suffer serious damage were East–West relations to sour dramatically. Hence they have a vested interest in arguing for moderation in Moscow – albeit after the main event.

For the GDR, again the case is more complex. It is unlikely that the present West German government will seriously disrupt intra-German trade relations. The GDR, for its part, was among the very first to support publicly the Soviet action in Afghanistan and welcome the Karmal régime. Although the GDR leadership initially fell into line with Soviet policy by postponing important political contacts with West Germany until the smoke had cleared, it is not clear whether current readiness to pick up the pieces and hang on to political gains at the intra-German level is inspired by East German or Soviet foreign policy goals. The contemporary German problem – meaning the evolving relationship between the two German states and its impact on the outside world – adds another element of uncertainty to the coming dangerous decade. From a Soviet perspective there is clear interest in maintaining open channels to at least one key Western power. In the case of West Germany, the GDR is uniquely placed to further Soviet foreign policy goals. It remains to be seen how the GDR would respond to overwhelming Soviet pressure for concessions at the intra-German level, designed to woo West Germany away from the Western bank to a midstream position in Central Europe. Again, the degree of conflict over this issue in GDR–Soviet relations depends much on the Soviet Union. This is a sensitive issue for the GDR and one where it has at least been prepared to stand and fight, even if the political battles have eventually been lost.

Each of these three states, therefore, has a different political stake in the future of East–West relations. All have a strong incentive to prevent any major disturbance of the political climate in Europe. Thus the calculation of the benefits versus the costs of future Soviet actions will come out differently in Warsaw, Budapest, and East Berlin from what it does in Moscow.

In other aspects the foreign policy of the GDR seems most closely attuned to Moscow's needs. In particular its policy towards *Africa and the Third World* seems closely co-ordinated with that of the Soviet Union, adding East German technical expertise to Soviet logistics and Cuban troops in support of primarily Soviet foreign policy objectives. On the other hand, the GDR has a long history of bilateral political and economic contacts with a number of African and Middle Eastern states, and has in the past lent active support to National Liberation movements which have subsequently come to power, e.g. Frelimo in Mozambique, the MPLA in Angola. This not only furthers the interests of the socialist community at large, it also provides East Germany with a foreign policy platform not readily available elsewhere, access to much needed raw materials, and a useful trading relationship to dispose of goods not easily marketable either in the CMEA or the West.

But commercial and formal ideological considerations aside, the GDR has always been a more acceptable ambassador of socialism to the developing world than the less tactful Soviet Union. Its aid programmes are well-organized, offering specific expertise from highly trained professionals in key areas, such as medicine, engineering, and communications. In some cases such aid programmes have suffered as a result of sudden changes in, or sudden reversals to, Soviet foreign policy. In the case of Somalia, however, the GDR still maintains youth brigade teams engaged in aid projects despite Somalia's abrogation of its treaty with the Soviet Union and despite the expulsion of all Soviet personnel from the country.

Far into the realm of speculation, it remains to be seen whether possible future Soviet blunders in foreign parts which undermine this painstaking and long-term GDR strategy will be accepted unblinkingly in East Berlin. Rather as in the case of Cuba, this close tie to Soviet foreign policy in Africa and Asia in particular may at some point prove dysfunctional.

A more immediate problem for all the East European states has been the recent Soviet practice of using the CMEA as a tool in its global foreign policy. Mongolia, Cuba, and most recently Vietnam are now full members. Even if a two-tier system is operated, leaving the non-European members out of the process of economic integration, these much poorer and less developed states will undoubtedly lay some claim to a share in the economic resources of their richer fraternal allies. As discussed in Alan Smith's essay, Czechoslovakia has already registered a clear objection to underwriting the economic reconstruction of the new Vietnam. Romania refused point blank to participate in the venture. Since the 1950s several of the East European states have been engaged in direct aid, contributing economic resources and manpower, to Third World countries. In this sense the policy is not new. However, the scale and pattern have changed. So far there is no indication that the CMEA as a whole will concede to what appears to be strong Soviet pressure to induce its East European allies to share the financial burden of Soviet foreign policy commitments. A similar pattern has emerged in respect of military aid. Although decisions to despatch military equipment and personnel from the East European states to such countries as South Yemen, Ethiopia, and Angola are possibly discussed in general terms in multilateral Warsaw Pact meetings, the impression so far is that participation in such activity is on a bilateral rather than a multilateral basis.

Conclusions

A glance back over the 1960s and 1970s and forward to the end of the 1980s would suggest that there are a number of important issues at stake in Soviet–East European relations. Judged by past experience, all the East European states are capable of defining national priorities within the context of the multilateral alliance. Far less certainty has attached to the inclination or ability to pursue them to a successful conclusion. The reasons are basically twofold: first, with the exception of the very early days of the Sino–Soviet dispute, for most of the East European states – Romania being the obvious exception here – the Warsaw alliance still represents the sole platform for foreign policy initiative. As a result, the pressure to co-ordinate policy under the Soviet umbrella is often intense. Second, short of threatening to collapse, the individual East European régimes lack direct and positive leverage over much of the foreign policy of their major ally. Unless their direct participation or acquiescence is required in the practical conduct of Soviet foreign policy (e.g. GDR participation in a negoti- ated settlement with West Germany; Romanian participation in CMEA or Warsaw Pact initiatives) the Soviet Union can normally proceed quite happily despite them. The SALT talks, Sino–Soviet relations, superpower relations in general, and the Soviet invasion of Afghanistan are all examples of the ability of the USSR to conduct a global foreign policy without reference to its allies, even when the repercussions of Soviet actions have a direct impact on East European security concerns.

No matter how subtle or crude the argument, the Soviet Union remains an important determining factor in the formulation and conduct of East European foreign policy. What *has* changed is the expectations on the part of the East European régimes of their Soviet ally. In each case the external (Soviet) environment remains a recognized input in the foreign policy process. Yet, just as clearly, its impact has varied considerably. For example, whereas the East German régime in particular has in the past consciously emphasized legitimate Soviet involvement, indeed responsibility for, East German domestic stability, it has done so in support of decidedly national goals. This has not prevented conflict in GDR–Soviet relations, when toes have been trodden upon on both sides. Romania on the other hand has skilfully manipulated change in its external environment to achieve a position of 'partial alignment' with the bloc[13] and a strikingly independent foreign policy. With perhaps the exception of post-1968 Czechoslovakia, arguably the remaining East European states, although subject to absolute if dangerously undefinable Soviet limits, enjoy more room for manoeuvre than they have thus far attempted (Poland and Hungary are two candidates here).

One way for individual East European states to counter such problems and take advantage of any room for manoeuvre over the long term would be to diversify as far as possible their foreign policy commitments and memberships of international organizations not directly subject to Soviet control. Romania has made this practice a consistent plank in her foreign policy. Poland, Czechoslovakia, Romania, and Hungary (1973) are members of GATT and several of the East European states have become heavily involved in trade and credit relations with the West. Although the Soviet invasion of Afghanistan may initially have caused nervousness in some East European countries due to their current economic vulnerability to Western displeasure, over the longer term this interlacing and over-lapping of interests may equally encourage the East European leaders concerned to argue the case for restraint and caution in Moscow over a wide range of issues.

The increasing complexity of the international environment, ensuring as it does that no single area of foreign policy can be effectively isolated from the rest, offers some prospect at least that issues nominally the exclusive concern of the Soviet Union will be subject to increasing East European comment and criticism – loyal or otherwise. Such changes in Soviet–East European relations as a result of long-term processes at work may be relatively slow and incremental rather than immediate and spectacular. Yet by downplaying the complexity of the policy environment of the 1980s within the Warsaw alliance, the more traditional focus on the primacy of Soviet power can easily miss the important nuances and understate the ability of the East European states to make their voices heard. Short of the hermetic sealing off of Eastern Europe from all contact with the world outside, the very process of integration, co-ordination, and inter-dependence which the Soviet Union encourages is increasingly likely to subject Soviet foreign policy to influence and modification by its East European allies – and not simply at the margins.

Unless the Soviet Union chooses deliberately to ignore some vital security interest of its allies, the coming years will see considerable co-ordination in public foreign policy statements by the members of the Warsaw alliance. Yet this need not reflect increasing Soviet domination, whatever the Soviet leadership's basest intentions. A more realistic assessment would be that such co-ordination will be the result of three developments: the partial resolution of some of the long-standing and highly contentious issues which have clouded alliance politics in the past, e.g. the German problem; greater consultation and *mutual* influence within bloc councils precisely because of the complex nature of the issues at stake and the potential repercussions on political stability of the policies adopted; and quite possibly a greater division of labour within the alliance, allowing individual states to press particular interests and concerns, but within a co-ordinated framework.

At the same time, however, there is no guarantee that behind the scenes the process of foreign policy formulation will be any smoother in the future than it has been in the past. There is a whole series of issues to be resolved and it is unlikely that the Soviet Union and its allies will all see eye to eye on any one of them.

Notes

1 Their significance is stressed by reference to them as the 'third generation' of such treaties. The second generation was those concluded between 1964 and 1970, based on the principle of 'socialist internationalism'. So far it has been the GDR that has made the running, it having concluded new treaties with all its allies except Romania.

2 This argument is put particularly by J. F. Brown, 'Detente and Soviet Policy in Eastern Europe', *Survey*, Spring/summer 1974.

3 For a useful summary of the factors for change and potential instability see Archie Brown, 'Eastern Europe: 1968, 1978, 1988', *Daedalus*, Winter 1979.

4 For a discussion of these issues see K. Jowitt, 'Inclusion and Mobilization in European Leninist Regimes', in J. F. Triska and P. Cocks, eds., *Political Development in Eastern Europe* (New York, Praeger, 1977).

5 This point is discussed more fully in Ross Johnson, 'Has Eastern Europe Become a Liability to the Soviet Union? II The Military Aspect', in C. Gati, ed., *The International Politics of Eastern Europe* (New York, Praeger, 1976).

6 This dilemma is posed by Ken Booth, *The Military Instrument in Soviet Foreign Policy 1917–1972* (London, Royal United Services Institute for Defence Studies, 1973).

7 This transition was first described in Z. K. Brzezinski, *The Soviet Bloc*, 2nd edn (Cambridge, Mass., Harvard UP, 1967); see also V. V. Aspaturian, 'The Soviet Union and Eastern Europe', in Aspaturian, *Process and Power in Soviet Foreign Policy* (Boston, Mass., Little, Brown, 1971).

8   GDR–Soviet relations over the German problem have a long and complex history not easily summarized for present purposes. For the author's own discussion of the detail see N. E. Moreton, *East Germany and the Warsaw Alliance: the Politics of Détente* (Boulder, Colo., Westview Press, 1978).

9   Some initial evidence of a change in public emphasis away from protestations of impotence on the part of the Polish régime is offered in Jeanne Kirk Laux, 'Intra-Alliance Politics and European Détente: the Case of Poland and Romania', *Studies in Comparative Communism*, Spring/summer 1975. It remains to be seen whether practice matches rhetoric in this case.

10   Details of this period remain sketchy but have been summarized in M. Kaser, *Comecon: Integration Problems of the Planned Economies* (London, OUP for Royal Institute of International Affairs, 1965); R. A. Remington, *The Warsaw Pact: Case Studies in Communist Conflict Resolution* (Cambridge, Mass., MIT Press, 1971).

11   The reasoning behind this conclusion is argued in Jeanne Kirk Laux, 'Socialism, Nationalism and Underdevelopment: Research on Romanian Foreign Policy Making', in H. Adomeit and R. Boardman, eds., *Foreign Policy Making in Communist Countries* (Farnborough, Hants, Saxon House, 1979).

12   Because of its seriousness, the Sino–Soviet rift in its impact on Eastern Europe could be considered 'largely consummated'. This point is argued by R. Löwenthal, 'China's Impact on the Evolution of the Alliances in Europe', in *'Western and Eastern Europe: the Changing Relationship'* (London, Institute for Strategic Studies, 1967; Adelphi Papers, no. 33).

13   This term was coined by R. L. Farlow, 'Romania and the Policy of Partial Alignment', in J. A. Kuhlman, ed., *The Foreign Policies of Eastern Europe: Domestic and International Determinants* (Leyden, Sijthoff, 1978).

12 Stability and Instability in Eastern Europe and their Implications for Western Policy
by Philip Windsor

THE considerations advanced earlier in this book suggest two major features of the present situation in Eastern Europe. First, it is probably a good deal more stable at present than it sometimes has the reputation of being. Second, that there is, however, a kind of downward spiral in the development of Eastern European affairs which implies certain long-term dangers. Before we review the factors for stability in the short term, it is worth examining the characteristics of this spiral.

Ultimately, they derive from the nature of Soviet rule in Eastern Europe, as laid down by Khrushchev, and reaffirmed in a harshly unambiguous manner in the guise of the Brezhnev Doctrine. Khrushchev had abolished many of the cruder forms of Stalinist control, but had also made it clear that there would be limits to Eastern European autonomy. Yet ambiguities had crept in during the years immediately after his fall. Soviet interest in European détente, skilfully exploited by de Gaulle, had seemed to lead to a growing possibility that the USSR would accept greater autonomy in Eastern Europe as the price for a greater West European independence from the United States. Indeed, Eastern European autonomy had come to be regarded in the West – and perhaps also accepted in Moscow – as an authentic Soviet interest: in that it provided the framework for a stable pattern of East–West relations in Europe. Until the invasion of Czechoslovakia in 1968 it seemed that economic, political, and cultural developments in the East were taking a form which could be encouraged in the West and accepted in the Soviet Union. But even during this period, there were signs of strain – at the time, for example, of de Gaulle's visit to Warsaw, when he and Gomulka engaged in some sharp exchanges in the Sejm about the kinds of relations that were, or were not, possible between a Western state and a member of the Socialist camp. The strains became increasingly evident during the Prague Spring; and it was at this time that the constituent elements of the Brezhnev Doctrine were gradually put together in the course of the meetings of the Central Committee of the CPSU and the various councils of the Warsaw Pact. The right of the Soviet Union to use all means necessary to prevent the erosion of socialism anywhere in the socialist commonwealth; the emphasis on the need for all Warsaw Pact states to maintain the leading role of the Party; the definition of security within the terms of universal adherence to the principles of socialist construction: all these were elaborated before the invasion of Czechoslovakia, and were merely stated again in more emphatic and public form thereafter. The scope for ambiguity left open by Khrushchev's reforms had been all but eliminated by the strains to which that ambiguity itself gave rise; and the system, and limitations, of the Brezhnev Doctrine have held sway ever since.

What do these imply for Eastern Europe? In the first place, it should be emphasized that the Brezhnev Doctrine still allows the socialist governments considerable latitude. Indeed, the conduct of the Soviet Union since 1968 suggests that it is anxious *not* to have to resort to force in its dealings with its European neighbours. It has tolerated a variety of experiments in economic terms, ranging from the New Economic Mechanism of Hungary to the modified 'balanced economy' policies of Romania to the U-turn from decentralization to re-centralization which have marked the policies of the GDR. It has not threatened to intervene, even at moments of considerable upheaval, as in Poland in 1970, 1976, and 1980, or the GDR in 1970, or Romania in 1978. It has preferred instead to conduct affairs in as co-ordinated a manner as possible through frequent meetings of the Political Consultative Committee of the Warsaw Pact, supplemented by other regular consultations, such as those of the Party Secretaries for Ideology. But while such latitude indicates a reasonable degree of Soviet tolerance, it obscures the truly disastrous legacy of the invasion of Czechoslovakia and the Brezhnev Doctrine – and also the point at which one may begin to identify the downward spiral.

It is that, bound as they are to the leading role of the Party, the individual régimes are no longer able to adapt to the social and economic demands that they must meet, for to abandon this role would indeed be to invite the ultimate threat of Soviet intervention. But what does it mean in practice? First, that the nature of party rule helps to cover up the natural antagonisms between a country's dominant intelligentsia and its working class. This might be very good at avoiding trouble, but it prevents creative and adaptive tensions from emerging, as well as destructive ones. Second, it helps to maintain control over pricing and distribution in a command economy – which itself makes it more difficult to meet real needs or direct activity into productive channels. The consequence of these two interacting considerations is that the party élites must cope with the demands of a sophisticated economy with very rudimentary means of direction and communication. The flow of rapid and effective information, the ability to devolve decisions to a level where they could be guided by such information, the flexibility of arbitrating between competing groups, either in the use of resources or in the allocation of consumer products, are all necessary features of a complex modern economy, and all are vitiated by the leading role of the party.

Yet the Eastern European régimes have come increasingly to base the legitimacy of their rule on the satisfaction of material aspirations. Their ideological basis is scarcely sufficient to win popular support, and has been clearly weakening in the conviction it carries. National-ism is not a substitute for economic growth. Indeed it can even strengthen the demand for economic satisfaction as the people in dif-ferent countries have become convinced (for the most part errone-ously, in the recent past) that they were paying to subsidize the Soviet Union – or, with rather more justification, a number of ill-loved Afghans, Cubans, Mongolians, or Vietnamese. In fact, economic dissatisfaction very rapidly acquires political overtones, as was the case in the wave of strikes in Poland in 1980. The criterion of stability in Eastern Europe is now very largely economic – and the governments concerned are increasingly liable to encounter economic difficulties.

It is here that the spiral can begin to take effect: economic trouble leads to a decline in governmental legitimacy, which in turn leads to a decline in political stability, which complicates European security and helps to promote international instability.

Such phenomena suggest that the Western powers have a strong interest in Eastern European stability, and in avoiding the kind of degeneration which could lead to the risks of East–West conflict. But the nature of Western interests will be discussed later: in the meantime there are reasons for expecting the short-term stability of Eastern Europe to continue.

Initially, it is true to say that the Brezhnev Doctrine, for all its repressive character, also indicated a Soviet anxiety to avoid the dangerous ambiguities which led to the invasion of Czechoslovakia. In this sense, it both helps to precipitate the dangerous downward spiral sketched above, and, in the meantime, to minimize the risks. There are also further general factors of interim stability. The most powerful of these is the manner in which most of the régimes of Eastern Europe have succeeded in assuming a national, or even nationalist character. Nationalism, as already suggested, is no alternative to economic success, and can even fuel economic dissatisfaction. But it is none the less indispensable to any régime which hopes to stay in power. Today, every government except that of Husak in Czechoslovakia presents itself as the authentic representative of a historical national tradition, and makes no bones about defending the national interest, even in competition with its 'socialist allies'. (And even Husak claims to represent at least the Slovak tradition.) In this respect, all the countries of Eastern Europe have to strike a balance between the national tradition and socialist internationalism in their internal politics, and national interests and those of the bloc as a whole in their external politics. One can find many examples of this perpetual attempt at equipoise in the politics of the CMEA. Since 1975, for instance, CMEA pricing policy has been the subject of fierce debate, in which there have been changing alignments against the directives of the Soviet Union, but also competitions for particular amendments or exceptions in favour of one particular country or another.

But nationalism goes further than the mere protection of national interest. Since, in Eastern Europe, it frequently takes the form of mutual antagonism, it has in any case generally been encouraged by the Soviet Union; and within this context the different governments have presented a variable profile of nationalism to their respective peoples. It can sometimes take the form of parochialism; of dislike of one's neighbours, as well as foreigners more generally; on occasion, of a revivied anti-semitism. It can take the form of intense cultural awareness and the glorification of a particular intellectual tradition. It can take the form of an emphasis on the military prowess of the past, and an attempt, through stressing the heroism of the universal fight against fascism, to link this with the emergence of the socialist present. In all these different and sometimes contradictory ways, nationalism can help to associate the régime with the society.

It also serves one further purpose: it can effectively limit the dangers inherent in détente. For on the one hand détente itself is a factor of stability. Particularly among the intellectual and professional classes the existence of contacts and relations with the West, and the sense that there is a European dimension to their activities which transcends the ideological rigidities of the two camps, are important in engaging their energies and in reconciling them to the system under which they have to live. On the other hand, détente can easily lead to enthusiasms which can take on an anti-governmental character – witness the mass acclaim which greets the visit of a Brandt to Erfurt or a de Gaulle to Warsaw. To the degree that national pride can be reconciled with the workings of détente, it helps Eastern governments to secure the benefits of good relations with the West without allowing these to spill over into anti-socialist sentiment.

A related element of stability is one which is not normally considered in the West, but which is of great importance. It is that there is no necessary relationship between internal forms of experiment and liberalization and the degree of contact with Western Europe. In Hungary, for example, a notable form of experiment has been carried out under the aegis of the New Economic Mechanism. This has been accompanied by heavy dependence on Western imports. And yet even Hungary is heavily dependent for its energy supplies on the USSR. In Poland, the government has been excessively reliant on Western credits, yet it has used these to maintain a highly conservative economy. The GDR is virtually a back-door member of the EEC through its special relationship with the Federal Republic, but also the closest associate of the Soviet Union in matters of military and global policy. As these instances suggest, internal experiment is not automatically associated with closeness to the West, is only one form of independence which is not necessarily accompanied by other forms, and is therefore more tolerable to the Soviet Union than if reform and Western associations were indeed to go hand in hand.

Similar considerations apply to the degree of internal liberalization and the question of independence from the USSR. Notoriously, Romania is the most independent state in the conduct of its foreign policy, but is also the least liberal in the conduct of its internal affairs. In Poland, a relatively liberal régime has been anxious to accommodate to the power of the Church and to give a certain leeway to the workers' movement, but has also been very careful not to alienate the

Soviet government over a whole range of matters, whether they be the official attitude to Eurocommunism or reactions to the invasion of Afghanistan. At the same time, Warsaw, like Budapest and East Berlin, made it plain throughout the crises of 1980 that it was most anxious to preserve the system of détente in Europe and to maintain an East–West dialogue. In general, there is no straightforward relationship between economic and social experiment internally and any particular attitude to the Soviet Union externally, nor is there any necessary relationship between economic policy, the liberalization of values, and attitudes towards Western Europe.

These are some of the general factors making for a greater stability in Eastern Europe than might sometimes be assumed; but it is also important to differentiate between the degrees of stability in the various countries. Here it is probably true to say that from the viewpoint both of Moscow and the individual capitals, the three most stable countries are Hungary, Bulgaria, and Czechoslovakia.

In the case of Hungary, the New Economic Mechanism appeared for a time to have been reduced almost to a façade but now seems to be expanding once more. It is also worth bearing in mind that economic re-thinking in Hungary has long been bound up with a conscious attempt on the part of the Kadar government to sustain a spirit of national reconciliation after the uprising of 1956. Such a combination was clearly shown in the Law on Enterprises in 1969. Today, alongside the New Economic Mechanism, the government is dedicated to continuing the importation of Western goods and keeping the shop-windows full, even though prices have been steadily rising for more than a decade. At the same time, Hungary attaches considerable importance to the instruments of the CMEA as a way of fostering internal economic growth. Such pragmatism indicates a certain self-confidence, and there is indeed no sign of serious opposition to the régime or any tendency on the part of the government itself to give way to what the Soviet ideologues might consider to be 'creeping revolution' on the model of Czechoslovakia.

In the case of Czechoslovakia, there is no sign at present of any organized challenge to the Husak régime. One reason is that the Soviet invasion of Czechoslovakia has ensured, in a manner opposite to that of Hungary, that Husak cannot hope to achieve any form of national reconciliation. For Czechoslovakia, uniquely in Eastern Europe, has an authentic bourgeois liberal tradition, and this tradition, even in

Novotny's last years showed signs of re-emerging as the country engaged in economic reform. It was certainly re-animated in 1968. But the consequence was the Soviet invasion, the disillusionment of the working class, and a permanent occupation force. Since then, Husak has felt obliged to maintain a rigidly repressive system, alleviated only by some measures of federal autonomy for Slovakia. There can be no risk of reviving liberal ideas – and by the same token, the economic reforms of the mid-1960s have been virtually forgotten. But repression of this nature has for the moment guaranteed a kind of embittered stability, sustained by the fact that the economy has been reasonably prosperous and that the Soviet Union has contributed to keeping it so. In these circumstances, intellectually and spiritually courageous movements like that of Charter 77 have not generated any widespread enthusiasm; and such opposition as there is appears to be readily containable. Moreover, the Soviet invasion had a disastrous effect on the Czechoslovak armed forces. They had in the past been highly effective – as far as peace-time manoeuvres and the indications of normal efficiency enable one to judge. But many of them had been willing, even anxious, to fight the Soviet forces; and the demoralization which was a consequence of their being forbidden to do so is still characteristic today. On the one hand, of course, this means that the Soviet Union has lost a small but reliable ally, and the Czechoslovak forces would, in the event of future hostilities, be of little use except for logistical purposes. But on the other hand it means that they do not represent any focus of opposition to the régime or, more important, any assurance of support for other opposition movements. In general, Czechoslovakia is unhappy, but unhappy in a stable way.

Finally there is Bulgaria. Bulgaria has the reputation in the West of being a docile Soviet satellite. This is not entirely true. From the mid-1960s onwards, it engaged in a number of remarkably sweeping economic reforms and went further than most East European states in restructuring the enterprise system to create greater management autonomy. But part of the reason for its reputation is that such changes led to no modification of its political system. This was partly because Bulgaria has the least developed working class in Europe, and is also the country which has the strongest attachment to rural and Slavonic traditions. By the same token, its historical experience is different from that of other countries which have also engaged in experiment: it has never known a Soviet invasion, and historically the Russians have been its allies against its enemies in the South: Turks, Greeks, Yugoslavs. In this sense, it is not historically part of the Warsaw Pact, which has clearly laid the greatest emphasis on the enmity of the West; it shows little concern for such susceptibilities (and has on occasion been prepared to affront those of the GDR); and Bulgarians have been able to preserve good relations with their Romanian neighbours on the basis of shared Southern concerns, even while Soviet–Romanian relations were at their worst. Finally, it is the only Socialist country ever to have experienced an attempted military *coup*. If it has no animus against the USSR, but is sensitive to the need for some measure of internal vigilance, it is most likely to ensure that no amount of internal economic argument is likely to lead to a change in the political system. For the foreseeable future, there is no chance of an organized opposition to the existing régime.

It is a striking indication of the lack of common criteria in Eastern Europe that the three countries mentioned here, so disparate in both their internal and their external politics, can be brought together as examples of stability. But in other countries the position is more problematic. The most important case is that of Poland.

During the summer of 1980 Poland underwent a crisis which was not merely one of government but a fundamental crisis of the régime. Strikes had been unofficially tolerated in the country ever since the Gierek government came to power in 1971; but the intermittent concessions that were made to the strikers were invariably couched in economic terms – as indeed, their demands were normally economic in the first place. What differentiated the events of 1980 from those of 1976 was that, as the strikers' movement grew, so their demands became more overtly political. In Lublin. the workers blocked the railway lines to the USSR; in Warsaw they demanded family allowances commensurate with those of the police and security services; in Gdansk they repeated this demand, but also agitated for freely elected representatives – including the recognition of those who had worked for dissident trade unions – and accurate reporting of the strikes in the press, in effect a partial abolition of press censorship. Demands of such political scope could hardly be other than a major challenge to the régime itself. Indeed, the government recognized that the time had come for one of its major readjustments which have characterized Poland as both one of the most volatile and one of the most flexible systems in Eastern Europe. While pretending to treat the strikes as purely economic in origin and intent, it also, through the person of the Politburo's chief spokesman on ideology, Jerzy Lukaszewski, recognized that, in future, relations between workers and management would have to be reconstituted, and that the trade unions would have to take account of this. Lukaszewski also referred, however, to the need to avoid creating any 'impression of instability among Poland's friends'. This clear indication of the danger of Soviet intervention was also no doubt intended as an appeal to the fundamental balance of forces in Poland, of which he singled out one as worthy of special mention: the Church.

In fact the Polish régime, which is so frequently reported as if it consisted of a communist party trying to rub along with the Church on the one hand and the USSR on the other, consists of four kinds of influence: that of the Soviet government, that of the domestic party leadership, that of the Church, and that of the emerging workers' movement. In one sense, these four forces have a mutual understanding. They all wish to avoid a bloody confrontation. But there are none the less inherent dangers. Polish history itself attests to one – namely the revival of Polish nationalism might seek to find a quasi-transcendental legitimation in terms of the Church. And there are also others. One is that in Poland, as opposed to other East European countries, the dissidence of the country at large begins among the workers, and is then supported by the intellectuals, and not the other way round. A second is that, in contrast to some if not all, the Polish party contains significant elements of what would otherwise be the opposition, and numbers powerful reformists in its ranks. A third is that the army, though in some respects it shares the traditional features of East European armies, namely those of providing an avenue of upward social mobility for peasants and youths from the provinces in general, also has distinctive characteristics of its own. The most fundamental of these is Poland's history during the Second World War, and the perpetual tension which still exists between the official account of what happened (where the People's Army was the only significant historical force) and the popular imagination (where the Home Army did all the fighting). The army newspaper, *Zolnierz Wolnosci*, tries to square the circle by playing on the heroic and intermittently xenophobic Polish tradition, but its attempts cannot deflect a powerful anti-Soviet sentiment. In this sense, the Polish armed forces represent a repository of historical ambiguity – and the judgement of most outside observers is that, if the Soviet forces were ever to intervene in Poland's affairs, these forces would fight. In one sense, this is clearly a factor of stability: in that it helps to deter the prospect of a Soviet intervention. In another sense, it is a factor of instability in that such very knowledge produces its own feedback effect. Polish workers, encouraged as they already are by the association between religion and nationalism, are also prone to calculate that the Russians would be reluctant to intervene anyway, and thereby to push their demands to the point where the whole balance of forces could be upset and an uncontrollable train of events could be set in motion.

In this sense, Poland is the joker in the pack. Both the general considerations outlined above and the particular considerations of other Eastern European countries indicate a fundamental interim stability. But Poland, though perhaps stable – at least because it has shown the ability in the past to reach its own accommodation with itself and to disguise a change of régime as merely a change of government – is also a country which *could* become violently unstable in a very short time. In turn, such a train of events could set off an immense chain reaction. The reasons for this will be seen more clearly after some discussion of the other members of the Eastern bloc.

They do not lie, as is frequently suggested in Western scenarios, in the relations between Poland and developments in the GDR. Such Western views tend to suggest that an 'upheaval' in Poland could trigger off a 'rising' in the GDR, which would make West German intervention 'irresistible'. This is nonsense. It is true that the GDR is more susceptible to events in Poland than the paucity of reporting might suggest: the wave of strikes in the Polish Baltic ports in December 1970 did help to produce similar phenomena in Rostock, which went largely unnoticed in the West. But, apart from that, the historical evidence is that East Germany is relatively stable, that movements against the régime are rapidly brought under control, and that the West German and the Berlin governments do all they can to prevent popular sentiment from turning to any form of intervention. The reasons for East German stability, in spite of a growing alienation between the Party and the privileged middle classes on the one hand and an increasingly disaffected and economically discontented working class on the other, are a curious blend.

In the first place, it is worth bearing in mind that economic discontent manifests itself at what is none the less a relatively prosperous level. Shortages of meat and consumer goods in the recent past should not obscure the fact that the GDR enjoys a standard of living which is in many ways more comparable to that of its Western than to that of its Eastern neighbours. In the second place, there are factors of coercion and prudence: twenty Soviet divisions on East German soil; a large, efficient, and heavily indoctrinated East German army; and an effective security service. But there are also elements of inducement. Among these is the very high degree of contact with the Federal Republic – eight million West German visits in 1979 for example. The security service appears to have had misgivings about such a volume, but visits are now seen as a way of keeping the population relatively tranquil. The same applies to the general East German habit of watching West German television. Finally, there is the curious success of the politics of *Abgrenzung*, not in the way originally intended, but in a manner which has now imposed a certain cultural self-sufficiency on the GDR and thereby obliged historians, philosophers, and writers to produce a more fundamental critique of German history and of East German society than anyone could reasonably have expected in the years after the building of the Berlin Wall. This has had two effects: on the one hand it has contributed to the renaissance of German literature in general, on which Western writers now draw heavily; on the other, it has helped to foster a sense of self-criticism, within some elements at least of the SED, and to encourage an intermittent flexibility. There is certainly, at times anyway, a sense of radical effervescence among the articulate sections of East German youth, but this should not be taken to imply a widespread readiness to engage in active revolt. In fact, the GDR presents a picture of tendencies towards instability which can be more or less permanently stabilized.

The real importance, however, of the forces at work in Polish society lies in the nexus of considerations affecting two other states: Romania and Yugoslavia. There are at present no indications of any imminent eruption in Romania. It has an exceedingly tyrannical and corrupt régime, and one which by the same token shows little sign of being sensitive to change except perhaps through a palace revolution within the party. In this respect, it is worth bearing in mind that the origins of Romania's 'declaration of independence' go back to its refusal to co-operate with Soviet desires for international economic planning and its own determination to create an all-round 'balanced' economy on the Stalinist model and one which would be as nearly autarkic as possible. The neo-Stalinism and the independence went hand in hand, and this has meant that, whatever Romania's dramatic gestures of defiance, it has never shown any sign of modifying the strictest possible interpretation of the leading role of the Party. It is also worth recalling that the apogee of Romanian independence in foreign policy was reached in the years 1967–8, with the unilateral opening of relations with West Germany, the pursuit of an independent policy towards Israel, and the vehement protests over the Soviet invasion of Czechoslovakia (which did indeed appear for a moment to tempt Soviet intervention in Bucharest as well). But since then, Romania has moved towards what might be called a selective co-operation with the network of relations of the CMEA and the Warsaw Pact. It co-operates, though sometimes grudgingly, in Warsaw Pact manoeuvres, while on the other hand there has been little overt Soviet pressure in the form of troop movements since 1971. There is no doubt that Soviet–Romanian relations improved considerably after the dismissal of the Minister of Defence, General Ionita, in 1976. On the level of the CMEA, Romania has virtually given up any attempt at autarky, and instead diversifies its measures of co-operation with that body by association with other international organizations – GATT, the IMF, the Group of 77 – and, of course, by agreements with the EEC and its individual members. But in all these respects, Romanian foreign policy is now considerably less adventurous than it looks. There is only one area of its foreign policy which is of real importance in judging the future potential of instability in Eastern Europe, and this is the nexus already alluded to, its relations with Yugoslavia.

Yugoslavia and Romania have long conducted a special relationship over defence policy. Under General Ionita, consultation between the two Ministers of Defence became a matter of routine, and it still remains so. They co-operate in some areas of defence equipment. Most important, there have been vague but repeated Yugoslav indications that if Romania were ever to be attacked by Soviet forces, it would receive Yugoslav assistance. Although the form this might take has never been specified, there is no doubt that Yugoslavia regards Romania as the front line of its defence against the threat of Soviet military force. This is not so much a geographical factor – Yugoslavia is at least equally vulnerable along its frontier with Hungary and around the Macedonian Salient which occasions so much contention with Bulgaria – as a political one. For if Romania is allowed to enjoy its tempered independence, Yugoslavia can calculate that its own real independence is pretty safe; if Romania's independence is threatened, so, ultimately, is Yugoslavia's. In this respect it is a Yugoslav interest to detonate any threats to its own independence into the wider risks of an East–West conflict – and Yugoslav officials have stressed on many occasions that this is the essence of their defence policy. It is here that one can begin to see the importance of developments in Poland.

For Poland, as suggested above, would be likely to fight against any Soviet invasion. A prolonged and bloody resistance would have incalculable effects elsewhere in Eastern Europe, but most particularly in Romania and Yugoslavia, the two countries which were so fierce in their denunciation of the Soviet invasion of Czechoslovakia. In these circumstances it is easily conceivable – not necessarily probable but easily conceivable – that the Soviet government would be tempted to take action against Romania, as there were signs that it was tempted to do in August 1968 and in the spring of 1969. And the point about any such action, from the moment that it came to involve Yugoslavia, is that it would transform an internal crisis of the Warsaw Pact into an international conflict of the gravest dimensions. The Western powers cannot afford to ignore Yugoslavia. Not only have they given repeated assurances of their interest in, and commitment to, its independence, and thereby created for themselves a test case of their credibility which could affect the very existence of NATO; they also have very clear strategic interests in the area. Yugoslavia dominates the Adriatic; in the north west, its land frontier also dominates the Venetian Plain. NATO finds it hard enough to defend the North German Plain as it is. Its difficulties would be redoubled if it also had to worry about Soviet divisions pouring through the Ljubljana Gap and into Italy.

In general, then, the particular importance of Romania lies, not in its occasional challenges to Soviet foreign policy but in its association with Yugoslavia and in the potential for this association to detonate a major international conflict in the event of an East European crisis. This question is clearly separate from that of developments inside Yugoslavia itself. Here, the least that can be said is that the months after Tito's death have seemed to demonstrate the stability of the system he created, his own success in de-fusing national tensions after the period of dangerous excitement in 1971–2, and the determination of the new collective leadership to maintain the structure he created. Here, the three great institutions of the army, the party, and the state are so interlocked that they virtually guarantee stability even while allowing for cautious reform. It is equally true that the Soviet invasion of Afghanistan reinforced the popular conception of the USSR as an aggressive and malevolent power, and helped to strengthen a commitment – if not to the idea of Yugoslavia itself, then at least to the working of the Yugoslav system. In all these respects Yugoslavia is a highly stable country, and has given the lie to the many Western prognostications of chaos after Tito's death. But there are dangers none the less.

The immense economic difficulties with which the country is now contending (an inflation rate estimated in 1980 at 21 per cent, an unemployment rate of 30 per cent) can have two effects. First, they can disabuse Yugoslavs of their enthusiasm for self-management, which is the basis of the whole system – and in any case this enthusiasm has long been waning. Second, they can accentuate the disparities between the different nationality groups, and thereby revive the nationality question. In a situation where, for example, Slovenia enjoys a standard of living approaching that of North Italy while the Albanians of Kossovo scratch out a subsistence corresponding to that of one of the less advanced countries in the Third World, the internal stability of Yugoslavia, as opposed to its involvement in the external relations of other countries, is reliable in the short term but highly problematic in the long. Unless, that is, the Western powers are prepared to acknowledge their interest in the country and to do something about it. A start was made, under the double impetus of the invasion of Afghanistan and Tito's mortal illness, early in 1980, when the EEC after many years of dragging its feet reached an agreement with the country, but this is not enough of itself. Further measures, such as credits or a possible EEC–Yugoslav trade agreement could serve both to demonstrate Western interest and to further the cause of Yugoslav stability. In general, therefore, Yugoslavia's *political* system seems to be in much better shape than earlier prophecies of doom might suggest, but its economic system can endanger its political survival. Its importance implies that the West has an active political interest in taking economic measures to ensure that this does not come about.

So far the argument has been that there is a tendency towards long-term instability in Eastern Europe, arising from the downward spiral of consequences which begins with the leading role of the Party. In the meantime, however, the condition of most East European countries suggests a period of short-term stability. But the problem is not merely one of time-scale, or of short-term against long-term interests. For the intermediate situation is characterized by unpredictable dangers, due primarily to the situation in Poland, but which could involve an East–West crisis if developments there were to spread their consequences into other parts of Eastern Europe, and could transcend the boundaries of the Warsaw Pact through the nexus of Romania and Yugoslavia. A discussion of the case of Yugoslavia has also suggested that the West has an interest in maintaining Yugoslav stability – primarily by economic means. But what, more generally, are the Western interests in Eastern Europe – and what can the West do about them?

At the beginning, it was suggested that the apparently promising ambiguities of the Gaullist era had been replaced by an unambiguous Brezhnev Doctrine, and that while this was not nearly so rigorous in its application as might appear at first sight, its principles were at the root of the present difficulties in the East. The implication, which should now be made explicit, was that the West no longer knows how to approach the East. The effects of Western actions are unpredictable; there is no necessary connection between internal liberalization and experiment in any Eastern country and the closeness of its relationship with the West; too great a degree of Western enthusiasm, for further room for manoeuvre or a higher degree of experiment, could lead to adverse social reactions – and possibly endanger the security of Europe as a whole. Yet, even while taking account of such security priorities, the West has distinctive interests in Eastern Europe.

In part these are economic: trade, credits, technology transfers, can help to stabilize the situation there anyway; and Eastern markets can also help to recoup on technological investment and maintain employment at home. But the West also has a more fundamental interest: namely, that of trying to restore the unity of European civilization and to recover a degree of freedom in the East. Such interest is perhaps the weakest in terms of immediate policy but also the most abiding, and the most important to the West's view of itself. It also corresponds to an Eastern interest in Western Europe – one which, as the foregoing argument should have made clear, does not depend on any strong

Eastern desire to join the Western system of bureaucratic liberal capitalism (for there is very little evidence of any such tendency among even the dissidents in Eastern Europe) but one in which the mere existence of the West is important. It provides that European dimension to the activity and life of the East which is of great intellectual and psychological significance. In these circumstances, the nature of Western policy clearly has to be based in the first place on an acknowledgement of the limits to action. In a context of unpredictable consequences, and with no guarantee that even the most generous economic approach will necessarily lead towards greater liberalization or avoid a crisis, the Western powers cannot hope to use economic instruments for a specific form of leverage. Such a policy might have appeared possible in the period of promising ambiguity; it is scarcely possible today. More overt forms of intervention are clearly ruled out. The only partial exception to such rules is in the case of Yugoslavia – but here, it must be recognized that the objective of Western policy is the opposite to that which applies elsewhere. In Yugoslavia, the objective of economic aid is to discourage nationalist diversity and thereby to promote stability. Elsewhere, the objective is to seek stability, but within that framework to do what is possible to create the room for greater diversity.

This raises one of the most important questions: what kind of diversity? One which attempts to produce greater fragmentation in the East, to play up the different forms of nationalism in the name of greater liberality, or one which accepts that a degree of integration has already occurred and cannot easily be undone, but which is not necessarily incompatible with Western interests or the promotion of Western values? In this connection, it is worth recalling the arguments advanced in the economic chapters of this book, which suggest that a high degree of East–West interchange, and of Western investment in the East might indeed help to encourage the process of Eastern integration anyway. In this sense, Western economic interest might help to stabilize the Eastern European situation, and indeed to promote greater liberality as well as greater stability. It might help to change the nature of the leading role of the Party, and to make the interpretation of a socialist society more flexible. But it would not necessarily halt the process of integration – and might indeed even foster it. In other words, a promotion of both stability and liberality might become more consonant in the long term – but only if they are clearly separated in principle and practice from resistance to the process of intergration.

This is perhaps an unpleasant proposition, and could easily be confused with the notion of making life easier for the Soviet Union. After all, a habit of mind associated with the history of the past thirty years – with the Polish October, the Hungarian Rising, the Prague Spring – suggests that the only hope for greater freedom in the East lies in national independence. But the same history also shows that the West is neither able nor willing to help when small nations come up against the power of the USSR and are defeated. In the strategic and geopolitical circumstances of the present, very little can be done to create the opportunity for full national independence. But something can be done to transform the conditions in which the peoples of Eastern Europe lead their lives.

The implicit conclusion here is the one formulated by Willy Brandt when he first defined the objectives of the Ostpolitik: 'Transformation through rapprochement'. But as his own formula implied, the process of rapprochement is itself competitive with the present position of the Soviet Union. There are, clearly, areas where interests both overlap and compete as in the process of European arms control, of creating a safer environment, and elaborating codes of conduct through such instruments as confidence-building measures. There are areas where interests are more directly competitive, as in the whole range of questions associated with the Conference on Security and Co-operation in Europe and in particular the 'Basket Three' proposals of the Helsinki Final Act. But in such areas, East European governments also have interests in common with the Western powers, even while they remain reserved or competitive about specific proposals. In the past, the West has won only modest victories, and the same can be expected of the future. But a combination of economic and security policy with a demonstrative diplomacy to show that the West still cares can make it possible to hope that greater respect for human rights and freer human relations can be promoted in the East in a context of autonomy – that is to say, of internal divergence and a reasonably pluralistic society – without creating the dangerous and unstable context of external divergence and the perpetual antagonizing of the Soviet Union.

Appendix: Selected Economic Statistics for the European CMEA*a* States in the 1970s*

A		Population
	A1	Population of the European CMEA states 1970 and 1978
B		Development Levels in the Late 1970s
	B1	GNP 1978
	B2	Per capita GNP 1978
	B3	GNP and per capita GNP of the European Community and the USA 1978
	B4	Proportion of the economically active population engaged in agriculture 1978
C		Economic Growth
	C1	Real GNP growth 1970–8
	C2	Real NMP growth 1970–8
	C3	Real GNP growth in the European Community and the USA 1970–8
D		Fuel and Energy
	D1	Production, consumption, and foreign trade in energy 1977
	D2	Energy production and consumption by main primary energy sources 1977
	D3	Eastern and Western Europe: percentage shares of main primary energy sources in energy consumption 1977
	D4	Importance of the Soviet Union as an energy supplier to Eastern Europe 1977
E		Foreign Trade
	E1	Importance of foreign trade in the economies of the European CMEA States 1978
	E2	Intra-European CMEA trade and trade with the West as a percentage of the total trade of Eastern Europe 1970 and 1978
F		Defence Expenditure
	F1	NSWP published defence expenditure 1970–80
	F2	NSWP defence expenditure growth rates in current and constant prices

---

* Compiled by Philip Hanson.
a Bulgaria, Czechoslovakia, the GDR, Hungary, Poland, Romania ('Eastern Europe'), together with the USSR.

A Population

Table A1 Population of the European CMEA states 1970 and 1978
('ooos, mid-year)

	1970	1978
Bulgaria	8,490	8,814
Czechoslovakia	14,334	15,138
GDR	17,058	16,756
Hungary	10,338	10,685
Poland	32,526	35,010
Romania	20,250	21,855
Total: Eastern Europe	102,996	108,258
Soviet Union	242,766	261,256
Total: European CMEA	345,762	369,514

Source: *Statisticheskii ezhegodnik stran-chlenov SEV 1979* (Moscow, Statistika, 1979), pp. 8–9.

B Development Levels in the Late 1970s

Table B1 GNP: US estimates for 1978 (bn US 1978 $)[a]

Table B2 Per capita GNP (US 1978 $)

	Table B1	Table B2
Bulgaria	24.8	2,814
Czechoslovakia	70.7	4,670
GDR	81.0	4,834
Hungary	32.1	3,004
Poland	108.3	3,093
Romania	67.5	3,089
Total: Eastern Europe	384[b]	Average: 3,547
Soviet Union	1,253.6	4,798
Total: European CMEA	1,638[b]	Average: 4,433

(The notes and sources for Tables B1 and B2 are at the head of p. 214.)

a Values in US dollars at 1978 US prices. Conversion into dollars is at estimated purchasing power ratios, not at official exchange rates.

b Totals are rounded to the nearest billion dollars.

Note: Per capita GNP is a measure of total production per head of population (including net income from abroad). It is not a measure of average consumption levels. Measures of per capita consumption place the USSR lower in the rank order of European CMEA states than do measures of per capita GNP.

Sources: Table B1 from CIA, *HES 1979*, p. 22. Table B2 derived from Tables B1 and A1.

*Table B3   For comparison: European Community and US GNP in 1978 (US 1978 $)*ᵃ*

	Total GNP (bn $)	Per capita GNP ($)
European Community	1,950	7,510
USA	2,107	9,650

a For the European Community, conversion to dollars is at average 1978 exchange rates.
Source: CIA, *HES 1979*, p. 10.

Table B4   Percentage of the economically active population engaged in agriculture 1978 (mid-year)

Bulgaria	26.9
Czechoslovakia	14.8
GDR	9.7
Hungary	19.5
Poland	31.1
Romania	38.6
Total: Eastern Europe	25.8
Soviet Union	23.4
Total: European CMEA	24.0

Note: These mid-year figures differ somewhat from the official CMEA figures for the share of agricultural and forestry labour in the economically active population. For Eastern Europe the divergences between the two series are small and are not in the same direction in all cases. For the USSR the CMEA data give a significantly lower proportion (20.9 per cent in 1978) than the US Bureau of the Census figures used by the CIA. Both series include, in principle, private-plot work as an element in the agricultural labour force. The CMEA figures include forestry, are averages of monthly figures for the whole year, and make less allowance for temporary (mainly harvest-time) employment.

Source: CIA, *HES 1979*, pp. 52–3.

C Economic Growth

Table C1 GNP growth in real terms 1970–8 (average % p.a., US estimates)

Table C2 Net material product[a] growth in real terms 1970–8 (average % p.a.)

	Table C1	Table C2
Bulgaria	4.0	7.2
Czechoslovakia	3.2	5.0
GDR	3.3	4.9
Hungary	3.0	6.0
Poland	5.2	7.9
Romania	6.6	10.4
Total: Eastern Europe	4.4	. .
Soviet Union	3.9	5.5
Total: European CMEA	4.0	. .

. . not available.

[a] National income produced.

Note: The growth rates in Table C1 are calculated from annual data in US 1978 $ (see Note to Tables B1 and B2). They therefore differ slightly from some other published CIA estimates of growth rates derived from GNP estimates with valuation in prices of a different base year.

Sources: Table C1 derived from CIA, *HES 1979*, p. 22. Table C2 derived from *Statisticheskii ezhegodnik stran-chlenov SEV 1979*, pp. 27–36.

Table C3 For comparison (with C1): real GNP growth in the European Community and the USA 1970–8 (average % p.a.)

European Community	2.9
USA	3.2

Note: Base data are in 1978 US $. See Note to Table B3.
Source: Derived from CIA, *HES 1979*, p. 22.

D   Fuel and Energy

Table D1   Production, consumption, and foreign trade in energy[a] 1977
('000 barrels per day [b/d] of oil equivalent[b])

	Production	Consumption	Imports	Exports
Bulgaria	154	591	442	4
Czechoslovakia	948	1,457	607	98
GDR	1,170	1,686	597	81
Hungary	292	549	297	40
Poland	2,479	2,319	472	632
Romania	1,133	1,244	259	149
Total: Eastern Europe	6,177	7,846	2,674	1,004
Soviet Union	24,290	20,600[c]	(470)[d]	(4,180)[d]
Total: European CMEA	30,467	28,400	(3,100)	(5,200)

[a] Coal, crude oil, natural gas, plus electricity from nuclear and hydroelectric power stations. Electricity generated from coal, oil, and gas is not double counted, and minor fuels (peat, shale, firewood) are excluded. The trade data include trade among the countries listed.

[b] 1 b/d = approximately 50 metric tons a year of oil. 1 metric ton of Soviet oil = (on average) 1.43 tons of standard fuel. 1 kg of standard fuel contains 7,000 kilocalories.

[c] Minor fuels included; figure given to only three significant digits.

[d] Approximate; compiler's estimate from Soviet data in standard fuel units.

Sources: Eastern European data from CIA, *Energy*, p. 5. Soviet production and consumption data from CIA, *HES 1979*, pp. 128–9. Soviet trade estimates derived from CIA, *HES 1979*, pp. 128–9 plus *Narodnoe khozyaistvo SSSR v 1978 g.* (Moscow, Statistika, 1979), pp. 44, 144.

Table D2   Energy production and consumption by main primary energy
sources 1977 ('000 b/d oil equivalent)

	Coal	Oil	Gas	Electricity[a]
Bulgaria: production	99.0	2.6	0.2	51.9
consumption	188.6	284.5	47.7	70.3
Czechoslovakia: production	904.4	2.5	14.4	22.2
consumption	900.0	382.7	132.7	41.2
GDR: production	1,076.2	1.0	53.0	40.3
consumption	1,190.8	340.6	111.0	43.4
Hungary: production	141.5	43.8	106.3	0.8
consumption	185.1	211.7	126.3	25.9
Poland: production	2,338.0	7.3	120.9	12.9
consumption	1,781.2	359.1	166.1	13.1
Romania: production	144.2	307.3	640.8	35.6
consumption	218.9	347.5	637.1	40.5
Soviet Union: production[b]	6,786.0	10,428.3	5,326.0	827.8
consumption[c]	(6,500)	(8,400)	(5,100)	(700)

[a] Electricity production from nuclear and hydroelectric power stations; electricity
consumption from nuclear and hydro plus net electricity imports.
[b] The total given in Table D1 exceeds the total of this row by the oil equivalent of
energy production from minor fuels.
[c] Compiler's estimate from *Narodnoe khozyaistvo SSSR v 1978 g.* and CIA, *Energy*;
approximate.

Sources: Eastern European data from CIA, *Energy*, pp. 21, 22, 31, 32, 41, 42, 51, 52,
60, 61, 69, 70. Soviet data derived from *Narodnoe khozyaistvo SSSR v 1978 g.*,
pp. 44, 144 and D. L. Bond and H. S. Levine, 'Energy and Grain in
Soviet Hard Currency Trade', in USA Congress, Joint Economic Committee,
Soviet Economy in a Time of Change, vol. 2 (Washington DC, 1979), pp. 244–90.

Table D3   Eastern and Western Europe: percentage shares of main primary
energy sources in energy consumption 1977

	Coal	Oil	Gas	Electricity[a]
Eastern Europe	57	25	16	3
Western Europe	20	55	14	11

[a] Hydro plus nuclear plus net electricity imports.
Source: CIA, *Energy*, p. 7.

Table D4 Importance of the Soviet Union as an energy supplier to Eastern Europe 1977

	Total energy imports as % of energy consumption	Energy imports from the Soviet Union as % of energy consumption
Bulgaria	75	70
Czechoslovakia	42	35
GDR	35	28
Hungary	54	44
Poland	20	15
Romania	21	2
Total: Eastern Europe	(34)[a]	26

[a] Derived from data in the second column and the share of imports from the Soviet Union in total energy imports given in the source.
Source: CIA, *Energy*, pp. 11, 12.

E Foreign Trade

Table E1 Importance of foreign trade in the economies of the European CMEA states 1978 (arithmetic mean of merchandise imports and exports, expressed as a percentage of estimated GNP in US 1978 $)

Bulgaria	27.7
Czechoslovakia	16.8
GDR[a]	19.1
Hungary	30.2
Poland	14.0
Romania	12.7
Total: Eastern Europe	17.6
Soviet Union	4.1
Total: European CMEA	7.3

a Including trade with West Germany.

Note: These percentages are only a rough and ready guide to the share of external transactions in total final output. Trade in services is omitted (including transport: all the trade data underlying these percentages are valued f.o.b. except for Hungarian imports, which are valued c.i.f.); capital transactions are also omitted; no allowance has been made for the fact that trade with different groups of countries is conducted at prices that are often very different; nor is any allowance made for the fact that trade values have been converted into US dollars at official exchange rates, while the US dollar valuation of GNP is at estimated purchasing power ratios.

For the share of the Soviet Union in Eastern European countries' trade, selected years 1960–78, see chapter 7 above, Table 7.1.

Source: Derived from CIA, *HES 1979*, pp. 11, 22, 106, 107.

Table E2   Intra-European CMEA trade and trade with the West as a percentage of the total trade of Eastern Europe 1970 and 1978

	1970		1978	
	Intra-European CMEA	West	Intra-European CMEA	West
Bulgaria	74	17	77*a*	13*a*
Czechoslovakia	64	23	68	21
GDR*b*	66	23	63*a*	25*a*
Hungary	62	27	62	27
Poland	63	27	56	25
Romania	49	37	40*a*	35*a*

a 1977.
b Including trade with West Germany.
Source: CIA, *HES 1979*, pp. 99, 106, 107.

F Defence Expenditure

Table F1   NSWP published defence expenditure 1970–80 (millions of national currency at current prices)

	1970	1971	1972	1973	1974	1975	1976	1977	1978	1979	1980
Bulgaria (lev)	324	354	391	422	483	548	596	653	668	683	—
Czechoslovakia (crown)	14,919	15,943	16,770	17,676	18,071	19,728	20,365	20,130	20,808	21,616	22,997
GDR (Mark)	6,733	7,167	7,625	8,328	8,732	9,564	10,233	11,023	11,570	12,148	13,086
Hungary (forint)	9,848	9,891	9,430	9,489	10,564	11,811	11,671	12,607	14,410	14,943	16,360
Poland (zloty)	35,700	37,665	39,868	41,066	45,209	49,872	52,928	57,282	62,264	65,299	70,378
Romania (leu)	7,067	7,424	7,710	7,835	8,744	9,713	10,575	10,963	11,713	12,000	12,500

Note and sources: *Bulgaria*—— 1970: planned budget figure; 1970–5: defence budget estimated at 6 per cent of total budget expenditure; 1975–9: defence budget estimated at 12 per cent of non-economic budgetary expenditure. *Czechoslovakia*—— 1970–8: actual defence and security expenditure figures taken from Czechoslovak statistical yearbook *Statistickà Rocenka*; 1979 and 1980: planned budget figures. *GDR*—— 1970–7: actual defence and internal security expenditure figures; 1978–80: planned budget figures; since 1977 the GDR has published separate figures for defence spending——1977: 7,868; 1978: 8,260; 1979: 8,670; 1980: 9,403. *Hungary*—— 1970–7: actual defence expenditure taken from *Statistical Pocket Book of Hungary* (Budapest, annually) and UN *Statistical Handbook*; 1978–80: planned budget figures. *Poland*—— 1970–80: planned budget for Ministry of National Defence, includes current and investment expenditure; published actual figures have not been given because after 1973 they cover actual *current* spending only. *Romania*—— 1970–8: actual defence expenditure taken from Romanian statistical yearbook *Anuarul Statistic*; 1979 and 1980: planned budget figures; the 1979 budget, originally set at 12,460, was reduced in early 1979 to 12,000.

Table F2 *NSWP defence expenditure growth rates in current and constant prices*

	(1)	(2)	(3)	(4)	(5)	(6)
Bulgaria	n.a.	n.a.	n.a.	n.a.	n.a.	n.a.
Czechoslovakia	154	4.4	2	2 (1970–7)	2.2	2.3 (1970–7)
GDR	194	6.9	1	3 (1970–5)	5.9	4.2 (1970–5)
Hungary	166	5.2	4	5 (1970–6)	0.8	−2.1 (1970–5)
Poland	197	7.0	7	7 (1970–6)	0.2	−0.2 (1970–6)
Romania	177	5.9	n.a.	n.a.	n.a.	n.a.

Notes and sources: (1) Index value of published defence expenditure in 1980 calculated from data in Table F1, i.e. current prices, 1970 = 100. (2) Average annual growth rate of defence spending in current prices 1970–80 (percentage). (3) Estimated annual average rates of inflation in Consumer Prices, 1970–8 (percentage). (4) Estimated annual average rate of inflation in the Machinery and Metal Working Sectors (percentage); the periods over which this average rate applies are shown in brackets. Source for the inflation rates in both Consumer Prices and Machinery and Metalworking is T.P. Alton and others, *Working Papers of the Research Project on National Income in East Central Europe* (New York, LW Financial Research Inc., Sept. 1978 and Sept. 1979). (5) Average annual percentage growth rates of defence spending in constant prices 1970–8, the Consumer Price Index used as a deflator. (6) Average annual percentage growth rates of defence spending in constant prices over the periods shown in brackets, the Machinery and Metalworking Price Index used as a deflator. Both the Consumer Price Index and the Machinery and Metalworking Price Index try to measure inflation in the civilian economies; it is likely that both overstate inflation in the defence sector.

Index

Abrasimov, P., 42–3
Adenauer, K., 52
Afghanistan, Soviet intervention in, 29,
    34–5, 42–3, 52, 184, 188
    effect on East–West trade of, 102–3
Albania, 35–6, 68
    Albanians in Yugoslavia, 67–8, 145–6,
    174–5
    Soviet attitude towards, 145–6
Altmann, F.-L., 132, 133
Armed forces, see Military factors;
    Warsaw Pact
Arms exports
    by Czechoslovakia, 98
    by GDR, 127
    by Poland, 98
    by USSR, 98, 127
Aspaturian, V. V., 82, 193

Behounek, O., 168, 171
Beria, L. P., 44, 53
Booth, K., 193
Brandt, W., 45, 199
Brezhnev, L. I., 19, 21, 26–39, 54, 60, 78,
    99, 104, 107, 119
Brezhnev Doctrine, 2–3, 19–20, 26–39,
    195–6, 198
    Afghanistan, Soviet intervention in, 29,
    34–5, 184
    applicability to Albania, 35–6
    Brezhnev's enunciation of, Nov. 1968,
    26–8
    Helsinki Final Act (Aug. 1975), 26,
    36–8
    main significance of, 29–30
    Romanian view of, 32–4, 38
    Treaty of Friendship between USSR
    and Czechoslovakia and USSR and
    GDR, 28–9
Bromke, A., 40
Brown, A. H., 193

Brown, J. F., 193
Brus, W., ix, 5, 23, 34, 84–9, 96, 106
Brzeski, A., 106
Brzezinski, Z., 24, 193
Bulgaria
    domestic situation in, 67, 201
    economic links with USSR, 127
    foreign policy, 50
    military reliability in WTO, 144, 154
    Western policy and, 201–2

Carter, President J. E., 24
Ceausescu, N., 32, 56, 58, 77, 129, 143–4,
    182, 188
Central Intelligence Agency (US), 104,
    122
Charter 77, 67–71, 182, 201, 206
Chervenkov, V., 53
China, foreign policy, 183–4
Church activities, 69–70
Cisar, C., 14
CoCom, 103
Connor, W. C., 83
Consumption levels in Eastern Europe,
    111, 128
Convertible currencies, 94–6, 98, 125–6,
    127
Corruption, 78–80
Council for Mutual Economic Assistance
    (CMEA), 46, 88, 90–133 passim
    complex programme of, 56, 88, 183
    joint investment projects, 94, 96, 112,
    119, 120, 130
    machinery trade within, 91, 117–19
    plan co-ordination, 96, 99, 112, 120,
    124–7, 183, 186
    terms of trade between USSR and
    Eastern Europe, 93–6, 98–9, 100,
    109, 113–17, 120, 129
Croat issues, 68
Cuba, 121–2, 150, 190

Czechoslovakia
  domestic situation in, 67, 71, 78, 200–201
  economic links with USSR, 126–7
  invasion of (1968), 7–26 *passim*, 55
    crisis, management of, 18–22
    economic reforms, 17–18, 128–9
    federalization proposal, 13
    Hungary, 1956, parallels with, 21–2, 25, 29
    lessons resulting, 22–5, 61, 65, 184
    military factors relating to, 142
    Prague Spring reforms, 14–18
    press censorship, 16
    reasons for invasion, 9–18, 78
    Writers' Congress, 1967, 12
  Military reliability in WTO, 142–3, 154
  Treaty of Friendship with USSR, 28–9

Dawisha, K., ix, 1–8, 9–25, 26
Defence expenditure, tables of, 187, 220–221
Demographic developments in USSR and Eastern Europe, 111, 131
Department of Commerce (US), 118
Détente, 24, 55–8, 188–9
Dimitrov, G. M., 46, 48, 50
Djilas, M., 82
Dubcek, A., 11, 17–18, 21, 25, 29, 30, 48–9, 55, 93, 182

Economic dependence
  between East and West, 101–3
  defined, 90
  of Eastern Europe on USSR, 90–107
Economic reform, 84–9, 97, 126
  Czechoslovakia, 86–7, 93
  GDR, 87
  Hungary, 84–6, 87–9, 97
  Poland, 86–8
  USSR, 85, 87
  Yugoslavia, 84, 85
Edwards, I., 106
Energy statistics for USSR and Eastern Europe, 216–18
Erdei, F., 83
Erickson, J., ix, 7, 148–69, 186
Ericson, P. G., 107
Eurodollars, 110

European Economic Community, 105, 130
Eximbank (US), 102
Export Credits
  by the USSR, 121, 132
  by the West, 102–3, 105, 110

Fabrikov, I. A., 139, 157
Federal Republic of Germany, 10–11, 41–60 *passim*, 52, 54, 59, 93, 179–181, 188–9, 199
Fiat (of Italy), 95
Firyubin, N. P., 160
Fischer, O., 43
Foreign policies of bloc countries, 172–93
  expenditure on defence, 187
  formulation, Soviet influence on, 176–9
  security issues, 176, 184–5
  towards
    Africa, 189
    China, 183–4
    German problem, 41–60 *passim*, 51, 179–81, 188–9
    West, 188–9
    Yugoslavia, 174–5
Foreign trade of Eastern Europe and USSR, 90–133 *passim*
  in agricultural products, 104–5, 127, 128–9
  in fuel and energy, 91, 94, 96, 100, 104, 108–9, 112, 113–16, 119, 122–5, 128–9, 130, 131–2, 186, 216–18
  in machinery, 91, 117–19
  of GDR compared with FRG, 93
  with the Third World, 95, 127
  with the West, 95–8, 100–104, 110, 112, 192
  see also Council for Mutual Economic Assistance

Gärtner, N., 106
Gati, C., 82
Gatovsky, L. M., 87
Gaulle, President Charles de, 195, 199
German Democratic Republic (GDR)
  domestic situation in, 56, 63, 69, 80, 180, 204–5
  economic links with USSR, 127
  foreign policy, 10–11, 42–3, 51, 57, 179–81, 188–90

German Democratic Republic – *cont.*
  military factors relating to, 144–5, 150
    153
  Treaty of Friendship with USSR, 28–9
Gero, E., 78
Gersimov, General I. A., 156
Gierek, E., 31, 56, 57, 88, 142
Ginzburg, A., 12
Gitelman, Z., 82
Gold sales by USSR, 98, 123
Goma, P., 80
Gomulka, W., 31, 55, 56, 77, 88, 195
Gosekonomkommissiya, 87
Gosplan (USSR), 87, 124
Green, D. W., 132
Gregory, P. R., 93, 106
Gribkov, A. I., 139, 157
Grishin, V. V., 20
Gromyko, A. A., 10, 43
Gross National Product for USSR and
    Eastern Europe, statistics of,
    213–15

Haase, H., 133
Halstein Doctrine, 52
Hanson, P., ix, 1–8, 84, 90–107, 108, 109,
    112, 116, 186, 212–21
Hayden, E., 106
Helsinki Final Act (Aug. 1975), 26, 36–8,
    211
Herspring, D. R., 170
Hewett, E. A., 95, 98–9, 106, 107
Hill, M. R., 106
Holzman, F. D., 110, 125, 126, 132, 133
Honecker, E., 42–3, 57
Hoxha, E., 46, 77
Hudson, C., 132
Hungary
  domestic situation in, 58, 64, 71–2, 200
  military factors relating to, 143, 154
  Soviet invasion of, 1956, 21–2, 25, 29,
    64
Husak, G., 56, 198, 200

Ideology
  competing ideologies, 66–72
  decomposition of official ideology, 64–
    66, 197
Inflation, pressure towards in Eastern
    Europe, 109–10, 111
Interatominstrument, 100

International Investment Bank, 100, 124
Intertekstilmash, 100
Intra-bloc relations
  basis of, 45–9
  détente, 24, 55–8
  future prospects, 58–60
  influence of West on, 41
  national interests, complications 48–58
  political culture as a factor in, 44
  political structure as a factor in, 61–82
    passim
  six phases of, 41–5
    1st, 1944–9, 44, 49–50
    2nd, 1949–55, 44, 50–52
    3rd, 1955–64, 44–5, 52–4
    4th, 1964–9, 45, 54–5
    5th, 1969–74, 45, 55–6
    6th, 1974–9, 45, 57–8
  Soviet intervention in Afghanistan,
    effects of, 42–3, 59
Ionita, I., 206
Ivanovskii, General I., 156

Jaksch, W., 49
Janos, A. C., 82
Jaroszewicz, P., 31, 58
Johnson, President L. B., 10
Johnson, Ross, 193
Jones, C. D., 171
Jowitt, K., 193

Kadar, J., 58, 77, 143
Kafka, F., 54
Kania, S., 77
Karlovy Vary Conference (1967), 24
Katrich, A. N., 157
Khoreshko, G., 157
Khrushchev, N. S., 12, 30, 34, 44–5, 52–4,
    78, 119, 124, 179, 181–2, 195–6
Kohn, M. J., 98, 107
Kolakowski, L., 82
Koldunov, A. I., 157
Konrad, G., 82
Kosta, J., 106
Kostov, T., 50, 53
Kosygin, A. N., 10, 20, 87, 119
Kovalev, S., 19, 22, 26–7
Kriegal, F., 14
Kulikov, E. F., 152, 157, 168
Kuron, J., 32

Laky, T., 83
Lavigne, M., 108
Leptin, G., 93, 106
Levcik, F., 106
Liberman, E. G., 54, 85
Lufsandorsh, P., 132
Lukaszewski, J., 203

McMillan, C. H., 96, 106
Mackintosh, M., ix, 6, 134–47, 186
Malenkov, G., 52
Marer, P., 106
Market socialism, 85
Markus, I., 83
Mayorov, General A. M., 156
Meissner, B., 40
Merezhko, General A. G., 157
Micunovic, V., 40
Mikhailin, Admiral V. V., 157
Military factors, 134–72
  Albania, Soviet military policy towards, 145–6
  border policy of USSR, 135
  buffer zone tradition in USSR, 135–7
  control over Eastern Europe by USSR, 135–7, 178
  defence expenditure of USSR and Eastern Europe, 186–7, 220
  dependability of NSWP forces, 141–5, 166
  Bulgaria, 144
  Czechoslovakia, 142
  GDR, 144–5
  Hungary, 143
  Poland, 141–2
  Romania, 143–4
  military preparedness of Pact forces, 148–71
  NATO, conditions for attack on, 137–141
  Yugoslavia, Soviet military policy towards, 145–6
  see also Warsaw Pact
Miller, R. S., 107
Mlynar, Z., 14, 25
Modernization in Eastern Europe, effects of, 61–4
Mongolia, 121–2
Moreton, E., ix, 7, 172–93
Motor industry in Eastern Europe, 95
Müller, F., 106

Nagy, I., 16, 21
Nationalism within the bloc, 66–8, 76, 174, 198–9
Nixon, President R. M., 45, 55
Novotny, A., 11, 54, 78, 201
Nyers, R., 58

Ochab, E., 77
Ochir, F., 133
Orenburg gas pipeline, 94, 102, 119, 124
Organization of Oil Exporting Countries (OPEC), 109, 110
Ostpolitik, 24, 45, 179–81

Panchevski, Marshal I., 138
Pastushenko, General Ya. Ya., 138
Peter, G., 86
Petrodollars, 110
Petrostudies, 122
Poland, 31–2
  domestic situation in, 58, 62, 64, 67, 69, 71, 74, 81–2, 185, 202–4
  economic factors affecting, 128–9
  foreign policy, 51
  military factors relating to, 141–2, 153
  Soviet response to domestic unrest in, 31–2
  Western policy and, 202–4, 207
Police role of USSR in Eastern Europe, 80–81
Polimex-Cekop, 103
Political pluralism and economic reform, 85–6
Ponomarev, B. N., 12
Population statistics of CMEA states, 213
Populism, as alternative ideology in Eastern Europe, 69
Prague Spring, *see* Czechoslovakia
Prchlik, General V., 15
Private enterprise in Eastern Europe, 86, 87
Pryor, F. L., 133
Pyjas, S., 80

Rajk, L., 50, 53
Rakosi, M., 53
Régime security and stability, factors affecting, 61–82 *passim*, 176, 184–5, 197–211
Religious issues, 69–71
Remington, R. A., 148, 162, 170

226	*Index*

Rokossovski, Marshal K., 138
Romania, 32–4, 38
  CMEA, approach to, 32
  domestic situation in, 64, 67, 205–6
  economy of, 129–30
  foreign policy, 181–3, 206
  military factors relating to, 143–4, 154, 187–8
  Warsaw Pact, approach to, 32–3, 143–144
Rubin, F., 170
Rybakov, O., 100, 107

Sakharov, A., 12
Samizdat, 66, 70–72
Schmidt, H., 42–3, 60
Schöpflin, G., ix, 4–5, 8, 61–82
Schroder, G., 45, 49
Schulz, E., ix, 3–4, 41–60
Shelest, P., 13, 55
Slansky, R., 53
Smith, Alan H., ix, 5–6, 106, 108–32, 186, 190
Smrkovsky, J., 78
Solzhenitsyn, A. I., 12
Sonnenfeldt, H., 56
Stalin, J. V., 30, 47, 50, 52, 85, 179
Stern, J. P., 107
Strategic embargo (Western), 103
Strougal, L., 78
Summerscale, P., ix, 3, 26–40
Suslov, M. A., 12
Szelenyi, I., 82

Technology transfer, West–East, 95–6, 97, 102–3, 112, 126
Tereschenko, M. N., 157
Tito, J. B., 44, 46, 48, 50, 53, 77, 145, 179, 207–8
Tokes, R., 83
Triska, J., 193

Ulbricht, W., 45, 46, 52, 53, 54–6
Ulbricht Doctrine, 54–5

Vietnam, 10, 122, 131, 190
Volgyes, I., 170

Warsaw Pact, 148–69
  advantages and utility of, 151–61
  Albania, 145–6
  and arms control talks, 42, 45, 56, 140
  armament levels, table of member countries, 153–4
  command structure, 138–9, 152–61, 165
  defence burden, 161–5
  defence expenditure, 187, 220–21
  East European contribution to, 151–61
  historical background, 137–8, 148–9
  military preparedness and Pact planning, 149–51
  modernization of weapons systems, 59, 140, 161–5
  NATO, margin of advantage over, 149–50
  role in war 139–41
  Soviet dominance in, 138–9, 157–8
  standardization, 161–5
  strategic assumptions, 149–51
  structure of, 138–9, 157
  use outside Europe, 184, 188–90
  Yugoslavia, 145–6
  see also Military factors
Weiner, F., 170
Western policy, implications for, 195–211
Wiatr, J., 83
Windsor, P., ix, 7–8, 195–211
Workers' councils in Eastern Europe, 86

Yugoslavia, 35–6, 67–8
  domestic situation in, 62, 67–8, 174–5
  foreign policy, 49–50, 174–5, 179, 206–208
  leadership in the Balkans, 50
  Soviet attitude towards, 145–6
  relations with CMEA, 130
  US security guarantees to, 23

Zhivkov, T., 144
Zielinski, J. G., 126, 133